About the Author

John King's ministry as a pastor and teacher spanned the years from 1969 to 1993. He was known in Western Pennsylvania for his knowledge of Koine Greek and Classical Hebrew, having taught in Western PA Bible Institute in Butler, The Lighthouse Ministry in Washington, and Faith Seminary in Bethel Park, PA in the 1970's. He also taught at the Charismatic Conference in 1979 at Duquesne University. He graduated from a four year ministerial program at Northeast Bible College, which is now Valley Forge Christian College, and later returned to complete a course of study for a B.S. in Bible. In 1982, he received a Master of Bible Theology from the International Bible Institute & Seminary.

Currently retired from the pastorate, he develops computer software at a financial services firm in Boston and lives with his wife in their townhouse in a nearby town. He occasionally speaks at area churches.

* * *

A letter written by my General Overseer, The Reverend Carmine Saginario, I think accurately describes his interests as a clergyman, Keep in mind the Reverend Saginario reserves the right to change his mind, but I like the candidness of the letter dated October15, 1982 to the then pulpit committee of a church on Staten Island. He was then a potential candidate for their pastorate.

> Brother King is an excellent Bible teacher. He is not only a student of the Word but an outstanding scholar. His exposition of God's Word will certainly serve to build up the faith of believers and nourish the life of both new converts and longstanding christians.
>
> His success, in the church he is now pastoring [Burgettstown, PA.] is an indication that he is not only a teacher but a preacher of righteousness and a pastor at heart.
>
> Your assembly would have to permit him to continue probing the depths of Divine Scripture, in as much as he is committed to proclaiming the Truth and allowing it to speak to his own life.

Reverend Saginario may have been too kind but he read John's heart's intentions and desires.

Jots & Tittles

Discovering Truth

from the Language of Scripture

Even when I am old and gray,
do not forsake me, O God,
till I declare your power to the next generation,
your might to all who are to come.
-Psalm 71:18

Unless otherwise indicated, Bible quotations are taken from The Holy
Bible, New International Version, © 1973, 1978, 1984 by Zondervan. For
full translation information, see under "Translations" in the back of this
book.

Most scripture quotations are set in a sans-serif font style, with words
underlined that are under examination or otherwise significant to the
discussion.

Pronunciations, where given, are expressed using the International Phon-
etic Alphabet.

Jots & Tittles

Published by J. Timothy King
http://www.JTimothyKing.com/

First trade paperback edition, February 2010.
ISBN 978-0-9816925-3-1

Printed in the United States of America.

10   9   8   7   6   5   4   3

To my three sons, who inspire me by just being themselves.

Front cover: The blocks we remember from our preschool days should constantly remind us of our need to learn more of the basics of Truth. When it comes to the wisdom of God, we have not left preschool. The Hebrew letters on the blocks represent jots and tittles, or tiny steps, in our quest to know God.

Table of Contents

Acknowledgments

It seems appropriate to give recognition to the man in white. One Wednesday evening back in my home church in Buffalo, New York, a visiting teacher wearing a white shirt and white pants presented a Bible study to us, around 30 congregants. I was about 15 years old.

I couldn't believe his presentation! I was used to the preacher/evangelist type, the screamer, the walker, the handkerchief-waver, but this man did none of these. He stood there in front of that small group and just talked. It was what he said and how he said it that had me sitting there awestruck. He had a way of explaining Scripture that made me then and there resolve to someday become a teacher.

He was my paragon. He, whose name was never known to me, to whom I was never formally introduced, was in the biblical sense of the word, an angel, a messenger, sent, I maintain, for me to hear and passionately want to emulate. I do not feel I crossed the goal line in that regard but I at least can acknowledge him for the effort I have put forth in the race to be as good as I could be as a teacher of God's Word.

I want to thank Professor Grazier from my Bible School days for acquiescing to teach us biblical or Classical Hebrew, when the school not only failed to offer the subject but—I am convinced—the Dean of Students did not want it on the curriculum. Professor Grazier was a true teacher.

I must acknowledge a dear friend, Rev. John Lathrop, for his instruction on documenting this work, as well as for much proofreading. He has an uncommon way of correcting me. I welcome his advice.

I am also grateful to my daughter-in-law, Cait, for proofreading an advanced copy. She dealt with the 'huh?!' factor—portions I needed to rewrite, so that they are more clear and interesting. This was no small task.

I want to acknowledge my son, Tim, for his work as editor-in-chief. It is no small task arranging anything for publication and sale. His knowledge of the book industry is invaluable. Tim also has been there for me when my frustration pushed me to the edge of my endurance. He is himself an accomplished author and has been a great encouragement to me in that area.

I am grateful to my son, Josh, whose counsel for the overall design for this book's cover was very much appreciated. His wisdom when it comes to graphics seems to be the very natural expression of the brush strokes of his genius. He inspires me to write, because his desire to serve God draws me back in time to relive my own. I am encouraged by his hunger for Truth.

I am grateful also to my son, Jim, who probably does not know the passion he instills in me to push ahead, studying the real message of Scripture, stripping away the bias of religious forms and dogmas that frankly cannot be found within the sacred pages. He inspires me to honesty, and for that I am very grateful.

And last but always first, I want to thank my dear wife for being there for me. I must admit that she took the initiative to purchase a laptop, so I could proceed with this book. I refused to scribble everything on paper first. The story doesn't end there. I needed a desk, too, so she encouraged me to join her at the furniture store and we got one—even though I am typing this acknowledgment from the dining room table.

Preface

Over the course of 24-plus years, I spent a career beginning a discovery of the Bible. Truth be told, the reason I went into pastoring was to find a paycheck while I busied myself studying the meanings of biblical terms, learning the history behind principles promoted within its pages. I also had an intense—and I might add primary—interest in sharing my discoveries with other believers. Together we might figure out how to use Bible instruction to better our lives.

I am not alone. Most pastors would probably prefer being back at the Bible school or seminary from which they graduated—back and on staff, so they also could wrap themselves up in pages upon pages of what we passionately believe was written by God Himself for our knowledge. Then standing in front of a group of eager-to-learn candidates for ministry, who need this knowledge, making a ministry or career out of presenting it.

Much of what we learn as amateur scholars, however, never makes the pulpit, because either it does not immediately promote what the denomination wants promoted, or it is too time-consuming to explain, or maybe Christians would find it just plain boring. Add to this today's use of simplified PowerPoint presentations, and religious terminology and phrases that don't necessarily explain what needs explaining, and Christians' interest in the simple message of salvation—which incidentally is commendable—and you will probably never hear about Moses' embarrassment over his grandson's idol worship, or Assyrian vulgarity which speaks to the realities of our own religious histories but which were written out of the translation we have come to accept as Bible.

"I wouldn't be bored!" you argue. "I am just as passionate about learning the Bible!"

Excellent! That must mean you'll be interested in this book.

Not everyone is, you must know, even though I do not plan to talk about the stuff you already know. I really want what I have to say to be different. My task is to make it interesting; so, I plan to use plain talk, not religious jargon. Some of what I have studied over the years—and I have copious notes—might knock your socks off.

And then there is the comment, repeated by many disillusioned former churchgoers, that the Bible is nothing but Israeli history and has no relevance to us. But history is very relevant if it teaches us something, and Bible history is very informative. Too bad we don't like studying history! Ralph Waldo Emerson correctly observed, "There is properly no history, only biography." And here we are wanting to take a look at God's through the language of Scripture!

Some Christians see Scripture as a record of miracles or Divine victory over demons or some other foe thought invincible. To them, if the account is not a sea-parting or a bush-burning sort of thing—no disrespect to Moses intended—they have no immediate interest in it.

My problem is that I don't live there. I deal with a modern life style, with its economic ups and downs. I contend with physical and emotional problems, and there are few miracles to rescue me from the pain of such experiences. I need principles that work for me, that I can live by, to stabilize me emotionally, to encourage me to get up one more snowy day and go to work when, God knows, I would rather win the lottery and retire.

Oh, there must be a few preachers who think I am full of myself, if I assume there is something worth telling God's people that they haven't already said. They might add that if they haven't said it in the pulpit, it doesn't need to be said, and that to listen to anything other than what they or their church promotes doctrinally would be to risk tolerating heresy.

Well, I guess I have been warned. But the truth is that I totally support their position on this point. Pastors, local pastors, have the responsibility of teaching truth: practical, livable truth, biblical truth. And no one should usurp their authority.

Here, however, in this work, I claim no new vision, no additional detail to the plan of Salvation, no doctrine that would not totally support the Christian position on the eternal plan of salvation. I intend to say nothing that would challenge any honest Christian pastor whose passion for his work, his people, and (above all) his God drives him forward to prayerfully prepare meaningful and inspired dialog with his parishioners and sermons worth listening to.

Bear always in mind that the visiting preacher, which is what I consider myself to be, is not always right. Be careful what you Google and what you read. And, incidentally, I went to the Blue Letter Bible on the web for a lot of my research.

The beauty of what I am saying here is that you are equally—yes, equally—as much a scholar as I ever hope to be. You may rightly disagree with me, but you have to read on first!

* * *

By the way, the title of this book, *Jots & Tittles*, references Jesus' words in Matthew 5:18: I tell you the truth, until heaven and earth disappear, not the smallest letter [jot], not the least stroke of a pen [tittle], will by any means disappear from the Law until everything is accomplished. Jesus was talking specifically about the Scripture that referred to His mission and His life. But isn't that all of Scripture? Sometimes the smallest word or piece of a word makes all the difference in catching the meaning God intended. Such an inquiry into why God chose certain words, and what that means, should excite our curiosity and impassion our longing to learn more at His feet.

I am not the teacher, here; He is. And we have the privilege of rehearsing and discussing His Truth in His presence. This is the vision behind this book.

* * *

You have a part in this discussion. You can even email me at jhking@comcast.net if you wish. I await your feedback and comments.

Introduction

Studying the Bible is an adventure of sorts, a journey into discovering things about God and His view of things that shock and awe us. Many books have been written and sermons preached on its topics and themes, and perhaps a few believers have heard so many sermons and homilies that they feel confident and comfortable with their level of biblical knowledge. I don't challenge them or their knowledge. I can only speak for myself, which I have already done.

Ahead of us in this book is a look into the meanings and uses of words that a devotional reading, which is usually a quick and cursory reading—-admit it—might not uncover. We are blessed with many translations of the Bible, which is a testimony to this fact, because another translation is another attempt, and often successful, at explaining something not clear in a previous one.

All we are trying to do here is to take one step further into the biblical language itself. There's no reason to be afraid of this—as if the whole idea was intellectually too difficult to understand—because even children can grasp the Bible's message. We must not forget this.

Nor is the subject boring, as some might think. Only its presentation might be boring. You may have heard the line, "It is tragic when someone in Church can be bored by the greatest story ever told!" I hope that such is not true here.

I am reminded of Dorothy Sayer's comment in Creed or Chaos on the life of Christ which works for the Bible as a whole:

> The people who hanged Christ never, to do them justice,
> accused him of being a bore; on the contrary, they
> thought him too dynamic to be safe. It has been left for
> later generations to muffle up that shattering personality
> and surround him with an atmosphere of tedium. We
> have very efficiently pared the claws of the Lion of Judah,
> certified him "meek and mild," and recommended him as
> a fitting household pet for pale curates and pious old
> ladies. [1]

I agree. The Word of God is far from boring. It challenges us: how we live, what we say and think, and even our intentions and motives. It realizes our humanity, but beckons us to a higher calling, to be like Him, God, its Author. We cannot go deeper into the message of Scripture without realizing this. Boredom is often a rationalization—pardon me—for an "I don't care" or "I don't want to know" attitude.

This doesn't imply that if you do not read this book, you are less of a Christian or less of a lover of Truth than someone who does. I am not going there. But what I do hope is that as a lover of Truth, if you read on, you will discover something here worth remembering, something far from boring, and something that encourages you in your quest to know God and to always look deeper into His Word.

* * *

Someone once said that cleanliness is next to Godliness and that this saying is in the Bible. That must explain how the children of Israel in the wilderness could be so incorrigible. I think they went forty years without a bath.

In plain truth, this saying is not Scriptural. We do tend to see things in the Scriptures that are not in there. We filter everything we read through our limited understanding, and even get excited over something God supposedly said but really hadn't.

I do it, too. We all do. Bias and the limitation of our personal brand of logic will cause us to translate Bible verses in even weird ways. Some meanings approach the absurd, but because we are people of faith and believe in miracles, they make sense.

I am careful here not to treat you to weird interpretations from my friends' teachings, because that wouldn't be fair to them. But I will tell you one of mine. Once still a teenager, I preached a rather detailed sermon about the locust in Revelation 3:9, from the last book of the New Testament. I described these insects crawling all over the bodies of their living victims, trying to capture the disgust in that scene. But now I think the verse in question is symbolic. Chuck Smith calls these creatures demonic, but you'll have to study that on your own.

Well, there is only one cure for this intellectual malady. We must always remain teachable and willing to revisit a Scripture and its meaning. If someone disagrees with us, we have to set our insulted pride aside and focus on the excitement of perhaps getting a bit closer to the true meaning. If the debate proves fruitless, we can always stay with our current view of things, but we must stay open and hungry to learn.

It is here we begin to ask some very good questions—and all questions are good; no question is ever stupid. (I heard that once in school.)

Introduction

We may wonder why something, which we thought should be in a given verse, simply isn't. Why, for example, is humility not a fruit of the Spirit?

* * *

What might you find, then, in the following pages? I hope to offer you examples of thoughts hidden in the original words and grammar, thoughts just waiting for someone like us to come along and start asking questions. I hope to offer examples of Bible thoughts that reveal something about God's personal way of relating to people. Some of these thoughts may start out mysterious, which is to say, they do not immediately appear from a casual reading of the text. With some Scripture, you have to meditate for a moment before the light goes on as to its meaning.

Here are the chapters in this book.

What's in a Name looks at the sources of some of interesting, and over-looked, Bible names, an example where an otherwise obvious meaning is overlooked because of translation.

Apples and Oranges looks at how differently words are used here than in other works of literature.

Awakened from a Sound Sleep observes what appears to be a spike in our Lord's emotional response—taking a closer look at how He must have felt, by observing His reaction. Jesus' feelings are often hidden by a casual reading.

Impossible! challenges human logic. It is an example of the Salvation story that shows it couldn't have been man-dreamed.

Perfect! explores the meanings of certain words in their historical setting. Greek like any language is constantly evolving and simplifying. We observe it here and discover why God made it the language of choice for the New Testament.

Whose Fault Is It? looks at the theological meaning of Scripture, an example of Pauline verses Scribal interpretation that clarifies why he was so hated by Jewry in his day.

Jot That Down takes a look at words whose meaning can be radically changed, sometimes by removing or adding the smallest mark.

Sin? I'll Drink to That! delves into—with perhaps surprising results—what the Bible calls sin.

I Can't Say That in Greek shows how difficult it can be to say something in another language. What did Paul or Jesus do when they wanted to quote the Old Testament, the *Tanakh*, and they had to say it in Greek?

Thy Speech Bewrayeth Thee looks at Hebraisms or Semitisms—a kind of Hebrew written in Greek—in the New Testament. The New Testament writers were Jewish for the most part. (And yes, *bewrayeth* is an actual word in the King James Bible, meaning "to disclose or betray.")

I Can't Believe You Said That! takes a shocking passage at face value.

Let Me Underline That takes a close look at the use of emphasis in the original languages. The order of words in a sentence should not be over-looked.

A Particle Of Truth looks at exclamatory words, so-called particles of excitement, which may or may not translate into English. Every language has them.

And... And What! is controversial but worth a closer look. It is an example of the power of just one word.

December 21, 2012 is a brief look at a doctrine that consumed Christian thought for generations, before it was considered not important enough to discuss anymore. Go figure!

Sign Here, Please takes a look at words or phrases peculiar to one writer. Some words and expressions are clearly a signature of sorts.

Threads takes a look at the development of a biblical idea or truth. We might even call this a progressive revelation.

Psychological Insight takes the nine ministries and ties them to the nine gifts of the Spirit, suggesting an organized approach to ministry.

Soteriology is the study of Salvation. Here we examine the biblical words that detail the plan of salvation, by applying the discoveries of the previous chapters. Note that the Greek language, in and of itself, isn't sufficient to explain all.

I Want to Speak in Tongues takes a look at the failure of our human language to describe the gloriousness of a Heaven we joyfully anticipate.

* * *

Professor R. C. Trench in his work *On the Study of Words, Lectures* introduces a series of lectures on the importance of the study of language in the history of thought. He remarked, "...words often contain a witness for great moral truths—God having impressed such a seal of truth upon language, that men are continually uttering deeper things than they know..."

Any study of God, when it begins to humanize the Creator or explain God in terms we can begin to understand, risks oversimplify the intensity of God's feelings, the strength of His passion, and the genius of His thoughts. But it is a heart-pounding exercise for us, nonetheless, watching our God in action. And that's where I want to go.

What's in a Name

...you shall call his name Isaac -Genesis 17:19

Professor Richard Trench who is renown for his study of words, especially in the languages of Scripture, wrote:

> The significance of names... are—or ought to be—the
> utterance of the innermost character and qualities of the
> things which they designate... They are not arbitrary
> signs, affixed at random, for which any other might have
> been substituted as well... [For example:] Stephen... the
> name signifying 'the Crown' was taken as a prophetic
> intimation of the martyr-crown... given to him, the first in
> that noble army to wear.[1]

God's choice of names can be revealing. In Exodus 6:3, God says: I appeared to Abraham, to Isaac and to Jacob as God Almighty, but by my name the Lord I did not make myself known to them.[2]

In Exodus 3:14, we read: And God said unto Moses, I AM THAT I AM: and he said, Thus shalt thou say unto the children of Israel, I AM hath sent me unto you. (KJV) A footnote in the NIV on verse 15 then adds, "The Hebrew for LORD sounds like and may be derived from the Hebrew for I AM in verse 14."

I agree. In fact the difference between "I am" and "He is" is only one letter: the letter for "I" is replaced in the Hebrew word with the letter for "He." Is it possible that God said, "I AM has sent you," and Moses turned to Israel and said, "He said HE IS"? This is too simplistic, granted; besides, God shared His name with Moses, not the other way around. That is, Moses didn't call Him 'Lord' until God shared this revelation with Moses. Even so —as we know—His name *is* significant and reveals His character to us.

Look into the Genesis account of God's announcement to Abraham that Sarah would deliver a son in her old age.

In Genesis 17:16-19 we read: "I will bless her, and indeed I will give you a son by her..." Then Abraham fell on his face and laughed... in his heart [reasoning]... "will Sarah, who is ninety years old, bear a child?" ... But God said... "Sarah your wife will bear you a son, and you shall call his name Isaac..." (NASB)

Take note of the word *laugh* in this portion of Scripture. In the other eleven places where this word *laugh* is used in this form, it is in the sense of scorn or mocking derision. Is it possible that here, it is not a laugh showing Abraham's joy or excitement over the news but—and I'll be nice—perhaps an expression of disbelief in what God just said. Sometimes, we do try to filter God's words and promises through the sieve of our own logic, and the promise gets altered in some way.

This might seem far fetched to some who want to believe that even if Abraham had a momentary setback in faith, it was incidental to the overall strength of his convictions and faith in God. But we can still raise the question that the use of the word *laugh* suggests. Abraham may have initially rested his faith—as genuine as that was—on Ismael's birth. The scriptural account suggests that Abraham never thought his lineage would come through Sarah.

The name Isaac means "laughter." It is generally assumed that Isaac's name was given him by God because he, Isaac, was a cheerful, sporting personality type. We might say he was sanguine. His name could mean "sporting."

Or we might take his mother's suggestion, at Isaac's birth in Genesis 21:6: And Sarah said, God hath made me to laugh, so that all that hear will laugh with me. (KJV) Since this word *laugh* is the same Hebrew word, it appears that Sarah is putting a good spin on her reaction to the pregnancy. But I think God sees it differently. His observation is in Genesis 18:13: And THE LORD said unto Abraham, Wherefore did Sarah laugh, saying, Shall I of a surety bear a child, which am old? Sounds like Sarah's laugh is not in joy, but in disbelief. Well, you decide.

You might find it informative that in Psalms 105:9—and a few other places in the poetic books—the spelling of Isaac's name is a little different. His name is actually spelled *Itsaac*—note the 'ts'—in God's conversation with Abraham. But it goes to *Isaac*—with an 's' instead— in Psalms 105 and when written later in Hebrew poetry. This softens not just the pronunciation, but the meaning as well. This word "to laugh" in—say—Ecclesiastes 3:4 ("a time to laugh") means, simply, "laugh." In Job 29:24, it's even translated "smiled" (in the RSV).

We may want to soften the meaning of Isaac's name to Smiley, but this does not adequately consider the obvious flow of the context in which God first shocks Abraham with this—actually exciting—news.

"Oh yeah," Abraham mocked, laughing. "I'm a hundred, and Sarah's in her nineties. And now we're gonna have a baby. What else you got, God?"

"What else? You will name him, 'He laughed!'"

If we are reading this correctly, God chiseled the moment forever in

Abraham's mind, by giving Sarah's son a name that would constantly remind him of this meeting.

It isn't difficult to believe this is possible, since a God-given name was always significant. After all, God changed both Abraham's and Sarah's names. In Genesis 17:15, God gave her the name Sarah, meaning "princess." And Abraham, whose name means "father of a multitude," before Genesis 17:5, he used to be called "Abram."

It is easy for me to believe that God, who knows Abraham, would want to touch the mind of His servant, to encourage his faith, perhaps to guarantee that this memory would instill a permanent faith in God, whatever the direction God took him in. Abraham would never again challenge God's wisdom, no matter how miraculous it would sound. And he would have a son —"Isaac," because Abraham laughed when God foretold Isaac's birth— whose name constantly reminded him of this conviction.

When Isaac was about 15 years old, God tested Abraham by asking for his son in sacrifice. Is it possible that Isaac's very name brought back to Abraham memories of an earlier time, when Abraham questioned God's wisdom? His "laugh" revisited brought afresh a strong conviction that God could be trusted. It might be easier now for him to follow God's instruction, because he Abraham had learned so well the lesson, even if he could not begin to understand where this winding road of providential guidance would take him.

Did God name Isaac, "He mocked"? Is this a possible interpretation? Would God do such a thing to one of His followers, to someone who has been instinctively—in a sense, blindly—obeying His every instruction? When God told Abraham to leave his homeland, he left. And we read in the account no indication that he was reluctant. He did perhaps delay at the town of Haran, to allow his dear old dad, Terah, to enjoy his final days without a lot of moving about. The old man was over two hundred years old when he died. (That's a good son!) But Abraham did not question God's instruction.

* * *

Would God do something, or say something, to somehow make an indelible impression on our faith?

God needs to encourage our desire to trust Him. He needs at times the means to make His point and chisel it for all time on our heart. He wants to put the instruction in the forefront of our minds, and make it a principle by which we live, once and for all.

You want more Scripture, right? Good for you! After all, this idea of sticking Isaac—let alone his parents—with such a name sounds like God might have gone too far. Maybe Isaac had a kinder nickname, one that his school chums gave him. Yeah, fifth graders always do that kind of thing!

But maybe it wasn't so bad, because back then names used to reveal character. Sometimes children's names remind the grownups of some moment in life that they did not want to forget. But the kids didn't reflect in that same way on the name.

Probably no one cared why his friend was called what he was called. Caleb's name means "dog." Benjamin's dying mother wanted him called Benoni, "son of my sorrow." What if she had lived? Hosea in his frustrated love for Gomer., his wife, called his daughter Loruhamah, "no more mercy." Shouldn't she have had a pretty name like Grace or Hope or something? And his son he called Loammi, whose name meant "not my people."

"Not-My-People! No-More-Mercy! Come in! It's time for dinner!"

Can you picture it?

Jacob was "a deceiver." A *jacob* laid traps for people to trick them out of whatever he wanted, and God named him right!

Another example comes from 1 Chronicles 4:9: Jabez was more honorable than his brothers. His mother had named him Jabez, saying, "I gave birth to him in pain." According to the footnote in one Bible, "Jabez" sounds like the Hebrew for "pain."

I was reading through the genealogies in 1 Chronicles 7, a regular treasure-house of names. And I read in verse 23 that Ephraim's wife gave birth to a son. He named him Beriah, because there had been misfortune in his family. And again the footnote reads: *Beriah* sounds like the Hebrew for "misfortune." The dictionary says: "There was a calamity in Ephraim's house. That calamity was the death of his two brothers in war." What it means is that this little boy was called "Calamity," a memorial to the heroism of the two brothers he would never meet, at least in this life.

* * *

Is God a God of drastic means? Laying aside a flood or a Babylonian captivity, would God ever do something drastic to an individual to get his attention for all time?

What about Miriam, Moses' sister? In Numbers 12:1 we read: Then Miriam... spoke against Moses because of the Ethiopian woman whom he had married. (NKJV) Oh the danger of the gossiping tongue! Oh, Lord, do something quick before the political climate turns on Moses!

He did. In verse 10, Miriam became leprous, as white as snow. (NKJV)

Leprosy was a disease which at the time could be diagnosed—how-be-it sometimes confusing it with a simple skin allergy—but there was no cure. So it was called leprosy, which simply meant in the language of the day, "smitten by God." This also fit well with the theology of the day, If someone got this illness, they were being punished by God. He, in effect, slapped them.

When Moses prayed for his sister, in verse 13-14, God's response was: "If her father had but spit in her face, should she not be ashamed seven days?" (NKJV) God healed her a week later.

How memorable is that? She probably made a decision to support Moses on every and any decision he made going forward. You think?

I think it is theologically safe to say that for some issues God has silver bullets. Now and then, He will fire away. He decides if a matter requires a dead Ananias and Sapphira, or if He can let an Apostle James go to his martyrdom without hardly a word said. He decides, too, in our experience, whether or not He needs to step in and do or say something to promote a lasting impression. Other times, we think He should move fast, and He does seemingly nothing.

You can say what you want, but I personally put nothing beyond God, if it is an expression of His holiness and love. God's love can be gentle but determined.

Perhaps, in later years, Isaac could have redefined his own name among his public, to reflect his playfulness or his love for Rebekah. But I want to believe that for his dad, the meaning was tied to the moment he laughed at God. The sound of his son's name would remind him of his momentary reaction, in his amazement, to God's promise.

Isaac was a good name to him. It had no bitterness in its sound or meaning. It was always a gentle reminder that God's promises are worth hanging onto, with excitement and hopeful anticipation.

So, is a name given by God worth studying? Does it carry a special meaning and weight of importance? I leave the rest to your thoughts.

Revelation 3:12: Him who overcomes I will make a pillar in the temple of my God. Never again will he leave it. I will write on him the name of my God and the name of the city of my God, the new Jerusalem, which is coming down out of heaven from my God; and I will also write on him my new name.

Apples and Oranges

the fruit of the Spirit is love, joy, peace, long-suffering, gentleness, good-ness, faith, meekness, temperance -Galatians 5:22-23

The fruits of the Spirit, enumerated by Paul to the Galatians, offers us a glimpse into the true character of someone who is a living example of Christ. After all, these are not the fruit of men but of the Spirit of God. And I say that only because Paul said it.

A closer look at each fruit reveals its divine character. Each of these words, in Koine Greek (the Greek of the New Testament), has a meaning not used in the same manner in Classical Greek—if, in fact, the word was used at all. This might sound a bit uninteresting, until we realize the task God has in relating these aspects of Christian character through language that we can wrap our minds around.

Remember, these are not traits of a good man or woman. These are not the niceties of beautiful people. But the actual behavior anticipated by a child of God. These are clear proof, if you will, that the Spirit of God does live within them, and has in fact made an increasing impact on how they think and act. Make any sense?

Should we be a bit interested in what these fruits of the Spirit really are? Should we go a step beyond Merriam Webster—no derogatory remark intended—to see what God is trying to say? Let's.

The first fruit mentioned is *love*. The word *love* was introduced through Scripture. No Greek writer ever used the term as an idea tied to human action until the Scripture was written. There are other words such as *affection* or *friendliness* or—yes—*eroticism,* which could describe the human heart, but God needed another word to describe His own heart. In fact, God's love is hardly definable, but it is to some degree describable. We have often studied 1 Corinthians 13 in this regard. But more about this word later.

★ ★ ★

Joy according to John 15:11, is God-given. So we must be talking about something uniquely Christian. This word according to its origins has more in common with the word *grace* than *happiness*. In the context of grace, it is God's gift of meaningfulness, fulfillment, and purpose. It has been called the divine spark that excites and lights our way emotionally to live above hardship and setback.

Perhaps Peter's epistle is a good place to begin our search for its meaning. The comment given by Peter is somewhat poetic, if not simply an emotional outburst that has to be seen to be described. 1 Peter 1:8: ...filled [he blurted out] with an inexpressible and glorious joy. That's the New International Version, which is generally an interesting read, but here it left out the word *rejoice*, which means to leap for joy. The King James Version reads: Ye rejoice with joy unspeakable and full of glory. Inexpressible joy. Or said another way, words are inadequate to either describe it or to adequately express it when you are leaping on the inside.

It is difficult to say for sure what Paul had in mind by the fruit of "joy." Maybe he was referring to a deep sense of fulfillment and satisfaction in living the Christian life. Look up Luke 1:28: Hail, O favored one, [the angel speaking to Mary telling her that she has been chosen to mother the Savior of the world] the Lord is with you! (RSV) Or John 4:36: He who reaps... and [he who] is gathering fruit for life eternal... may rejoice together [over a fulfilling ministry]. (NASB)

To the Greek mind, the opposite of joy was regret. Think about it. This is a profound thought and at the same time full of psychological insight, to connect one's joy with one's sense of meaning in life. When you can answer the question, *Why am I here?* and you draw the satisfaction that you have reached that high calling; when you can say, "I know me, and that was me at my best"; when at last in old age you are able to look back on your life, without regret for the final outcome, but cherishing the memory of the adventure, well, then you may know what joy is. It is the Christian's contention that such a level of fulfillment and meaning is inextricably bound to what God intends for one's life. So there you have it.

It may be a deep sense of a believer's personal liberty in Christ. How about, say, Isaiah 51:11—Old Testament, yes, but it speaks of a future time, so it counts: The ransomed of the Lord will return. They will enter Zion with singing; everlasting joy will crown their heads. Gladness and joy will over-take them, and sorrow and sighing will flee away. It is almost self explanatory.

And it may describe the absence of fear, of dying, for example. Luke 10:20 is also a good verse: Rejoice, because your names are written in heaven. (KJV)

This may be as strange to the natural understanding as what Paul testified to in Romans 5:3-4: We also rejoice in our sufferings, because we know that suffering produces perseverance; perseverance, character; and character, hope. Can you relate to this?

Of course you can, as a believer in Christ. If you can sense that somehow God has used you, in some way, to help someone, anyone; if you can read His Word with a hunger to know it, and with a passion that finds you meditating on its text; if you burn with desire to meet again with another believer, to talk about it, and it spills out of your conversation at odd times, like a cup that overflows its contents... That is joy. At times, it may even bubble up over a sudden inspirational moment, when God's truth crashes in on your thoughts, and if you are not prone to too much free and unfettered self-expression, it may even frighten or embarrass you. If you get too excited over God and what He is doing in you, doing for you, and doing through you, get yourself to a ball field. Because there, they won't care if you shout a bit.

Just a thought.

* * *

Peace is not a strange word in Greek writings. What is worth noting is that, whatever the Bible means by *peace*, it is specifically a God-given quality. Let me toss a couple familiar verses your way.

John 14:27 quotes the Savior: My peace I give to you; not as the world gives do I give to you. (NASB) And in Philippians 4:7, Paul calls it the peace of God, which transcends all understanding. Wow!

This word means believers getting along, working together, having in common Christ and the life of faith He died to provide for us. It is harmony, not merely a truce. It is being in one accord, and working toward a common goal, or having a common interest in God's coming kingdom.

I know, I am rambling, but I am trying to suggest—as painful as it might be to accept—that this is a spirit of reconciliation and commitment to unity which comes with maturity. 1 Thessalonians 5:23: May God himself, the God of peace, sanctify you through and through.

I maintain that church infighting is a childish activity that denies the peace we are supposed to exhibit. It is about time somebody said it! Right? I do not believe that there is any such thing as righteous indignation among Christians toward Christians.

But I also maintain that the harmony Paul is talking about here, it can only come about because first we are at peace with God, and at peace within. This is fellowship, as God intended it to be, when He introduced the idea on Pentecost in that long-ago upper room, at the birth of His church.

If the turmoil of guilt has been calmed by forgiveness; if the nightmare of yesterday's mistakes, the traumatic hurts of the past, have somehow been reconciled; if you can somehow learn to hug again, learn to recognize kindness for what it really is, with no attached strings or hidden agenda; somehow, if you can learn to accept others and be accepted by them, this is peace!

* * *

Longsuffering is also a uniquely defined term, and it may help to say first what it is not. Longsuffering is not patience, as we picture it, say, singing a happy tune while waiting at a traffic light, or wearing a smile when you bump your head on an overhanging cabinet door (instead of daydreaming about taking it out with a sledge hammer and a few choice expletives). My son tells me this might be the word "forbear" or "tolerate" found in Romans 2:4. Here, Paul speaks of the riches of God's tolerance. I don't think God was upset with red traffic lights, but He was tolerating people and their sinfulness.

And how do we interpret 2 Timothy 2:24? The servant of God must be... patient. (NKJV) This word means patient of ills and wrong. It is a general term that might hate red lights but accept them as an unavoidable municipal mistake.

Longsuffering is not hanging in there under stress or pressure, instead of turning and running. That is another word, also translated "patience," not in our list here. Scholarship defines this "patience" as a bravery "with which the Christian contends against the various hindrances, persecutions and temptations that befall him."[1] Patience—distinguished from our word long-suffering—depicts a man who is unswerved from his deliberate purpose and loyalty to his faith. Luke 21:19: By your patience possess your souls. (NKJV) Or in the NIV, if you prefer: By standing firm you will gain life. Patience in circumstances, as Professor Lightfoot says, means not easily succumbing to suffering.[2] Again, though, this is not our word *longsuffering*.

Longsuffering is not staying on the job instead of quitting when the fun has gone out of it. The closest I can get to that idea is in 2 Thessalonians 3:11-12: We hear that some among you are idle. They are not busy... Such people we command and urge in the Lord Jesus Christ to settle down and earn the bread they eat.

Why study what longsuffering isn't? The simple truth is that we are prone to give our local culture's meaning to common terms like *patience* and *longsuffering*. We think we know what these words mean, from regular use, and inject those meanings into our interpretation of Scripture. We might be a nuance or so off the mark. Christians might feel that they are on track with God, because they don't curse the traffic light; they might have stress management down to a science, and confuse that with being spiritual. We hope here to point out the difference.

Longsuffering here, as a fruit of the Spirit, means patience with people. It is the opposite of outrage; it is being slow to anger. Not tolerating people; that's forbearance—another word and not in our current list. Longsuffering is a sustained peaceableness toward people who do not deserve such a warm welcome or verbal hug. It is the ability to keep the victory, instead of "losing it"—as Mom used to say from time to time, when we kids tried her patience.

A good look at longsuffering is found in Ephesians 4. The first three verses are one piece. Don't chop it up! I like the New King James Version which maintains a bit of the poetic flow of the text that we find in the King James: I, therefore, the prisoner of the Lord, beseech you to walk worthy of the calling with which you were called, with all lowliness and gentleness, with longsuffering, bearing with one another in love, endeavoring to keep the unity of the Spirit in the bond of peace.

I'm not preaching a sermon on this text, but I'll just make a note of the fact that it starts with lowliness or humility—not a fruit of the Spirit. So we can get there from here regardless of who we are. It might take a little hard luck, knocking us down a peg or two first, though I hope not. But then it proceeds through gentleness, which is a fruit of the Sprit, and ends up with love and peace—also fruits. This verse is a veritable fruit salad of Christian conduct, a walk worthy of the name we bear, Christ.

Bishop Lightfoot understood longsuffering to refer to "self-restraint which does not hastily retaliate a wrong."[3] Professor Trench says it is "holding out under provocation."[4] Yes, I went a bit further in suggesting that for believers this word denies any retaliation. "Vengeance is Mine," says the Lord. I read that somewhere in the Bible.

I have another confession to make. The two words *patience* and *longsuffering* are sometimes interchangeable in Scripture. So if you want to believe that the fruit of the Spirit, longsuffering, keeps you singing at red lights—a bit far-fetched—or that it means you will keep your current employment nonetheless, I can't deny you that grammatical right. I would ask you, however, to add the note that you are convinced this is the will of God concerning you. But it makes far more sense to me in the context of love and peace to understand this word as referring to people, and in particular to other Christians. Longsuffering, if correctly exhibited, provides a bit of heaven in our gatherings. This word has a meaning in the New Testament that was not found earlier.[5] It has been called "an attribute of God"[6] and rightly so since it is a fruit of His.

But wouldn't Aristotle have guessed all of this? Let's look. We can't actu-ally speak for our literary friend Aristotle. But in general, to glean from J. Horst, who contributed to a dictionary in my library edited by Gerhard Kittell, our word and its many forms—verb, noun, whatever—are latecomers to non-biblical Greek, and they are also rare. In one writing, *longsuffering*

14

means "resignation," and in another, it refers to leaving no stone unturned in trying to stave off the inevitable end. In a good sense, it is a physician treating a chronic illness with only a doubtful hope of recovery, or a soldier putting up with hardship, or swimmers in the sea seeking safety on the shore. And in one case, it means "persevering in one's task."

So the short of it is, I believe, that when God got a hold of this word, He breathed inspiration and life into it. He resurrected a word of little use in philosophical thought—and incidentally, of no use to the stoics—and made it a first-string team player in the believer's character.

If you want a real example of longsuffering, take a look at God in the Old Testament—in the *Tanakh*—in His relationship with Israel. Talk about suffering long and retaining your love for someone!

And talk about grace! "The wrath and the grace of God are the two poles", says Horst, "which constitute the span of His longsuffering." It reminds me of the words of the prophet Jeremiah, in Lamentations 3:22: It is of the Lord's mercies that we are not consumed, because his compassions fail not. (KJV)

Christians need to maintain the same level of commitment to the principle of God's love that He does. This trait or quality is from Him, and it can only be extended to others to the degree we allow Him do it through us! It is a fruit of the Spirit.

If forgiving comes easier for you than punishing; if seeking revenge or retaliation is hardly worth the daydream, because it just isn't your style; if blessing comes easier than cursing; and if you find it simply not in your nature to harm those who intentional and repeatedly and knowingly cause you pain, but conversely all you want to do is to love others as Christ would love them, that is longsuffering.

* * *

Gentleness is a word I wouldn't have guessed would be in this list. I might have guessed "zeal" or "jealousy for God and Truth." In devotional reading, Numbers 25:11 told of Phinehas, whose faith and zeal the Lord credited with saving many lives during His wrath. The Lord explained: He was zealous for my sake among them. (KJV) Well, this talk of "zeal for the right" is a fruit of the Spirit—not under the term *zeal*, but under the heading of "goodness," which we have yet to look at. For now, bear in mind that even when zeal swings a sword, it is the gentle spirit that is wielding the sword of the Lord, and we have yet to see how that goes together.

Gentleness is a certain mellowness of temperament or warmth about a Christian, whose words and deeds place a soothing balm on emotional pain and the injuries of the heartbroken. It is a sweetness. It is a nature without harshness or gall. This word is assuaging, softening, soothing, tension reducing. It is benignity, the cradling arms of a loving mother. It is kindness shown, and is in places coupled with words like mercy, love, humility of mind, and grace. And elsewhere in Scripture, as here, it belongs in a list that includes words like longsuffering and meekness. It's the opposite of severity, roughness, and sharpness in behavior, according to Romans 11:22.

The Greeks undeniably had a problem with this word *gentleness*. The only things that were gentle for he-men, who almost crave another war, is a good, aged wine and a woman. The word actually means, in the King-John vernacular—that's me—to be able to do as advertised. Gentle food is good food, not poison but nourishing, A gentle bee is a worker, not a drone. A gentle house is set in order, not disarray. A gentle end is a favorable outcome. A gentle offering is acceptable to God. You get the idea. *Gentle* means "useful." A gentle soldier is brave, and a gentle man is a worthy citizen. Well, on and on we can go but this hardly fits our word *gentleness* as a fruit of the Spirit.

Our word gentleness is more like "pleasant," as opposed to surly, "magnanimous," as opposed to ill-tempered and unfriendly.

Our word needed to be raised above the human condition, to a place much higher if it ever was going to keep company with the grace of God.

What did David mean, then, when he wrote in Psalm 119:39: Turn away my reproach which I fear: for thy judgments are good? (KJV) "Good" here is our word *gentle*, at least that's how the Greeks translated it. The original does say "good," but the translators felt *gentle* was the best Greek word to capture its meaning.

So what does this mean, that the Lord's judgments—NIV and others say, "ordinances" or "laws"—are "gentle"? I think David saw the Lord's laws as expressions of his kindness and forgiveness. Philo, a well-known Jewish philosopher from Alexandria, Egypt who lived during the time of the early apostles, felt that God was particularly kind and gentle when His discipline was reasonable, and when it lacked intense severity.[7]

Isaiah 61:1-3 says it best about our Lord:

The Spirit of the Sovereign Lord is on me, because the Lord has anointed me to preach good news to the poor. He has sent me to bind up the broken-hearted, to proclaim freedom for the captives and release from darkness for the prisoners, to proclaim the year of the Lord's favor and the day of vengeance of our God, to comfort all who mourn, and provide for those who grieve in Zion—to bestow on them a crown of beauty instead of ashes, the oil of gladness instead of mourning, and a garment of praise instead of a spirit of despair.

That's gentleness! His yoke is easy, or gentle, and His burden is light. That's grace.

If you change the first 'i' in *Christians* to an 'e,' it becomes *Chrestians,* which in Greek means "professors of gentleness." This is a play on words that early Christian literature used repeatedly—referring to Christians as "Chrestians," or professors of gentleness. How cool is that?

So what can we say?

If you are driven by a desire to be part of the solution and not the problem; if you want to be an instrument of God's grace instead of His vengeance; if you are prone to soft answers instead of harsh debate; if you would rather embrace the tearful than discipline the incorrigible (even if you have to do the latter on principle); if you have a cooperative spirit that wants more than anything else to work side by side with other Christians in a common vision to promote the Gospel message—be honest—that's gentleness.

⋆ ⋆ ⋆

Goodness is a word found only in the Bible and later church writings, so we do not need to ask the Greek philosophers what it means. The word is simply the word *good*, with the Greek equivalent of *-ness* attached to the end, which means "the quality or trait of being good," whatever that is. Professor Trench helps us out by saying that it refers to a zeal for truth. A very good example is Jesus' cleansing the temple in Matthew 21:12.

The King James text works for us here: And Jesus went into the temple of God, and cast out all them that sold and bought in the temple, and overthrew the tables of the moneychangers, and the seats of them that sold doves.

Paul referred to the Roman believers as being full of goodness, but that's not much to go on. Bishop Lightfoot referred to it as an active benevolence as an energetic principle.[8]

And in 2 Thessalonians 1:11, the King James talks about the good pleasure of his goodness. But since the word *his* is not actually there in the original, the NIV translates it: By his power he may fulfill every good purpose of yours. So whether it's God's goodness or your goodness from Him, Paul prays for its fulfillment, and that is our only clue as to what he meant.

I like Professor Grandmann's comment in Kittell's Dictionary, that it's "the Christian's radically new possibility of life."[9] However, let me take a stab at it, while leaving you the reader to capture its meaning in your own Christian experience.

If your actions demonstrate Christian love; if your responses to life's crises are tethered to an inner commitment to wait prayerfully on God for answers and direction; if hurting others in word or deed is not your forte, and seeing others in pain drives you to prayer, regardless of who they are to you; if you treat others as you want them to treat you; and if following in the steps of the Savior is your heart's passion; in short, if the principles and directives of God's Word are your standard for living, and if you are resolute about that, then that is goodness.

* * *

Faith is a term used by Christians in everyday speech, so I could probably shorten my comments here to a few words. No one should insult your know-ledge of this word or your intelligence, by trying to suggest an angle or perspective that you didn't think of already. Faith is a well-known concept. It is what makes a Christian a Christian. It is your trust that God rescues you from the consequences of your own sins and mistakes, and saves you from a few other things as well. It is probably strengthened by a personal history of "May Days," where God came through for you, and now you know what you know about His inevitable ability to get you out of tough scrapes, as well as your growing expectancy that He will. Well, that's faith. And we have a few examples, each of us do, which we call "testimonies," that are constant reminders of God's continuing involvement in our lives, His total truthful-ness to keep His word and His promise.

My only real point here is to remind us of Peter's comment in 2 Peter 1:1, that we have obtained *like precious faith... through the righteousness of God and our Saviour Jesus Christ.* (KJV) The NIV, I think, isn't as strong: *To those who through the righteousness of our God and Savior Jesus Christ have received a faith as precious as ours.*

I contend that Peter is reminding us that the faith you have is essentially the same as the faith I have. They are not two different things. They are not defined differently. And what is more, God gave each believer the faith that makes him a believer. We didn't invent it, or conjure it up, or produce it by some emotional or intellectual means.

Faith has two sides. It is active as a trust in God, and passive as a faithful-ness to God. The active side is predominant in the Old Testament. That is what Habakkuk 2:4 is saying: *See, he is puffed up; his desires are not upright —but the righteous will live by his faith.* The prophet reminds us that pride has an impossible time admitting any dependence on God's solutions, but those who trust Him are doing the right thing.

Faith is also faithfulness. Perhaps the clearest example is in the poetry of Psalm 89:37. The Psalmist refers to the moon, *the faithful witness in the sky.* Is there any fear that the next full moon will not appear? Is there fear that maybe tomorrow there will be no morning sun? God calls them faithful witnesses to His promises. We could argue scientifically that it might nova someday, but that is not relevant to God's point here. What we are saying is that if there is faith, there is faithfulness. If we trust God, we serve God. Nothing could be simpler to understand and yet so profound.

Just as a footnote to all of this consider a few interesting uses of the word *faithful* in the Old Testament. Depending on the context, it might be translated "sure" approaching the meaning, "guaranteed"; "established"; "confirmed"; "enduring"; "lasting" or "of long continuance"; and lastly "verified," which reminds us of Hebrews 11:1, which calls faith evidence.

If you are sure that God's Word was written for your instruction, even though it may be difficult to understand or follow; if you are sure of God's promises, that somehow they are—or many of them are—for your benefit; if you are convinced that God has rescued you from whatever, and will again should the situation arise; if you can look at that historical moment when Christ died on the hill outside Jerusalem, and somehow, in some way, you know He did that for you, so that your communion with a God—you now know—loves you could be restored; regardless of how things are going, or how circumstances are playing out, or how good or bad your fortune appears to be, if you are at peace, because you trust Him—God—to get involved and do something that will ultimately be to your benefit, well, that's faith.

* * *

Meekness has a simple meaning, and it is even recognizable in non-biblical writings. It represents a gentle disposition. One Greek author, named Theophylact, referring to this fruit of the Spirit, commented, "meekness forgives everyone of everything."[10] Some say it's a synonym for being quiet or peaceable. But Professor Richard Trench distinguishes meekness from quietness, by pointing out that the meek man is never agitated or disturbed, whereas the quiet or silent man, though quite disturbed, endures in silence.[11] After comparing the secular meaning or virtue of this "grace" with its higher calling in the New Testament, he added that one has to "feel that revelation has given to these words [*meekness* and *meek*] a depth, a richness, a fullness of significance which they were very far from possessing before."[12] Meekness is quietness of spirit. It is a tranquility on the inside that becomes evident in speech and action. It is more spontaneous and natural than just grinning and bearing someone's alleged abusiveness.

If we compare meekness and humility, which is a recognition of one's utter dependence on God, we can quote Trench again: Meekness "is the inwrought grace of the soul; and the exercises of it are first and chiefly toward God... It is that temper of spirit in which we accept His dealings with us as good, and therefore without disputing or resisting, and it is closely linked with [humility], and follows directly upon it... because it is only the humble heart which is also the meek; and which, as such, does not fight against God, and more or less struggle and contend with Him."[13]

I have no trouble believing that meek persons will not be quick-tempered, so it goes hand-in-glove with temperance, a word we have yet to look at. But meekness also suggests a soul at peace, and that sounds like the fruit of peace, which we did look at. But these two ideas are siblings from the same parent, love. They have the same spiritual DNA, if you will, that identifies them in the same family of traits, coming from the same divine source.

Meekness is also a synonym of the word *gentleness,* found in Paul's second letter to the Corinthian church, where he refers in 2 Corinthians 10:1 to the meekness and gentleness of Christ.

Let's first look at *gentleness* as a synonym of *meekness*. The word *gentleness* in this verse in 2 Corinthians means "sweet reasonableness," and in a sense is a meek spirit, but—and this is hugely important to note—of a superior toward an inferior, a boss toward a worker, a master toward a slave, a parent toward their child. Makes sense. The one with the power needs to be reasonable and sweet, not the one who is under their authority.

This word for "sweet reasonableness" didn't make the list of the fruits of the Spirit, although it came close, being linked to meekness. Unlike gentleness, with meekness there is no hint of "rank" or social status in Christian relationship. Meekness applies to relationships with no reference to rank or status. It works best among equals. Gentleness or "sweet reasonableness" means that the person in power must not be pushing their authority around or lording it over those who are under them. Standing up for and pressing to get the last tittle of legal rights is the privilege of superiors, but it isn't Christian. Sometimes in the spirit of grace and mercy, if it is our privilege to make the decision, we forego the literal meaning of the law and honor those who are under our authority, by honoring their suggestions and their input. Sometimes it is better not to seek our rights over our relationships. Does that make any sense?

The pattern of sweet reasonableness is found in God. God backed off from exacting His rights against man, His creation, who tormented Him with a cultic devotion to idols. Old Israel tempted God's infinite grace with countless excursions into heathen practices, including the sacrifice of their own children, as unbelievable as that may sound.

What did God do? He did not require the last tittle of His divine right to their worship. If He had, who could have argued their defense in His court? He punished them, yes, but ultimately He punished Himself, in the person of

Christ, to satisfy the requirement of His offended holiness.

If God were unreasonable, He would have no cause to be merciful. And perhaps He might even have chucked the whole idea of man on this planet and headed off in another pursuit. Is not this the message behind Matthew 18:27? In the parable of the servant who owed his master 10,000 talents, probably silver talents—so that would be millions of today's dollars—the master took pity on his servant, canceled the debt, and let him go scot-free.

So Jesus taught—read verse 35—that we should forgive. I suppose we can ask for borrowed money back—that's not the point, as well we know already. But we are indebted to God for the terrible things we have done to Him, and to one another for the terrible things we have done to each other, over our lifetime, in our at-times ruthless exercise of being right.

But meekness is a little different. Meekness is a disposition to obedience and, in particular, to obey God. There is in meekness an intentional desire to follow Christ; given opportunity, the one possessing it proceeds with spontaneous abandonment to His will. It becomes a natural interest of the meek to serve the higher cause of God, when they know what that higher cause is. Either through insight into His Word, or simply by the peaceful acceptance of who they are, they are in love with Him and want to follow Him. This comment would make a good "if" at the end of this section.

But first, I am hoping to pin down its meaning in a way that shows why the Greek playwright or philosopher would never have preached this sermon.

The Greeks knew *meekness* to refer to a mild temperament, easily appeased. A softy. In one writing, referring to a sore that had been "appeased," the word meant "soothed," perhaps by some ointment.[14] So how could I say that this word is special? How does a word that has such a basic meaning and is used all over the place, of persons who are easy to get along with, how is this word special enough to be listed here as a godly attribute?

To make the question stand out even more, consider the opposite of meekness, that is, downright wild in spirit, quick-tempered, selfish enough to go after everything one feels he deserves, regardless of the expense to others. A meek animal is tame, and some people need to be kept on a leash, if you get my drift.

What is Paul trying to tell us about this word that makes it stand out as something that particularly should ID a Christian?

I could give up the quest at this point trying to figure it all out since our Professor Trench says, "We have no words in English which are full equivalents of the Greek."[15] But I want to say something to support my original idea that the fruit of meekness is special, and that it is from the Spirit of God.

I think what defines it here in Galatians is the fact that it so readily lends itself to a spirit of obedience to *God's* will. The spirit of meekness is seen in Psalm 37:4: Delight yourself in the Lord. Here, the word *delight* means "to be happy about or take exquisite delight in someone." For a woman—take no offense ladies, please—it is the word *coquettish,* the amorous gestures in looks and walk that girls show when around a guy they like. Is not this when the young lady feels right at home waiting on the beau of her choice? She would do anything for him if she could.

Maybe I am off base in my insight about women, but not about a believer who is crazy, as it were, about the Lord.

So if you find it most natural to follow the instructions in God's word, as you understand they apply to you; if you find yourself wanting to want to obey God, and any struggle is because temptation is so real and not because you have given up on wanting to follow Him; if you find yourself wanting to forgive, and even when you confuse forgiveness and forgetting—which happens—you would rather be reconciled than to be estranged from other believers; if you find yourself wanting reconciliation, and you are tired of church-hopping, as they call it; if heaven means fellowship with other believers, as much as it means sitting under your favorite oak or pine—whatever—listening to Jesus talk; if you would readily give anything to follow the Lord's will, providing it is crystal clear to you, even if it means giving up fame, fortune, family, even health, that's meekness.

* * *

Temperance means self-control, and as such is as common as the air we breathe. But—stretching this analogy—it is just as vital to our survival, spiritually speaking. Moulton, whom I mention in the appendix, calls this trait "moral strength."[16]

Aristotle viewed this virtue as a control over pleasure. That might be worth mentioning to the teens. Self-control doesn't mean no fun, just fun in moderation. Fun that satisfies, not fun that becomes addictive. In his writings on ethics, he asked the question, "When water chokes you, what do you take to wash it down?"[17]

The difference between satisfaction and addiction is that with addiction, the person is controlled by the pleasure, and in that case no satisfaction is possible, since the addiction grows and keeps the satisfying feeling always out of reach, like a carrot on a stick hanging a foot in front of a walking jackass.

Am I getting rude?

Sorry about that. But satisfaction is possible only when the person controls the pleasure and administers it in reasonable—ethically and morally reasonable—doses, to an otherwise dull and stressful existence. Make sense?

John Milton's *Paradise Lost* (book 4, lines 325-340) describes the bliss of the first couple, and it does show why Eden—which means "pleasure" in Hebrew—is Eden.

> Under a tuft of shade that on a green [325]
> Stood whispering soft, by a fresh Fountain side
> They sat them down, and after no more toil
> Of thir sweet Gardning labour then suffic'd
> To recommend coole Zephyr, and made ease
> More easie, wholsom thirst and appetite [330]
> More grateful, to thir Supper Fruits they fell,
> Nectarine Fruits which the compliant boughes
> Yielded them, side-long as they sat recline
> On the soft downie Bank damaskt with flours:
> The savourie pulp they chew, and in the rinde [335]
> Still as they thirsted scoop the brimming stream;
> Nor gentle purpose, nor endearing smiles
> Wanted, nor youthful dalliance as beseems
> Fair couple, linkt in happie nuptial League,
> Alone as they. About them frisking playd [340]

Before sin, Adam and Eve didn't need to fear pleasure or think in terms of self-control. It was all natural. They would engage in whatever pleased them, whatever appetite hungered. And once satisfied, they would stop, until within the reasonableness of time, in a sinless world, they would hunger again. Forbidden fruit-eating ended that, and I would have had a few choice words for Adam, except Paul made me see that it was his humanness, something I share with him, that came to sin. In Adam, I myself somehow took a bite. I know that isn't clear, theologically speaking, but you'll need to ask a minister for an explanation, because this subject is not about that.

It is about self-control. It is about subduing one's thoughts.

Paul, according to Luke, presented the message of truth to Felix, then-governor in Judea, when he spoke to the governor about righteousness and judgement to come. And in between these topics, he mentioned self-control. I would not have thought to go there in my dialog with a political leader, not because I would fear offense—the Gospel itself takes care of that—but because I would have his ear for so short a time. I would want to highlight the Gospel message before he sentenced me. But temperance was important to Paul in his conversation with Felix, and I have always wondered a bit, *Why?* In the language of Judaic teaching, self-control means containing one's feelings, affections, grief, anger. You get the idea. Maybe Paul wanted Felix to do what the governor knew in his gut was right—not listen to the mob—and release him.

Temperance is a divine fruit. It comes from God and distinguishes the believer in some sense. In what sense is that? If I could be so bold as to venture a guess... Maybe it isn't a guess so much as an opinion...

But hopefully you won't buy that. You need to come up with some answers yourself in prayerful meditation on God's Word. I can offer some insight, perhaps. But the final answer—as the quiz show tells us—is yours to make.

This is my final answer here. I think Christians are—or maybe "should be"—led by a higher calling, an eternal plan, the vision of becoming more and more like Christ, as Paul says it in Romans 8:28-29, conforming to His image according to His purpose. This should decide which pleasures get fed and when. This should guide our interest in things and passions. This should help us put a value on all of our feelings and decide which get vented, if at all, and when.

I don't subscribe to scream therapy, and I am no therapist. I do not think control means holding back or suppressing anything. I think self-control, which says time to love not hate, time to embrace not push away, is expressing natural feelings in the right proportion and at the correct time and place. Some Christians maintain that this is an application of grace, and I cannot disagree.

Still, I maintain that as believers, we are blessed to have the word of God to give us insight into the new person we are becoming in Christ, and that insight means recognizing the gift of moderation, moderation over very natural feelings and passions.

Christians do not cease to be human when they get saved. They don't become stoics, or turn against pleasure, as thought it were a hedonistic impulse that must be destroyed. You don't cease to love caressing your life-partner, now that you are a believer. And if you imagine that all Christians do for fun is pray and read the Bible, think again.

All things in moderation is the thought here. It is pleasure with a divine touch. We were made for Eden, is how I read Genesis. *Eden* means "pleasure," and there was nothing painful about the life our first parents lived before the fall. Christians can find a life full of clean fun and still enjoy their Christianity. Nothing is more natural. But true, fulfilling, satisfying enjoyment is always and only pleasure in moderation, reasonable doses of good times. God's people should be able to return to Eden, or at least find the road that leads back. To me, it is walking with my bride among fragrant flowers and all sorts of delicious eatables. To you, it might be something different, but be careful not to condemn a biblically legitimate impulse that simply wants a vacation.

Peter speaks highly of temperance in his second epistle. In 2 Peter 1:6, we are told to diligently add self-control to our knowledge; and perseverance to our self-control. He sandwiched temperance in between knowledge and perseverance, and if you think about it, it is the perfect place to mention this godly trait. In plain English: first, know what you should and shouldn't do, and then decide to do it the right way. Exercise the necessary control over your feelings to do what is right, and then after doing it once, make this a habit for life. Persevere!

What Peter didn't say in this one verse, but I believe needs to be emphasized, is that this control means exercising our right to deny temptation. It means exercising our privilege to freely cooperate with whatever God is doing in us. Once we become a living example of Romans 12, which has been referred to as "the secret to living the Christian life," we can look back over the years of our spiritual education and thank our teacher, temperance, for every instruction it barked at us, every scolding, and every encouraging feeling it engendered.

If you say "No!" to temptation, not because someone said you should, but because that is what you want to say; if you find it easier and easier—-granted, over time—to do the right thing, and the temptations of the past are becoming a distant and fading memory, not because you are getting older, but because you are getting closer to God and His word; if you find yourself refraining from reacting to things or situations that once drove you to rage and again, not because you've resigned to give up trying, but because it just isn't your nature anymore to yell and throw tantrums; if (on the positive side) you still find pleasure in life, you still eat potato chips, but not the whole bag at once; if you still love your spouse, more than ever, in every sense; if you enjoy life and its simple pleasures, and if they tend to draw you closer to God; if guilt is less and less an issue in your life; that's temperance.

* * *

Love sums up everything one might say about the fruit of the Spirit. It has been said that these eight fruits are the real definition of the first one—love. I tend to agree.

C.S. Lewis wrote a book called *The Four Loves*: eroticism, friendship, natural affection, and *agápê* or God's love, which is our word *love* here in this chapter and in Galatians 5.

God is love. This elevates the definition of this type of love to a place outside our language, and yet we need a word to at least say it. Lewis refers to this love as "divine energy." He also defines it as a giving love, that is, a

25

love that needs nothing but offers everything.

In Lewis' words:

> The primal love is Gift-love. In God there is no hunger
> that needs to be filled, only plenteousness that desires to
> give. The doctrine that God was under no necessity to
> create is not a piece of dry scholastic speculation. It is
> essential. ... God, Who needs nothing, loves into existence
> wholly superfluous creatures in order that He may love
> and perfect them. ...Divine Gift-love—Love Himself
> working in man—is wholly disinterested [unselfish] and
> desires simply what is best for the beloved [you and
> me] ...Divine Love in a man enables him to love what is
> naturally unloveable; lepers, criminals, enemies,
> morons,the sulky, the superior, and the sneering.[18]

Lewis goes on to link such love to grace which must make sense to a believer.

So we may glean love's "if's" from the other eight sets of "if's": if you can sense that somehow God has used you in some way to help someone, and it was a disinterested act on your part, no "thank you" necessary or sought; somehow, if you can learn to accept others, simply because they are God's children, and to give no negative value to the differences that otherwise would separate you; if forgiving comes easier for you than punishing, and blessing, easier than cursing; if you are driven by a desire to be part of the solution, and not the problem; if you want to be an instrument of God's grace, instead of His vengeance; if hurting others in word or deed is not your forte, and seeing others in pain drives you to prayer, regardless of who they are to you; if you can look on the cross of Christ and see the love of God; if you find yourself wanting to forgive, and you would rather be reconciled than estranged from other believers; if you find yourself refraining from reacting to things or situations that once drove you to rage, because it just isn't your nature anymore; if guilt is less and less an issue in your life, that's love, gift-love, God's love. Or put simply, that's God.

The reality of salvation as provided by and through Christ is recognizable in these nine fruits of the Spirit. That is why they are part of our character. That is why Paul listed them here, to clarify to us that salvation is not a religion or a philosophy, but a genuine manifestation of God at work. Salvation and Christ make a difference, which is best described as "newness of life" or "the born-again experience." The Bible message offered in the fruit of the Spirit is not a random list of good ideas, or of characteristics of especially good people. In fact some of God's people struggle with these nine, because they have not realized yet that living them means the freedom to be who they are. They have not discovered yet the fuller benefit of God's salvation.

Nonetheless, it is a discovery worth pursuing. It is a message of His love worth realizing. It is worth going beyond the sermon and beyond the theology, and learning God, who He is, and how He moves among us, by learning that these nine fruits of the Spirit are His way. They are God at work in and among us.

The best witness Christians could possible show are these nine. I call them the nine ways God has to say "I love you" to a spiritually dying world.

* * *

Perhaps you noticed a certain degree of difficulty defining the fruit of the Spirit. Not only can we say that the other eight sum of the first, love. But also, we can see overlapping among the eight as well. It is like a rainbow effect, where one color blends or washes into the next, and yet they are somehow distinct.

We might also agree that where one is visible in someone's life, all are, that it is not possible to live part of them perfectly, unless we live all of them perfectly, and I think no one other than Jesus did that.

We can also promote the idea that one fruit supports the next. Learning to live one encourages living the next and the next.

And no matter how you categorize them, they are all relational. They all deal with our dealings with others, with God, and even with ourselves. That's the primary reason why I didn't think the traffic light important.

And they are spiritual. They define godliness and holiness. They are inspired behavior, virtuous thinking, and holy living.

This is the whole point in this chapter: that the nine fruit of the Spirit are in fact fruit of the Spirit. These are special traits or characteristics that persons who do not love the Lord cannot claim in their psychological makeup.

Terms like *humility* and *zeal* and *patience* (in stressful circumstances) and *forbearance*, to name a few, are missing from the fruit of the Spirit. It is not because they are not good things to have. They are. But these are human conditions and can be produced in anyone's experience, if the circumstances are right. Or should I say, "wrong," because it is the unwelcome or undesirable experiences in life that better us as human beings. There are a boatload of ideas we can tie to the human condition, and many of them have a good side. Many of them indicate healthy behavior and a good life. But I maintain, Paul singles out nine which distinguish the child of God as a child of God.

Awakened from a Sound Sleep

Peace, be still -Mark 4:39

No two words of Scripture seemed so at odds or disjoined as these two words spoken by Jesus during a Galilean storm. In Greek they are just two words: "peace," and "be still." And although their meanings may be somewhat similar, their use represents feelings that no one should expect to hear spoken in the same breath.

And yet once we learn something about these two words—and I am tempted to simply teach you the Greek words; why translate them?—we can begin to question Jesus' use of them. This one moment at sea is more dynamic than might appear by the translation.

The word "peace" in Greek is *siópa*, pronounced " ' sço.pa."

The word "be still" is *pefímoso*, pronounced "pe. ' fi.mo.so."

Here's the thing about these words. The first word, *siópa*, is used at the dinner table to minimize the children's chatter while the adults want to eat in peace. It is a very gentle term similar to our word *hush*. It is found a few times in Scripture, meaning "hold your peace." It is intended to alert someone that the speaker would be interested in a little less noise, but it carries no warning or threat. It doesn't even require an immediate response, when used as it is here. It seems to more envision the hope that some positive silence will follow, and maybe soon. It is a nice word. You should use it the next time the kids are too noisy and you just want to alert them to your interest in some peace and quiet, but you are doing it with a smile.

The second term, *pefímoso*, is a strong word, filled with emotion and determination. It is demanding, and requires immediate action. The term is so emphatic that this word in this form, with the *pe-* on the front of it, is not used elsewhere in the Bible, and for that matter nowhere in Greek literature that I could find.

The form usually represents action that is immediate, complete, and permanent. I think it is safe to say that we do not have a corresponding form in English. What is also interesting here is the fact that this form is used in a command. So we have a command that is to be executed immediately and completely, with results that are said to be permanent. Actually, these three qualifying terms make good modifiers. So because—say—in Acts 5:28, the

Apostles are accused of having filled Jerusalem with [their] teaching, we could translate: "You have *completely* filled Jerusalem with your teaching." Logically, since Jesus' death and resurrection was the talk of the town, we could also use the word "immediately" to describe it, because it isn't a fear that it might happen; it has happened. And I wonder if there isn't a hint of deep concern that this religion, later called Christianity, wasn't about to go away, that the rumors of a Jewish Messiah, which the religious leaders were probably troubled about, would not die down, but would have a permanent impact on the minds and hearts of many who heard. Well, they were perfectly right about that.

Let me try to paint a verbal picture for you. If I see the door left open and want it closed, but if I am only asking if you could give it a nudge closed, I would use the form of the first word, and ask if you could close the door. You almost can hear me say "please," even if I don't say it.

But maybe you forget, or simply ignore me, so I get emotional and a bit demanding. Maybe I am tired of this door being kept open time and time again, and I have had enough of the draft it lets in. So I yell, using the second form, "Shut the door, **NOW**. Latch it, completely closed. Lock it if you must. I don't ever want to see it open again. Got it?!"

What a grumpy grouch!

In Jesus' case He went from requesting the wind to begin to cease, all the way to "I want the sea like glass—**NOW!** That's it! Enough is enough!" The storm was over, and a state of utter calm followed. You could almost hear the gulls chattering.

Why the emotional leap? Why go from "hush" to, as some translate it, "muzzle your mouth"? Do you think Jesus took a moment to rub His eyes and wake up fully, before He realized the situation, and His first remark was made half-asleep, but when He fully composed Himself and realized that the storm had disturbed His needed rest, He blew up at it?

Neither do I.

Let's see if we can get some answers from a few scholar types.

Chuck Smith remarked: "Tremendous power!" And then added on the next verse:

> First He rebuked the wind and the waves, and then He
> rebuked the disciples. He rebuked them for having no
> faith. Why would He do that? The ship was full of water;
> it looked like it was going to sink. Why would He rebuke
> them for not having faith? Because you go back to the
> beginning, what He first said, "Let us pass over unto the
> other side." He didn't say, "Let's go under." He said, "Let

29

us pass over to the other side." And when Jesus said, "Let us pass over to the other side," there's no way they could go under. You see, this is God speaking, and God's Word must come to pass. And that's why He rebuked them; for little faith. Because they had His word that they were going to go over to the other side.[1]

I enjoy his comments but they don't address my question.

But listen to Matthew Henry now:

The word of command with which Christ rebuked the storm, we have here, and had not in Matthew, v. 39. He says, *Peace, be still*—**Siopa, pephimoso**—*be silent, be dumb.* Let not the wind any longer roar, nor the sea rage. Thus he *stills the noise of the sea, the noise of her waves;* a particular emphasis is laid upon the noisiness of them, Ps 65:7 and 93:3, 4. The noise is threatening and terrifying; let us hear no more of it.[2]

If I read Henry right, he is applying the word *peace* to the wind, or more precisely the noise, and the word *muzzle* to the waves. This isn't bad! These words were important to him, and since he was a prolific writer, he took the space and ink to say something. This doesn't belittle Chuck Smith's thought, or for that matter, anyone's. I am just looking for a little discussion around these two words, and since they are Scripture, and we maintain they are inspired, I get excited over such a use of language.

Don't you?

If we look at Matthew's account of the storm, Jesus mildly reprimands the disciples first, before addressing the sea or the wind. Actually, the Scripture simply narrates that He spoke to them. It is what He said, "Oh you of little faith!" that led Chuck Smith and others to use the words *reprimand* and *rebuke.*

Johann Bengel—I am reaching back here into the 17th century—taught that the Lord rebuked the storm in the heart first, "peace," and then the storm in nature, "be still." Dr. J.J. Oosterzee, who wrote for Dr. John Lange's Commentary on Luke, was led to conclude as much, and we can agree because it brings out the dynamic meaning of both terms.[3]

It makes sense to me to picture Jesus rising from sleep, sizing up the situation, and then first looking to the disciples with sensitivity, and yet stern instruction, whispering into their huddled trembling circle, "Shush." Then with raised and demanding voice, yelling toward the waves, "Muzzle it!"

Jesus is the master of the inner storm, which I think is more to the point of Matthew's story. There is no conflict between Matthew and Mark, although in Mark's record, it appears that the Lord spoke first to the sea and then to the disciples. Putting both recollections together, Jesus simply could have repeated His lesson in faith to the disciples, before and after rebuking the sea. He might have said it twice. Either that or Matthew, who has repeatedly shown his individuality, was reminded primarily of Jesus' masterly way of calming the storm inside of him.

To be accurate, Matthew was most likely not in the boat at this time, but there would be another boat and another storm later for him.

I want to place a footnote here about Matthew. The account of his calling was recorded by Luke, in Luke 5:27. But Luke doesn't relate the story the way Matthew does in his own gospel—Matthew 9:9-13. Matthew adds our Lord's conversation with certain scribes, who objected to Jesus choosing him as a disciple. He remembers Jesus saying with authority in verse 13, "I will have mercy..." Matthew's gospel account is not just history, it is his own personal history, and we see this reflected from time to time in his writing. This is how it is easy to reconcile Mark's account of the storm with Matthew's. Matthew's individual style comes through, as he recalls the warmer moments of his journey with the Savior.

What I didn't expect to read was, according to Mark, Jesus said, "Peace," to the sea. This doesn't seem to fit our interpretation. I wish He would have spoken that soft word to a group of frightened men, which says what we want to hear. But we surrender to the text. So how is this word "hush" to be addressed to six-foot swells? Did He tell the wind, which was no doubt very noisy, to hush up? That's what Matthew Henry and others believe.[4]

I interpret this to mean that Jesus did say "Quiet!" to the sea, and He would have been perfectly content to see the violence of the storm gradually subside. But after noticing His disciples, and how the least disturbance suggested danger to them, He reached a point where He wanted instant peace. Then they would also be at rest.

If this is so, it suggests that Jesus allowed a pause to separate the two statements, in order to emphasize their need for faith. He was saying in the pause, "Let's test the strength of your faith." This isn't cruel. It is a touch of reality, for Christians to experience the pause between their prayer and the answer. We need to learn to stop trembling, because we prayed, not because we have answers. One of my daughters-in-law put it this way, "as if He says 'Hush' to our inner storms for a time, and we must wait in faith for Him to say, 'Hush up!'"

1 John 5:14-15: This is the confidence we have in approaching God: that if we ask anything according to his will, he hears us. And if we know that he hears us—whatever we ask—we know that we have what we asked of him.

31

The thing to note here is Jesus' ability to separate His feelings, and direct His comments in an appropriate manner to the proper listener. I don't believe He yelled at His disciples, "Faithless idiots!" although *I* might have. And as far as the waves might have disturbed my sleep, I might have yelled a few choice words their way before slapping them back down into the sea. But Jesus never lost it. He never lost focus. In fact, the word *rebuke* can refer to anything from a mild admonishment to a sharp rebuke or charge. Regardless, Jesus did not rebuke His disciples, not in that sense. He spoke to them. He questioned them about their faith. And He did that because it was all part of today's lesson. In fact, I think this whole episode was a lesson in faith, and as we know, it was a vital part of their education as future apostles.

Jesus never spoke out of turn. He always remembered not only where He was, but also who He was with and who He was speaking to. He has always known how to address His disciples. He knows what to say and when to say it, and He says it passionately—even now, to us, through His Word.

The lesson for us here is from time to time to take our focus off the storm and listen carefully to Him say, "Hush." That's for us. And then watch Him in action, turning to whatever it was that was wearing on our faith, or driving us to such worry and fear. Psalm 46:10: Be still and know that I am God.

A short time later in the story of their developing faith, the disciples would find themselves again on the stormy Sea of Galilee, without the Master. This time, Peter ventured out of the boat when Jesus walked up. Peter was learning, sinking into the sea, yes, but he was briefly standing outside the boat. That says volumes to me about a man who wants to learn to trust, and is willing to step out into the unknown as long as he can see the Master, through the mist and darkness.

There are storms and then there are *storms*.

Listen to the Savior. *Siópa!*

Impossible!

Who, being in the form of God, ... and took upon him the form of a servant, and was made in the likeness of men: And being found in fashion as a man, he humbled himself, and became obedient unto death -Philippians 2:6-8

Christian thought is fragmented because of differing views and interpretations, but we should spend more time on our common belief, which is my topic here: "What happened at Calvary?" Or, "The day Christ died." I entitle this chapter, "Impossible!" looking at Calvary through the natural mind, because the natural way of thinking finds it impossible for such an event to occur, followed by an even more incredible resurrection of our Savior. Our logic is incomplete when it comes to figuring out God's plan for our salvation, and this is no surprise, because it tells us that God, without our help, had to think up the plan after Adam—and all of us—blew the Garden-of-Eden chance at perfection.

It is because of the difficulty of guessing what God would do that it became necessary to accept at "faith" value—if I may say it that way—what the Bible tells us about God's activity on our behalf. One commentator, perhaps exasperated by countless opinions and debates over truth, blurted out, most memorably, "Let's surrender to the text!"

Let's. And to me, surrendering means focusing solely on what is, according to one grammarian, written simply, clearly, and emphatically, as the underlying or overriding message of the Scriptures. You get the point. This is—yes, plainly, simply, and emphatically—the message of Calvary.

Let's always remain hungry to know God, to look more closely at Golgotha, to stare up at the Cross, and ponder what might be happening. Let's remain passionate about learning truth that, by definition, we know we don't know yet, at least not as completely and with depth of understanding as we should and ultimately want to know it. Did I say that clearly?

I knelt once at an altar, a high schooler with a backward and somewhat withdrawn personality, when I found myself face to face with Davey Wilkerson. Many know of Davey as the one God used to start Teen Challenge. He was the visiting preacher that evening at church. Less than a foot from me, nose to nose, he asked me if I read my Bible. I sheepishly stumbled out a "yes," at which he replied, "Not as much as you should."

I have never forgotten that admonition, "Not as much as you should." I think this is the heart of every believer, to go a little deeper, a little further into the message of Scripture. We need to say that up until now, we have not read or studied or followed the Bible as much as we should. When someone says this to us, it can be offensive. But when we say it to ourselves, it becomes a desire to focus on, opening us up to the message of Scripture. As the belief goes, the blood line is the red thread that links the entire text together! It is Calvary that should be the sole proclamation of the preacher. No argument here, but we have only begun to meditate on this miraculous and unfathomable dogma—as Dorothy Sayers calls it.[1] The whole pattern for our behavior, the entire conduct of our life and the essence of our faith as Christians is embodied in what happened on that Cross, on that day, at the turn of history.

This is why I keep referring to my desire to know, and that my knowledge of Scripture lacks the depth of understanding I wish it had.

What happened the day Jesus died? I have a comment or two, but I need your heart to debate it and challenge it. If it just sets well in your spirit. your heart can confirm that I am on to something.

It is with this in mind that I want to revisit a familiar text, where Paul shocks our logical sensibilities, by giving God credit for doing three things, which according to the ancient Greek philosopher were impossible. I think we need to reevaluate the benefit of our powers of reason when our understanding is limited. When it comes to God, He is always capable of knocking our mental socks off. He is admittedly capable of thought, and a kind of wisdom that escapes our ability to catch on to what He meant. He is *GOD!*

Do I need to throw Scripture at you? Of course not, but just for the record, look at Romans 11:33-34:

> Oh, the depth of the riches of the wisdom and know-
> ledge of God! How unsearchable his judgments, and his
> paths beyond tracing out! Who has known the mind of
> the Lord? Or who has been his counselor?

I guess we need at times to go by faith. Faith doesn't mean we are ignorant of what God said He would do, or even what He did do. Faith is accepting God's promise to do it, or giving Him the credit for doing it, even though we can not imagine how He is able to pull it off.

Can I philosophize a piece, here? Logic is simply the ability of our minds to accept things based on their common occurrence, not based on our ability to understand what happened. So we believe in birth and death as a logical part of life even though they remain somewhat mysterious—especially, birth. This is why people can imagine reincarnation as believable. It's an idea defined as repetitive. But a resurrection at the end of time, once and for all, happens only once. Therefore, it doesn't fit the logical pattern.

Lee Strobel in his work The Case for the Real Jesus quotes the historian N.T. Wright in saying, "It is no good falling back on 'science' as having disproved the possibility of resurrection... science observes what normally happens; the Christian case is precisely that what happened to Jesus [His resurrection] is not what normally happens."[2] So when God does something once and only once, which is what Calvary was and means, it blows our minds.

In Hebrews 10:10, we read: The sacrifice of the body of Jesus Christ [was] once for all. In Romans 6:10, Paul clarifies: The death he died, he died to sin once for all; but the life he lives, he lives to God. He would not die again, nor would God ever come again, incarnate, as a man, to die.

I am sure the regular sacrifices made daily, weekly, monthly, at feast days, and year after year, all made some sense to Israel, and for that matter to the world, as it observed and practiced similar ceremonies. But when Christ died on the 14th of Nisan (1 Corinthians 5:7), while the passover lambs were being prepared in the temple courtyard, his death went unnoticed by the philosopher and logician, not to mention the religious mind.

God did three things we knew by our logic could not be done. And these are recorded in Philippians 2:6-8. Keep in mind that He was and is God, or as Paul put it: Who, being in the form of God... Jesus, in summary, became what He needed to become, in order to provide our salvation on Calvary's cross. He:
1. took upon himself the form of a servant,
2. was made in the likeness of men, and being found in fashion as a man,
3. humbled himself, and became obedient unto death.

"What's so unbelievable about that?" you ask? What's so unusual about the route through humanity that God needed to take that led to Golgotha and to our reunion with Him?

Think about it. Jesus was in the form of God. The word form indicates what is essential or intrinsic—in Jesus' case—to being designated as "God."[3] Jesus was God incarnate, and even though we might credit some things to his humanity, such as His learning obedience and growing in grace or wisdom, He was and remained, all the while, God in the flesh.

The rub is simply this: God's humanity is beyond the philosopher's reasoning. The philosopher maintains that God cannot be "commensurately hypostatized," which simply means that God and man are totally separate beings. So the greatest part of this mystery of godliness, according to 1 Timothy 3:16, was that God appeared in a human body. So everything Jesus did, He did as God, as well as man.

This is the Christian doctrine. This chapter is not, however, about theology. It is not about our logic that cannot figure God out, but about God's logic, which concluded a Calvary experience that He required somehow in His wisdom for our Salvation.

Countless books no doubt have been written, arguing back and forth—for and against—the Christian view of who Jesus was. Some argue that Jesus being the "Son of God" did not make Him divine.[4]

Some use simple logic that cannot transform, in their thinking, a single and only God, of Jewish and Old Testament theology, into a Trinity of three persons, which is the Christian position. If Jesus is God, and if His Father, the God of the Old Testament, remains God, we have at least a two in one. The Holy Spirit is also divine, according to Scripture, and thus the Godhead becomes a Trinity. The Trinity, however, is illogical to some "scientific" minds, and that is more to the point of this chapter. It is true—and we will mention this again—that the Trinity, as a well-understood and well-defined belief, is not found in any one verse of Scripture. One needs to study the body of truth to see it.

It is as unwarranted, we maintain, as it is wrong to split the Savior somehow in two. When we say He was totally God and totally man, we mean that His humanity and His divinity somehow shared in everything, everything He was and everything He did and said. This challenges our powers of reasoning: it is logically beyond our mental grasp. And that is why we depend on our faith.

Some would like to separate His humanity from His divinity. So they reason that He grew in wisdom as a human, but that He raised the dead as God. Sounds good, but only because we have neatly compartmentalized His actions in our understanding, not because we have made any less mysterious the reality of who He is. I am anxious to jump ahead in my thoughts here, but I shall try to stay the course and simply say, when you think *Jesus,* think *human* and think *divine;* think *man* and think *God.* And if this becomes a mental struggle—like the Trinity, you just can't explain it—allow your faith to accept it, only and simply because it is in God's Word, as it was drawn up in His heart and thoughts for your salvation.

If this seems unfair, remember, we are trying to figure out a plan God drew up when all else failed to provide for our reconciliation to Him, after Eden. We are trying to figure God out. Can't be done! We can only learn and know what He gives us to learn and know. Deuteronomy 29:29: The secret things belong unto the Lord...

Paul says He, Jesus—God—took upon Himself the form or essential nature of a servant. If I were to argue from a non-Christian point of view, I might simply maintain that there is not sufficient logic in this belief to explain it. I might maintain that it is impossible for God to become anyone's slave, let alone grow in wisdom and eventually die, which is what Paul is declaring to the Philippian church. I might argue that these things are humanly possible, but since Christianity argues that Jesus was God in the flesh, their position is untenable.

Think about it.

1. He became a servant to someone over Him, who had to be greater in rank than He. How can God do that? Who can possibly be over God? Jesus was and is—by grammatical implication in the word form—by nature and in fact, God. But also, He is subject to God, as a true slave or servant. We have called this a "kenosis," from the Greek meaning "to empty." Philippians 2:7 reads: ...made himself nothing, taking the very nature of a servant. God was "emptied" and became in essence God's slave. Jesus was a servant of God in every sense, which makes the logician roll his eyes.

2. Jesus, though God, was in the likeness of man. *Likeness* means "similarity" or "sameness." I freely maintain, this refers to his humanity. He had a human nature, but without sin. In Luke 2:40 we read: And the child grew and became strong. God grew and became strong! This Scripture emphasizes Christ's humanity, but this is God, and He is growing. In the letter to the Hebrews we read (Hebrews 5:8): He learned obedience from what he suffered.

How does God grow and learn? It is also interesting to hear the Scripture say that a sinless Jesus learned to obey. Doesn't this suggest that what we are reading about couldn't have come from the mind of the philosopher? Learning generally includes fumbling, tripping up, making mistakes, but getting better and better at whatever it is we are learning. It suggests a purely human experience. Growing and learning were part of our Savior's human nature. He was truly God and truly man, two natures, one person. None of this truth lends itself readily to Greek thought or logic. Later we'll see that this truth cannot be put into clear doctrinal form using the Greek language. But it is Bible!

3. He was found in fashion as a man, Paul instructs. *Fashion* means "appearance." He had a human form or body. This was His incarnation.

And why?

To die!

Paul told us here what we have known all along. God died. An obvious philosophical stickler.

The idea of God dying was not unique, though it was uncommon in the writers and thinkers of antiquity. However, the idea that God, any god, would take punishment meant for someone else, this was totally foreign. Dr. Gregory Boyd, a professor at Bethel College, St. Paul, Minnesota, wrote:

> There is no other belief which does this... Only the Gospel
> dares to proclaim that God enters smack-dab into the middle
> of the hell we created. Only the Gospel dares to proclaim that
> God was born a baby in a bloody, crap-filled stable, that He
> lived a life befriending the prostitutes and lepers no one else
> would befriend, and that He suffered firsthand, the hellish
> depth of all that is nightmarish in human existence.[5]

The idea? God, in the person of someone named Jesus Christ, took on Himself the punishment for our sins. The Greek philosophers and the great thinkers of ancient civilizations never wrote about it, and that is important to note. The foremost idea is that Jesus the Christ was put to death, on a Roman cross, for a crime he did not commit. In God's mind, we maintain, he paid the penalty for sins or crimes against God, crimes that *we* committed. We call this "the vicarious atonement."

Since this idea is in the Bible only, this book must be God's book, I conclude. He must be the author of it. If you accept this, the vicarious atonement, even if you cannot explain it, you are a Christian.

Dorothy Sayers, in her play *Man Born to Be King,* has Mary the mother of Jesus looking up at Him on the cross and saying, "From the beginning of history until now, this is the only thing that has ever really happened."[6] She went on to say that when we understand this, we will understand all prophecy and all history. A profound but accurate statement.

On point two, Christ's humanity, "Larry King made a very perceptive comment," says Ravi Zacharias in *Can Man Live without God,* "when he was asked who he would most like to have interviewed from across history. One of those he named was Jesus Christ... 'I would like to ask him if he was indeed virgin born...' Larry King was absolutely right in identifying the hinge upon which all history turns."[7]

Dorothy Sayers, in Creed or Chaos , summarized thusly:

> So that is the outline of the official story—the talk of the
> time when God was the underdog and got beaten, when
> he submitted to the conditions he had laid down and
> became a man like the men he had made, and the men he
> had made broke him and killed him.[8]

I don't like lengthy quotes, but I have to throw a few more of Dorothy

Sayer's comments your way:

> If Christ was only man, then He is entirely irrelevant to
> any thought about God; if He is only God, then He is
> entirely irrelevant to any experience of human life.[9]

Elsewhere in her writings, she shares the profound thought that if Jesus is God, then when Jesus died, God died. And if Jesus is totally man, then when He was raised again from the dead, man was resurrected. And this sums up the major points of our singular and common faith.

If we are right about this, that the plan proposed and carried out on Golgotha's hill was provably a divine one, then Christians do have a message worth sharing with their world. We should not buy the bill of goods that argues that ours is just a belief, with equal weight as any other belief in any other religion. The Christian message outweighs the thoughts of men.

I could not have said it any better than Dr. Lin Yu Tang, a well-known Chinese scholar and author, who was quoted by H. Kerr Taylor, retired Presbyterian missionary. His reference is to Jesus' teachings, more so than His death, but I for one cannot imagine a disconnect between the two. Jesus' words and His work, His philosophy, if you want, as well as His actions, all lead ultimately to a fulfillment at Golgotha's hill.

Keep in mind that any reference to the teachings of Christ should include the message of the Cross, which closed his prophecy, fulfilled his life, and made ultimate sense out of everything else He said or did. These words should close every Christmas Eve candlelight service, because (admittedly) He came to die.

When the great Emperor Yao of China mounted the throne, an ancient philosopher of the time in that land is said to have remarked, "Blow out the candles: the sun is up!" Centuries later when in New York City, Dr. Lin Yu Tang, after a lifetime of study, made his profession of faith in Jesus Christ, he wrote:

> The world of Jesus is the world of sunlight by compar-
> ison with that of all the sages and philosophers and the
> schoolmen of any country. It is like the Jungfrau which
> stands above the glaciers in the word of snow and seems
> to touch heaven itself. Jesus' teachings have that imme-
> diacy and clarity and simplicity which puts to shame all
> other efforts of men's minds to know God or to inquire
> after God.[10]

(Let me interject a question to try and tie this together. Impossible? Illogical? Not at all! It is God.)

Then Dr. Lin Yu Tang added, quoting the ancient philosopher, "Blow out the candles! The sun is up!"

Perfect

It is Finished -John 19:30

Some thoughts lay themselves out in such a logical connection of ideas that they roll from the pen across the page like a ball rolling down a hill. Our intellectual exercises, our schooling, our upbringing, and our language all join in cooperative effort to make these thoughts so easy to understand. The writer who relates them, if he or she is not hindered by temporary writer's block, will not be able to type fast enough. The mind races to get the words on paper. The reader, too, finds the story hard to put down because like an avalanche of intriguing dialogue, it comes in one furious moment of excitement, a story like a dream filled with the meaning of a lifetime.

But—and this is a biggie—some ideas are not this easy to grasp but are, none-the-less, worth capturing on the page. Some parts of the Bible are definitely worth the reader's time even though they are difficult to get our minds around. They must be learned the hard way, starting at the kinder-garden level of our understanding of things, and gradually piece by piece adding concept on concept, until a brand new way of thinking is introduced. A brand new reasoning may be needed to shape our logical conclusions and even our theologies. Isaiah 28:10:

> For it is: Do and do, do and do, rule on rule, rule on rule;
> a little here, a little there.

This entire book, you may have observed, has been in large part commissioned with the burden of doing just that, of introducing ideas to you that you may not have thought about before. It isn't heresy to ask questions about our salvation or our God—even new questions. Our learning should not be the rubber-stamped image of someone else's theories. We can think for ourselves. It is a God given faculty.

Yes, there is in any discipline a basic understanding, which is common knowledge and the basis upon which that profession is defined and operates. Else we would have no professional understanding at all, and the benefit it intends to offer would simply not exist. If, for example, nurses decided to toss their training away for some ingenious way of caring for patients, a way not proven to benefit, well, I, for one, do not want to be at that hospital!

Setting aside nursing for now lets talk Bible basics This basic understanding is for us, here, a belief in the substitutionary death of Christ for our sins. And ministers of the Gospel message must never tamper with that message. It is a common truth among all Christians, and as such, it defines what Christianity is all about. It is the Christian's faith. Change it, or offer a purely humanistic explanation of evil in man, where our Jesus' death becomes irrelevant, and you have destroyed Christian faith. Offer a theory that offers hope in man's science alone (which, incidentally, is the practice of some would-be philosophers), and you have destroyed Christian faith.

The believer's hope is alive. It is known as a living hope for reasons the preacher can admirably expound upon. Faith is an unshakeable confidence in a loving God's driven passion to bring us to His heaven, to His level of existence. "If Christ be not raised, your faith [is] vain", Paul argued in I Corinthians 15:19, "we are of all men most miserable." It is trust that the plan of Salvation, be it little-understood and impossible to explain—so be it —nevertheless, God will pull off as He has historically related it, through our Savior's death and resurrection.

Some things should not be questioned. If we do, my prayer is that we are ingenious enough and godly enough to get divine direction. I wish to live in the playpen of basic truth. Deuteronomy 29:29 says it for us: The secret things belong to the Lord our God, but the things revealed belong to us and to our children forever. Put it on a plaque in your living room as a constant reminder that God has intentionally, in His wisdom, placed limits on what He will explain to us, at least until we are old enough to understand.

There are other things worth knowing, however, that just might invigorate and excite our faith. They might put a little skip back into our Christian walk! Unfortunately, some learning does take a little effort, a little brain power—just a little. Some truth needs to be mined, so to speak. We need to dig! We need to think! We need to spend a little of our meditation time on the pursuit of some thoughts seemingly buried deep inside the language of the Bible.

If you are fortunate enough to know the languages used in the original writing of Scripture, well, you have a big head start on the rest of us. In the mine of biblical knowledge, you're using heavy equipment, while the rest of us have simple pickaxes. I am not deterred or discouraged over this. I have all eternity to keep digging and I shall.

* * *

I said all of this to introduce you to the so-called perfect tense in biblical Greek and how this tense relates to the message of our common faith. I thought if I outright threw this idea at you, you might close this book, and that would be that. I want you to allow me to rattle out a grammatical idea and then apply it, hopefully in a way that you will find meaningful to your faith.

We all know what a "tense" is, even if we don't use the word *tense* to describe it. Examples are the present tense (what is happening) and the future tense (what will happen). In English, tense represents the time when something has happened, is happening, or shall happen. The English "tense" is a bit different, however, from Greek. There's the rub, as they say.

What is interesting about the perfect tense in Greek is that it has disappeared from modern Greek. It has a history. It came and then went, and it appears to be at its height of usage around the time the New Testament was written.

What should we make of that? To me, it's a big deal, since I am convinced that when it comes to the Bible, the history of God's language of choice had to be under the control of Providence. It cannot be, in my thinking, that seven dialects merging into one—as they did two centuries before Christ—is a mere coincidence in time. The dialect known as the koine or common Greek, which appeared between the years 200 BCE to 200 CE, just happened to surface in the fullness of time spoken of in Galatians 4:4. It was a synthesis of sorts, of Ionic, Doric, Aeolian, Attic, Epic, and the dialects of the Peloponnese. The Greek language after 200 CE once again split up into several dialects, which is what language tends to do. Meanwhile, the literary language took on a classical tone. The next known spoken form of Greek was Byzantine Greek, in about 600 CE, and we're missing the link between it and the Greek of the New Testament.

Anyways, when have you ever heard of many dialects merging into one common one? When has one dialect been created in the arena of ordinary speech, borrowing spellings and pronunciations and terms from seven others? Koine did. Koine, the Greek dialect that our New Testament was written in, was the language of the streets. (I have added an appendix to further explain this point.)

Again, it was during this period that the Greek perfect tense came into vogue. I find this fascinating, and curiously providential. It was as if the language of the Bible was frozen in time and meaning.

That's a coincidence?

No way! At least not from where I view it.

* * *

E. D. Burton, in his grammar book on Greek tenses, has a little to say about the perfect tense.[1] You probably do not want a lesson in grammar. Understood! But let me grab some of Burton's examples, and shed a little light on this delightful New Testament form. What a discovery!

God <u>has poured out</u> his love into our hearts, in Romans 5:5, is a perfect tense. In English, this usually means, simply, that God poured out His love. But in Greek, it means more. It means that not only did He pour out His love into our hearts, but also there it remains. Our hearts are characterized by this abiding and full love.

How about 2 Timothy 4:7? I <u>have fought</u> the good fight, I <u>have finished</u> the race, I <u>have kept</u> the faith. Paul was sitting in a prison cell when he wrote this. In English, we might say, I have been fighting the good fight, and *I have won*. I have *all along* stayed true to the faith. But finishing the course says something more, even in translation.

Paul is at the end of his ministry. He has finished fighting, and looking back, he concludes a good fight, and his faith is intact. So what are we saying? Just this, that the perfect tense "have finished" indicates a remaining condition or state of affairs. Having completed the marathon, you can't un-cross the finish line. This is the pivotal point of this chapter. The perfect tense shows that it is completely, finally, and forever done. We may say, "Done, done!"

The perfect doesn't say what is now happening as much as it tells us what state or condition something is in as a result of what happened. I know, this is as clear as mud. But let me keep sputtering out an explanation. I think you will get it.

It's hard for us, because we are not used to thinking in terms of states but of actions. We can sympathize with Moses and the other Old Testament writers, who also thought in terms of actions. Even sitting was an activity to them according to Thorleif Boman.[2] As my wife says often to me, "Sit up straight." Anyone who sits this way knows that it is work! It isn't a state unless you are in a brace. It is a conscious activity and I find myself slouching again.

When we are speaking with someone from a different culture, who is used to thinking in a different language, we can be surprised at their inter-pretation to what we say. So, *to stand* in Hebrew could mean "to take one's stand" or "rise up." *To lighten* might really mean "to illuminate," which is the effect of light. Something is happening; light is causing things to appear out of the darkness.

"So what?" you ask.

Well, a certain dynamic is hidden in the words when we are not used to interpreting them the way they were meant to be interpreted. As was pointed out to me in the course of my studies, every language is intended to say certain things clearly, but that clarity might not translate directly into our language or thought.

* * *

The Greek perfect tense represents a state or condition, not just the activity that produced it. Let's look at a few more examples.

Matthew 27:43: He trusts in God. The Jewish leadership got that right! *Trusts* is a perfect. This was the unchanging condition of the Savior's heart throughout his life here.

What do we make of 1 Corinthians 11:2, where Paul points out with delight that the Corinthians remembered him? *Remembered* here is—you got it—a perfect-tense verb, that he is in their thoughts and knew this. He was not merely recalled at some memorable occasion or in relaxed conversation; he was on their minds constantly.

I love the phrase: *It is written.* You can find this in Luke 24:46 and Revelation 19:12, to mention two instances. The Word of God and His purposes and promises, as stated, stand irrevocable and unchanging.

I like this one, too: the perfect is sometimes used for emphasis. We could call it an intensive use. In John 6:69, Peter could have said, as in English, "We believe and know that you are the Holy One of God." But he actually got a bit more emotional and emphatic than that. Both *believe* and *know* are perfects. "We have believed with unshakeable faith, and most assuredly and convincingly know, that you are the Christ!"

* * *

Jesus' last saying from the cross was a perfect, "It is finished!" (John 19:30) There is no disagreement in Christian theology, across all Christian faiths, that Jesus died on Calvary for our sins, and that He did it only once and will never do it again. The absolute finality of the work at Calvary is unmistakably the pivotal point of the plan of Salvation. The ultimate goal was the resurrection of all believers. Logically, there is no resurrection where there is no death. So when Christ was called "the first fruits," a Jewish concept meaning simply the first, that meant He was the first to be resurrected from the dead.

The plan of Salvation had to be executed to the letter, with co-ordinated effort between Father and Son, and with precise timing—in the fulness of time—in order to make a reality of the resurrection of believers into eternal life. This isn't the place for a lesson in theology, but the verse that comes to mind is Romans 4:25: He was delivered over to death for our sins and was raised to life for our justification. Our sin killed Him—the negative side of Calvary—but when He rose from the dead, the promise of our justification became real. The plan for our salvation was proven workable when He came back to life. This is the positive side of it all.

Jesus knew all of this, so when He mustered the strength for one last outcry, it was one word in Greek, and the period on the end of the sentence of His life, "*Tetelestai!* It is finished!"

Jesus' final word on the cross, as John relayed it to us was *tetelestai* (pronounced "te.ˈte.le.ste").

This is another example of a use of emphasis that carries meaning for Christian dogma. In the language of this single word, Jesus' work as finished was finally done, completed at last. Tomorrow, He could go on with something else. That something else would be a ministry of intercession, from His position of authority at the Father's right hand. So says Paul: Jesus became our high priest, first to reconcile us to God (Hebrews 2:17), and then to make intercession for us (Romans 8:34).

Secondly, His life's work was complete, with nothing left to do, nothing left undone, all loose ends tied up, all details tended to. All prophecy regarding His mission fulfilled. In retrospect, in His mind, He did not forget or fail at any part of His reason for coming.

Thirdly, His life's work was at that moment finally over. The moment had come, finally come. This is the exclamation point at the end of the thought. *Finally! Done!* If His life's work was done, this moment could be tied to His death in peaceful resignation. With His mission complete, He could breathe His last breath without regret or irreconcilable sadness. There is no change-of-life panic here. Death was not a frightening prospect in life, but a necessary part of it. As strange as that sounds, it has validity for anyone who comes to the end of their days and can say that the things they wanted to accomplish, and the places they wanted to visit, that they have.

We know what His death means to Christianity, but what about viewed from His personal perspective. After walking from one end of Palestine to the other and back again for two-plus years, weary and exhausted, He finally could exit this world, satisfied that He had fulfilled what He came to do. His work and reason for coming was finally, completely and at last DONE! *Tetelestai!*

What does this message mean to our understanding of Calvary? One word, *tetelestai,* makes this the fulcrum of human history, the pivotal point of our theology, the center of our experience as a believer. Calvary was the culmination of three years of ministry, and an eternity before that of planning. It was the dynamic conclusion to the drama of the ages, which unfolded at the center of God's universe.

We do not know whether there were moments when it just might not have happened. We claim that Jesus learned obedience, that He was as human as we, and tempted along the way, to the very limit of His ability to endure. We understand that He asked God to find another way, in the garden of His agony, and that He was in enough pain to want to die. We know how overwhelmingly real the tempter can become. We all know in the history of human experience how many skirmishes the enemy of our souls has won; how often our best intentions succumb to temptation. We know that even in the history of the church, Satan came all too close to bringing God's vision to an end. But we rest in the confidence we have, in our understanding of God's power and promises, that the enemy of God cannot win.

Jesus mustered one more breath in His exhaustion—some maintain that He could not physically go any further—and let us know that He had made it! *Tetelestai!*

Whose Fault Is It?

Cursed is every one that hangs on a tree: -Galatians 3:13,
for he that is hanged is accursed of God -Deuteronomy. 21:23

Did you ever wonder why the Jewish world in Paul's day didn't like Paul? They pursued him and hunted him down to harm him. The word *persecute* means "to pursue or hunt down"—as they do in Pennsylvania and Massachusetts (we have lived there) to deer, during hunting season.

Why the hunt?

In a nutshell, Paul disagreed often with the scribes' interpretation of certain Old Testament verses—and remember, we are talking here in Hebrew, a language both he and they knew well. From a purely logical point of view, either one could have been correct.

Only inspiration could decide. Christians think that favored Paul. The rabbis do have a legitimate claim to their view, however.

A simple example of Paul's way of interpreting things could be found in Galatians 3:16: The promises were spoken to Abraham and to his seed. The Scripture does not say "and to seeds," meaning many people, but "and to your seed," meaning one person, who is Christ. There is no separate plural form of the word *seed* in Hebrew, just like there is no separate plural form for *sheep* in English. So Paul took some liberty with the grammar in his comment to the Galatians. What he said was possible, but unlikely to get the rabbinical seal of approval.

Dorothy Sayers was right when she wrote:

> It [is] a grave mistake to present Christianity as some-
> thing charming and popular with no offense in it. Seeing
> that Christ went about the world giving the most violent
> offense to all kinds of people, it would seem absurd to
> expect that the doctrine of His Person can be so presented
> as to offend nobody... Nobody need be too much
> surprised or disconcerted at finding that a determined
> preaching of Christian dogma may sometimes result in a
> few angry letters of protest or a difference of opinion on
> the parish council... At the risk of appearing quite

insolently obvious, I shall say that if the Church is to
make any impression on the modern mind She will have
to preach Christ and the Cross.[1]

The message of the cross hinges on one's interpretation of a verse found in Deuteronomy 21:22-23: If a man has committed a sin worthy of death and he is put to death, and you hang him on a tree, his corpse shall not hang all night on the tree, but you shall surely bury him on the same day (for he who is hanged is accursed of God), so that you do not defile your land which THE LORD your God gives you as an inheritance. (NASB)

The Jewish position is found in the Jewish Publication Society: "for he that is hanged is a reproach unto God."

But Paul gave it a different meaning in Galatians 3:13: Christ hath redeemed us from the curse of the law, being made a curse for us: for it is written, Cursed is every one that hangs on a tree. (KJV)

So, the question is, does God's curse mean cursed *by* God like Paul saw it, Christ taking the curse of God in our stead? Or does it mean *cursing* God, the curse or reproach that the hanged, in his mode of death, is spewing in God's face? In Hebrew grammar, you can have it either way just as in English.

Consider the phrase, *a man's troubles*. Are these troubles he causes? Or troubles he experiences that others cause him? You say, these are problems he has with others. Well, what about, *a man's help*? Now, you probably think it means the help he gives, not the help he receives. Trust me, it goes both ways, and there's the theological rub.

Consider, the "faith of a man" is faith he has in God, but the "faith of God" is the faith or belief that a man has in God. Both phrases mean the same thing, even though one is "God's faith" and the other is "a man's faith." We say one is "active," and the other is "passive."

Which is which? Does it even matter?

If you want to enjoy of few "this of that's" in Scripture, keep in mind a simple rule regarding the beautiful word *of*, that it is like a two-way street. You can drive down it in either direction, as long as it makes sense to do so. Look at the "of that" in the phrase. Now ask yourself, "Is that person or thing *causing* whatever action is implied in the phrase?" (In other words, "active.") Or is he the recipient of the action? (In other words, "passive.")

Take *the faith of God*, as an example. Is God the recipient of the faith? Or the one causing it? Is He receiving it? Or is He the author of it? If He receives it then that is like saying, "faith in God." If He is the author of that faith, the giver of faith, as we might read in 2 Peter 1:1, then is it a belief we obtained *from* Him. Well, both are true.

How about the old hymn, "Faith of Our Fathers"? I think the song commends them for having faith. This is not our faith in them, although that might not be such a bad idea, politically.

"Cursed of God" is the phrase Paul used from Deuteronomy. Now, you see it can be active—God is pronouncing the curse—or it can be passive—God is being cursed.

Which is it?

If you are Paul, it is active. God is pronouncing the curse on Christ, or to put it in Christian terms, Christ is dying for our sins. The curse of sin, or the punishment for sin, is on Him. Isaiah kind of said this, hundreds of years earlier, in Isaiah 53:5: The punishment that brought us peace was upon him.

Isaiah didn't "kind of" say it, actually. He came right out and said it. But in rabbinical terms, every man is punished for his own crimes, not those of another. The idea of a vicarious substitute for a crime was unheard of. In simplest terms, in old Israel, if something bad happened to you, and that bad thing was punishment, it was because of your own sin. It was your own fault for not obeying God.

Now, here comes Paul talking about the only perfect and sinless man, who was punished by God, "cursed of God," so that you would not have to be. And Paul saw the stones start flying at him. That literally happened at the town of Lystra in Asia. They nearly did him in.

* * *

I am not surprised anymore when I find out that one Scripture can have multiple possible meanings, and that all of them would be reasonable. Here is where scholarship depends on a good hermeneutic, a good set of rules by which to interpret the verse, in the context of the overall message of Scripture and what we affirm we believe about God its author.

Here we are talking about multiple possible meanings for a given verse. When this is possible, there is nothing wrong with taking your pick, as long as you can live with it. But when we support differing interpretations for argument's sake, we do a grave injustice to God's word. And please, if you are Christian, stay true to the central truth of Christ's death and resurrection, and all it means in Christendom.

One of my favorite verses with more than one meaning—and perhaps we can end this chapter on this inspiring note—is Philippians 1:7 where Paul says to the Philippians with affection, I have you in my heart.

Not to bog us down in a grammatical quagmire, but the word *have* is actually "the act of having," which in English grammar is called a "gerund." What that means is that the word *I* (which is actually "me" in the original) and the word *you*, both are equal candidates for the act of having. The word *my* actually isn't even there.

What all this means is that this verse could be saying, "You have me in your heart."

Which is it?

I am a romantic. Must I choose?

I want to think that it is both. The affection between Paul and the people of this church is mutual, as it should be. That's the way God would want it.

You are probably saying that the context clearly says Paul had the church in his heart. Paul said:

In all my prayers for all of you, I always pray with joy because of your partnership in the gospel from the first day until now, being confident of this, that he who began a good work in you will carry it on to completion until the day of Christ Jesus. It is right for me to feel this way about all of you, since I have you in my heart; for whether I am in chains or defending and confirming the gospel, all of you share in God's grace with me. God can testify how I long for all of you with the affection of Christ Jesus. And this is my prayer: that your love may abound more and more in knowledge and depth of insight, so that you may be able to discern what is best and may be pure and blameless until the day of Christ. (Philippians 1:4-10)

But take that phrase and flip it. No harm; no foul: "... since you have me in your heart; for whether I am in chains or defending and confirming the gospel, all of you share in God's grace with me."

Does any translation flip me and you? Only John Nelson Darby does in his translation around 1890.

I still like both.

Do you think maybe God intended such ambiguity? Paul could have made his thoughts clearer, even in Greek. In Hebrew, the rabbis, I believe, like to call such phrases "pregnant": the inner idea is carried by the one we see. Take both together for a fuller meaning.

Jot That Down

...not the smallest letter, not the least stroke of a pen,
will by any means disappear from the Law... -Matthew 5:18

T he Old Testament is replete with examples of words in Hebrew
that could radically alter the meaning of a text, just by adding or
removing the smallest mark or dot, which is part of its meaning. The
Society of biblical Literature—you can use the Google search engine to
find their website—provides articles that deal with problem words in the
original Hebrew text. This shouldn't overly concern us, as if to suggest
that the Bible record is garbled somehow. The message is clear. In the
Savior's interpretation, the jots and tittles are precise, and it is up to our
love of truth to see it as He does. This is a workable idea, which we will
begin to investigate in this chapter.

Now, we know that when Jesus referred to "not a jot or tittle" falling short
of fulfillment, He was referring to the types and prophecies that outlined and
foretold His incarnation, His time on this earth, His death, and His resurrection. But must we not also show an interest in the literal jots and tittles, when
they teach us something about the God we serve?

Let's talk about dots.

One of my favorite dots is the so called *dagesh forte,* or "strengthening
dot," that is placed in the middle of a Hebrew action word to intensify its
meaning. Take the word *kneel.* In its strengthened form, it means "to bless."

Take the word *speak.* דָּבַר With the dot it can mean "to speak eloquently"
or "to promise." דִּבֶּר (See the dot in the middle letter?)

The example that comes readily to mind is in Psalm 18:1, where David
exclaimed, I love you, O LORD. That's nice. But did you know that if you put a
dot in the middle of this word *love*, strengthening the pronunciation, it means
mercy?[1]

However, the strengthened form, "to have mercy," is only used about the
Lord in the Old Testament, not about men. Now we have a glimpse into
God's love that we didn't have before. His love for us is more intense than
ours for Him—that can go without saying—but He shows mercy when He
expresses it.

The only place I know of where the strengthened word perhaps refers to someone else is in Isaiah 49:15, where God's love is compared to a mother's for her nursing baby. And the verse says, God's love is stronger.

In the New Testament, this is the same word as "bowels," believe it or not. Have you heard of bowels of mercy? The bowels were said to be the seat of intense emotions, according to the Greeks. But when God got hold of the word, its meaning became the seat of tender affections and compassion. And the verb refers only to God, Jesus, and Christians.

1 John 3:17 is another good verse: But whoever has the world's goods, and sees his brother in need and closes his <u>heart</u> against him, how does the love of God abide in him? (NASB) The word is translated "heart" here.

God's love is far stronger than ours. We love cars and boats. But substitute the idea of showing mercy, and see what happens to that kind of love.

* * *

I love dots. And I love those little squiggly or curlicue thingies on the end of some letters that change the sound of them or turn them into different letters.

I remember in grammar school a teacher returned a paper to me ungraded. She wrote across the top in red ink "chicken scratch." I guess she couldn't read it. Well, one has to observe closely when one reads Hebrew, because although they are inscribed very carefully, one must still watch the curlicues. Otherwise, one might mistake a Z for an N, because in Hebrew the two look very similar. Or he might not be able to tell a B from a C, or an M from an S or T, or H from Ḥ, or— You see what I am saying. But this suggests the question: how big of a deal is this? After all, in English, if I use the word *zoo*, you can't mistake it for *noo*, because there is no such thing as a noo, except in Dr. Seuss' world.

An example might be Ezekiel 21:14, and I underlined the words in question.

Prophesy therefore, son of man; clap your hands and let the sword come down twice, yea thrice, the sword for those to be slain; it is the sword for the great slaughter, <u>which encompasses them</u>, that their hearts may melt. (RSV)

In the KJV, the underlined phrase is translated, "which entereth into their privy chambers." The ancients, on the other hand, translated it, "the sword that terrifies," which more closely resembles what the Greek Old Testament says, "strike them with amazement."

Which one is it? Encompasses? Enters into chambers? Or terrifies? This whole question hinges on a squiggly, which I have to show you. There are two words in Hebrew which look similar. Can you tell them apart? Here they are: חדר חרד

Look closely, and you'll see that the two letters on the left are reversed. Let me blow up these two letters so that you can see them better.

ד ר

On the letter on the left, can you see the little burr on the corner, where the other letter is rounded? When these letters are flipped, the meaning changes, because they form a different word. The ancients read it with the letters in the order you see them enlarged, חרד, and that is the word that means "terrified." If we reverse them, חדר, the meaning is "to surround," and then in the context of Ezekiel 21:14, the noun refers to a chamber, like a bedroom.

An overview of Ezekiel's prophecy in chapter 21 might simplify things for us. The Lord was alerting Ezekiel to the Babylonian's conquest of Jerusalem, and to the subsequent destruction of the temple. The king Zedekiah would be taken, and he would then watch his own sons being butchered, and then his eyes would be plucked out, in 2 Kings 25:7.

This portion of Scripture also references the last days, or the end times, in Ezekiel 35:5, "the time of the iniquity of the end," which refers to the anti-christ. You can study this sometime, but our point here is the little tittle on the corner of that Hebrew letter.

It is clear, in any case, that God's judgement is a terrifying nightmare of punishment upon an unjust and sinful world. The commentary says, "God shows us the sword and waves it over our heads, so that we should be time-lessly and profitably alarmed."[2] This way we can take both spellings into consideration.

It might help with the interpretation of any prophecy to understand in general what prophecy was ultimately all about. 1 Peter 1:10 clarifies the general truth, that all the prophets spoke of the coming salvation, which was provided on Calvary. Peter reminds us: Concerning this salvation, the prophets, who spoke of the grace that was to come to you, searched intently and with the greatest care. Ezekiel's prophecy here is no exception, and whatever translation we give it, it should reflect and exemplify this truth. So prophecy is ultimately a message of grace. Discussing judgement, however, doesn't immediate scream,"Hallelujah!"

"Grace to come," Peter said. But we are talking about a divine sword in Exekiel's prophecy. How can all scripture somehow embody the message of grace, when we are talking about wielding swords and cutting enemies down?

A sword of grace?

Grace to one becomes a sword to another. A sword to one provides grace to another. To defend one person, you may need to fight another. It is God's mercy that has to bring judgement. Jesus had to cry out to God, "Why have you forsaken me?!" and experience the pain of Calvary, in order for you and me to enjoy the peace of heaven. I don't know a better way to say it.

Whenever the prophet, therefore, speaks of judgement or a sword, it is grace, because judgement must precede peace. Mercy for one is a form of revenge on another. To give to one means taking from another sometimes. In God's courtroom, judgement for the plaintiff must go against the defendant, or vice-versa.

The prophet Nahum's name means both "mercy" and "revenge." The words *mercy* and *revenge* in English have a Hebrew word in common.

In terms of the final outcome of prophecy, a heaven for some must mean a hell for others, and God cannot right wrongs in a final period of tribulation without someone feeling the pain of it all. If God has a right side, where the sheep are gathered, there must be a left for the goats.

My immediate point here is to note the interesting challenge for whoever interprets the Bible. Sometimes a slight change in the spelling of a word can engender all kinds of discussion. For my money, the idea of being terrified by a wielded sword fits the context better and is more to the point than the idea of being surrounded by it.

God's sword is about to be unsheathed again and wielded above His head, since—we maintain—the end of time is nearing. And that should be enough to make even God's people tremble at the thought.

* * *

Let's look at another letter change. There is something known as the "*qeré and ketív.*" This was created by the Masoretes, groups of scribes and scholars working between the 7th and 11th centuries, in the Muslim world.[3] *Qeré* is Aramaic for "read," and *ketív* is Aramaic for "write." The *qeré* and *ketív* are comments—one might loosely call them—in the margin of the Hebrew Bible. When the scribe copied the Scripture, he would add these notes to suggest a different pronunciation (*qeré*) or a different spelling (*ketív*) for that part of the text.

One of my favorite examples—it must be the little boy in me that remembers this—is found in 2 Kings 18:27 where Rabshakeh is threatening Hezekiah with frightening consequences, unless Jerusalem surrenders to the Assyrians. His language is vulgar, to say it as gently as I can. The translation talks about the men sitting on the wall—who will have to eat their own filth and drink their own urine. The word "filth" caught my attention, because the word found in the text differs from the word found in the margin, the *ketív*. According to Gesenius—he is a favorite scholar of Christian expositors—the word originally used in the text was from an obsolete verb which meant "to ease oneself."[4]

Hebrew critics have placed in the margin a less offensive expression. This marginal reading made its way into our translation. Like English, Hebrew had a far more vulgar term for "filth." The Bible's realism sometimes challenges and offends our sensitivities, especially when it quotes a Rabshakeh, or tells it like it actually was.

* * *

Another interesting "tittle" of sorts—and I am using the term loosely, to represent some of the interesting tweaks we read or might find in the text—is what has been referred to as a suspended letter.[5] This is a letter added to the spelling of a word to change it into another word. Take, for example, Judges 18:30, which reads: There the Danites set up for themselves the idols, and Jonathan son of Gershom, the son of Moses. The footnote on the name Moses reads, "An ancient Hebrew scribal tradition, some Septuagint manuscripts and Vulgate; Masoretic Text Manasseh." The simple fact is that some scribe added the letter 'N' in the Hebrew name for Moses (*Moshé*) and changed it to Manasseh (*Manshe*). This conversion works smoothly in the Hebrew. The scribe knew enough not to actually modify the divine text, so he put the "N" in as a kind of superscript. The scholars called it a "suspended N."

How utterly embarrassing for all Israel to admit that a grandson of Moses was instrumental in introducing idol worship into the tribe of Dan! It is far easier to say someone from the tribe of Manasseh was to blame. But the text is the text. I for one am grateful that in an age of political correctness, with cyber-crime and Ponzi schemes and other new ways of inventing crime, in a society that has taken litigation to a new level, where lying is an art, and hiding incriminating evidence is a necessary part of any legal defense, there is the Bible with its openness and transparent honesty about sin, and its historical frankness, without bias, about life. Idol worship was introduced into Dan by the grandson of Moses.

* * *

Another interesting change that can occur in the text is in our translations. Sometimes one translation sounds better to us than another. Take, for instance, in the love chapter, 1 Corinthians 13:5 (in the King James): love is not <u>easily provoked</u>. The word means "to provoke or rouse to anger." I get that, but where did "easily" come from? The *New* King James translation takes it out.

I recall in school when we were in this chapter in our studies. The class, almost to a person, thought that this kind of love was too much for God to ask of us. We maintained that such a description of dedication and affection is beyond normal human behavior. I didn't know at the time, because I hadn't read C.S. Lewis on the four kinds of love, that we wanted to alloy this divine love with a little eros. It is human to experience three different kinds of love: eroticism, natural affection for family, and friendship (what we call "liking someone.") For the Christian, God wants to add the love from 1 Corinthians 13. In my humble opinion, since this is the case, this love has to be expressive of a much higher or loftier experience in relationship. If you ask me, the word "easily" does not belong here.

And then there are all the italicized words found in the King James Bible. These represent natural gaps in the wording of the original, which the translator thought should be filled in, in order to make sense in English out of what we were reading. Some of the gap-filler is warranted by rules of grammar, and those don't interest us here. But what about the words that were added because the original writer left something out, for one reason or another?

My favorite epistle for this observation is 2 Corinthians. Paul seemed to be so emotional in relating his thoughts that he left out words that would make the flow of his thoughts clearer to us. In 2 Corinthians 2:10, Paul writes (translated directly from the Greek), "To whom you forgive anything, I also —" Correctly, the translators wrote: If you forgive anyone, I also <u>forgive him</u>. They added an extra word or two for clarity.

How about the word *give* in 2 Corinthians 4:6. The King James Version reads: For God, who commanded the light to shine out of darkness, hath shined in our hearts, to <u>give</u> the light of the knowledge of the glory of God in the face of Jesus Christ. The NIV reads: For God, who said, "Let light shine out of darkness," made his light shine in our hearts to <u>give</u> us the light of the knowledge of the glory of God in the face of Christ.

This word *give* is not in the Greek. The Greek says, "His light shines in our hearts *toward* or *for the purpose of* shining forth the knowledge of God's glory, seen in Christ and His death and resurrection." This idea is possible if you take the "give the light" to be the same as "for shining." This is grammatically legal.

So what's the difference? It more clearly explains Paul's point that God "gave" him the revelation to share, as his testimony with everyone else. Our experience in Christ is public information. The light should not be hidden under some bushel. The city is set on a hill, elevated on the horizon, so that all travelers may be more easily able to find it.

The word "give," though, suggests to me a private thing, a gift of knowledge, which might be treated as personal insight, but which others do not—

and perhaps cannot—know or understand. In Bible days, this idea was called "gnosticism," and it should be avoided, because no truth is of "private interpretation," Peter warns us in his second epistle (2 Peter 1:20).

* * *

What have we really learned? We have discovered that there is much to learn, much we do not already know, much that we cannot intelligently relate in debate with the skeptic, to prove our faith. But this is okay. We have learned enough to prove to us the reality of our salvation, and that is sufficient for now.

What about debates that lead to hurtful estrangement with other believers? Don't I have the right to defend my opinion and my beliefs, even if I don't know what I am talking about? Or what if I do know what I am talking about? Well, maybe, according to some of the discoveries we've made in this chapter, maybe we can't be so positive about some of the minutiae—the fine edge of the sword—with which we parry our angered and passionate responses.

I for one want to stop the futile exercises in meaninglessness. It is a waste of my time, which these days is at a premium. Colossians 4:5: Walk in wisdom toward those who are outside, redeeming the time.

Let's just keep reading and learning—together.

Sin? I'll Drink to That

...everything that does not come from faith is sin. -Romans 14:23

If you think about it, if we could pin down the meaning of *sin*, and if we could just avoid sin altogether, we should be good to go... to heaven, that is. But the church has found this all-important subject a bit challenging to define.

Perhaps, sin is not easy to determine or describe, because it—like love—is not a concrete term. By concrete, I mean—with respect to "sin"—something we can see as always wrong. If you want concrete examples of sin, ask a young child what is bad to do, and they might offer a few examples. The problem with this approach is that life isn't that simple, and what is wrong for one person may not be so wrong for another. Sometimes the kids are flatly misinformed.

So what is sin? Drinking? (Thus the title of this chapter.) How about smoking? Pantsuits for women? Jewelry? Fighting? I think we taught the children that one. Watching movies? Any movie? Or just anything not rated G?

These are concrete ideas, and if it were that simple, I think I for one would be considered almost next to God. Okay, I like crime scene investigation shows on TV. That's my only vice... I think.

I want to ask Robert G. Girdlestone, who wrote a book on synonyms of the Old Testament, what sin is. He addresses the topic of evil, and his first two paragraphs in his chapter on sin are worth repeating here. Perhaps, you can take his comments and skip mine because his insight speaks for itself, and I think maybe through them we can get a handle on this all-important subject.

> The pictorial power of the Hebrew language is seldom exhibited more clearly than in connection with the various aspects of evil. Every word is a piece of philosophy; nay, it is a revelation. The observer of human affairs is painfully struck by the wearisomeness of life, and by the amount of toil and travail which the children of men have to undergo to obtain a bare existence; he sees the hollowness, vanity, and unreality of much that seems

bright and charming at first; ...

> The Hebrew Bible meets us with a full acknowledge-
> ment of these manifold aspects of human suffering, and
> blends wrong doing and suffering to a remarkable
> degree, setting forth sin in its relation to God, to society,
> and to a man's own self...[1]

We could study each word in Girdlestone's list of synonyms for *sin* or *evil*, as well as their Greek counterparts, but that isn't the burden of this chapter. Word studies abound, and I recommend that every believer study these words, in an effort to more fully appreciate God's contention regarding sin. Words like *evil, unrighteousness, sin, rebellion, wrong, transgression,* and even *pain* and *wearisomeness* you should observe, as part of this overall malady that has estranged us from God and from each other, and has torn from us the reality of who we are and what we are suited to become, both as a contributing human in our own society and as a member of God's creative genius.

The burden of this chapter, rather, is to assign some concreteness to this concept of sin. It is an effort to give shape to a somewhat ethereal idea that has appeared in all kinds of shapes and sizes of "wrongness."

In a desire to give substance to what sin is, Christians have created a lengthy list of no-nos, some of which are probably okay things to do. As a church, we have attempted to give people a sense of spirituality, based on the things they do, or should do and shouldn't do. So we say, go to church, and give money, and don't wear jewelry, and don't kill anybody—I like that one —and you will be spiritual. The list often resembles the profile of the person who prepares it. We tend to understand spirituality in human terms, and form our theologies, based on our own experiences.

As a working idea, that is excellent. But the preparer has to be God, and the profile should be God's. So we ask: Can we find such a profile of holiness in Scripture? Can we learn the true meaning of sin by reviewing the biblical record of what God doesn't do and won't do? And can we call this list sin? We often enough ask, "What would Jesus do?" And then we make our decisions and live our lives as if we didn't have a clue.

Well, there is a biblical list of no-nos, or "don't's," that we should be avoiding in the practice of our Christianity. And this list isn't so long or so mysterious that we cannot get our minds around it. The more likely problem is that we have only cautiously glanced at it, just long enough to say that we know about it, but we see no immediate need to underline any of its items in our own experience. "*My* Christianity is intact, but I might know a few people who should take a closer look!"

The general breakdown of sins in the Bible theologically follows the outline given by John the Apostle, in 1 John 2:16: For everything in the world —the cravings of sinful man, the lust of his eyes and the boasting of what he has and does—comes not from the Father but from the world. So here we have three major categories of sin: (1) cravings, (2) lusts connected with sight, and (3) pride. The difficulty with this list is that it employs only two terms: *lust,* which is also the word *cravings,* and *boasting* or *bragging,* which is the word *pride.*

There are three words for "pride" in Scripture; so, I think a further breakdown of this idea is in order. And the word *lust* is simple "desire" or "longing," but used for a bad end. Both words should be further researched if we want to get more specific about sin. Put another way, if bragging and wanting things which we should not have are the only sins, most Christians can breath easier, even if their behavior is characterized by bitterness or hate, and what they say displays a tongue that is, as James said (James 3:6), set on fire by hell.

Let's look at three areas of sin which when avoided, can make us be reasonably comfortable with our commitment to truth.

* * *

The Word of God does not cut corners or shortchange an idea, especially if it is germane to the main theme of its message. God is well capable in this record of calling sin, sin. It is unfortunate that here and there, a teacher of God's truth would tweak the message of sin, or redefine it, either to improve their own apparent chances at perfection, or to encourage their followers through guilt into a decision thought to be in the will of God, even if in fact it was only in the will of the preacher.

I know I almost sound angry, but I'm not. I want to underscore the idea that sin is not a mysterious or cloudy biblical concept. It is concrete in Scripture. When the Bible mentions stealing, or murder, or covetousness, or adultery, or any of the ten commandments—and that is just one list of no-nos found within its pages—some have decided to philosophize away the simplicity of its convicting message. Some prefer to look for synonyms, to say, for example, that killing in war is not murder. This may be true, but we know when it is "killing" and when it is "murder." Other times, a preacher might explain away the obvious meaning of sinful behavior, for reasons that are more socially acceptable or politically correct in today's world. The plain truth sometimes lacks popularity, and brings a price tag with it that could get a minister fired, or bring persecution to anyone who shares his belief in it.

We know that today's world of thought disowns the standards of a holy God. They disown God, Himself, as even a being out there on the fringes of our reality. If He exists in their minds, notwithstanding, there still is no standard to follow. This precludes them even looking in Scripture for such a standard. But Christianity still maintains that there is a God, and by attribute His holiness means a divine standard for us to hold high as the banner of truth. And where there is a standard, the breaking of it is sin.

I have taken the opportunity to say as much, because in my humble opinion, the Bible does define sin, and it isn't drinking wine or wearing a wedding ring.

So, what is sin?

I have found—or think I have discovered—three major categories of sin in Scripture. And if this be true, it just got a lot easier to discern right from wrong. There are sins of the tongue, or what we say and why we say it, such as, blasphemy, false accusing, slander, cursing, all forms of verbal abuse, which includes gossip and just plain lying. Another category is pride in three forms: proud speech—giving oneself full credit for some good outcome—or bragging, proud thoughts, and hubris. (*Hubris,* by the way, comes from a Greek word that has found its way into our language.) The third general category I find is lust, which starts with selfish interest and works its way to intractability or addiction.

Before I run the risk of boring you with details—if you have read this far without coercion—it seems incredulous to me that someone might assume they don't know when they are breaking one of the rules that leads to verbal abusiveness, self-deception about their worth, or desires out of control. Of course, a person with no moral center might not, but then again they require hospitalization—and I say that lovingly. But for the rest of us, there is no real mystery when our lives are coming apart, because we have crossed the line in what we say or think or do, and that line was visible to us all along.

* * *

One verse that, no doubt, is overlooked is Deuteronomy 32:15:

> But Jeshurun grew fat and kicked—
> You are grown fat, thick, and sleek—
> Then he forsook God who made him,
> And scorned the Rock of his salvation. (NASB)

He was the Old Testament prodigal, scattering his inheritance, or living in riotous living, and if rich, faring sumptuously, until like an ox he became intractable through such good feeding, and refused to bear his master's yoke. Jeshurun, a tender and loving appellation of God's people, refused to follow God's laws. Too much free manna?

Now I must give you homework, or we will never get through this chapter. Research the words *pleasure* in 1 Timothy 5:6 and *luxury* in James 5:5.

Also, the words for *riotous* (or *wild*, or *loose*) *living* in Luke 15:13, and *faring sumptuously* (or *living in luxury*) in Luke 16:19. Look into the idea "lacking in self-control," which is being undisciplined, uncontrollable, ungovernable, and self-indulgent, found in Matthew 23:25 and 1 Corinthians 7:5. And how about *lasciviousness*—what a word!—or *excess,* found in Galatians 5:19 and Ephesians 5:18, which describe a loose and profligate habit of living. And note lastly that the opposite of these terms is "a sound mind," or "self-discipline," in 2 Timothy 1:7.

Look these up if you want, or just refer to the appendix in the back, entitled "I Said No!"

"It is easy to see that one who is excessive," says the professor, "in this sense of spending too much, of laying out his expenditures on a more magnificent scheme than his means will warrant, slides easily under the fateful influence of flatterers and all those temptations with which he has surrounded himself , into a spending on his own lusts and appetites of that with which he parts so freely, laying it out for the gratification of his own sensual desires."[2]

And yes, that's in the Bible!

The person who wastes his goods, wastes everything else: his time, his faculties, his powers, and himself. Now, I understand what Jesus had against wealth. It wasn't wealth at all that He objected to. Rather, it was the soft living and the "I will do what I want" attitude that such wealth meant to some rich people. I also know now why I am better off without a winning lottery ticket.

Peter called it brutish behavior in 2 Peter 2:12-13.

Teach the children self-discipline, through loving parental discipline, and include a savings account and a Bible. Free advice.

There is also a biblical no-no, love of money, greed, avarice, in love with gain and profit, which we should be aware of. 1 Timothy 6:8, and the verses that follow, talk about contentment with God's provision. Now, if God provides you with a good stock portfolio, I think that's cool. But when the market takes a dive, get back into 1 Timothy! The Pharisees, according to the Savior in Luke 16:14, didn't understand this simple truth.

Lastly, on this topic, there is self-love. There is a healthy kind, which Mark 12:31 alludes to. But there is a sign of the times which Paul prophesied about in 2 Timothy 3:2. We can thank the Puritans and our pilgrim fathers for the word *selfish,* which they coined and which goes a long way in translating the Greek term here. Selfish people want things easy and pleasant for themselves, and they reserve harshness for others. This has been compared to the hedgehog who, rolling himself up in a ball, keeps all the soft and warm wool for himself, but sharp spines to those without.

We are—by way of summary—maintaining that the Bible encourages discipline, both self-discipline and divine discipline, as well as parental leadership, because the lack of it together with a few misplaced resources — spoiled children with money—leads to pleasure gone awry, and eventually addictions. Winning the lottery, with exciting dreams of pure amusement, beyond the rest all busy lives require, is a mistake. It is God's grace, no doubt, that protects a believer from this scene. Can we handle a lot of money? Could we manage ourselves as well as our resources if such fortune smiled upon us? If not, sin, like a hungry beast, lies crouching at the doorway of our lives.

* * *

Pride is another bad thing, because it is lying to oneself, and then to others. We must not take credit for things we don't deserve credit for. We must take a lesson or two from David and give God some of the praise. Besides, humility, as we said already, recognizes our dependence on God.

Pride exhibits itself not just in bragging, but also in an arrogance or self-exultation, even in secret or in one's own thoughts, that lifts oneself above others in his estimation of his own accomplishments and worth. This is the word *pride* (or *arrogance*) in Mark 7:22. It is a very bad thing, according to the company it keeps in that verse.

Hubris you can look up in Websters. It is a pride that now walks over people and steps on them, as it climbs the social ladder higher and higher, and doesn't care who it hurts or how, in its advancing self-importance.

I think we got the point, and we know what pride is, and what it isn't. So this is a word that should never be explained away, if we are serious about following Christ.

* * *

And at last the end of this chapter draws near. We just need to mention the third category. We have saved the worst for last: the tongue gone awry. I recommend for every Christian a course in communication and listening. The wisdom of this world has a good handle on what *not* to say to people, and church people need to hear about it.

Did I say something nasty?

If so, how did it feel?

We need to see that shaming, scolding, putting another down, belittling (especially our children), insulting, slandering, blurting out misplaced sarcasm, condemning, lying, speaking evil of someone, projecting blame, accusing (which is Satan's job), humiliating, using abusive and scathing language, purposely trying to say something you know hurts, and even being unthankful, all these are spelled out in Scripture as what *not* to say. And aren't you glad God takes His own advice here?

There is such a thing as constructive criticism. Criticism needs three things to be constructive, rather than destructive: (1) It must look ahead, not back. (2) It must reference a situation that is correctable, and endeavor to do just that. And (3) it must be said in love, as a positive encouragement. That's my two cents worth.

Let me give you your homework assignment, verses to look up, but I warn you, it is like squashing bugs. After a few, I start to get sick to my stomach. Instead of looking up all these verse, you might want to just take my word for it and continue to the next chapter. But those who are a glutton for punishment: Isaiah 52:5; Leviticus 24:11; 1 Corinthians 4:12; 6:10; 10:30; 1 Timothy 1:20; 6:1; James 2:7; Romans 15:3; and there's more where they came from.

* * *

You can see that the Bible is full of psychological insight. It and its author, God, knows what's in the heart. And God, being the counselor that He is, comes right out and says it. He tells us what is right and wrong. His interest is in sharing His wisdom, not scolding us. So His approach is positive and healing.

From time to time, we all will say and do the wrong thing, and some of our regrets last and last. We need a God who can free us from yesterday's guilt, as well as tomorrow's temptation. I am glad that He has spelled out what is sin. I can at least discard the self-loathing that is based on misplaced and misread social norms—so-called hand-washing in wheat fields—and not Bible principle. At least, I can look more realistically at my shortcomings, and ask forgiveness for what really is sin in me, and live above the accusing tongue.

Paul wrote to the church in the Greek town of *Thessaloníki* (1 Thessalonians 5:14): And we urge you, brothers, warn those who are idle, encourage the timid, help the weak, be patient with everyone. Good advice. When it comes to the no-nos in our lives, there are four approaches: exhort, warn, comfort, support. By "comfort and support," we understandably refer to the need at times to help up those who have stumbled. Not everyone needs to be warned, and I think we can safely say that we should treat no one always and only like a truant to the plan or will of God. That diagnosis goes too far. But we might say now and again, what Paul called a "warning." This delightful word means to get it through their thick skulls. This is my inter- pretation, but it's accurate, since it means to put something in someone's mind, or to admonish him. The Germans say *"an das Herz legen,"* lay it on the heart. This reminds me of the Old Testament phrase in Haggai 1:7, consider your ways. It means, "lay it to heart."

Isn't it theologically safe to assume that with different believers, or at different times in any believer's life, God may have to use—now more and now less—gentler means to get His point across?

Sometimes, as in Haggai's account, God thinks we should be able to apply to our lives the instruction He knows that we've already heard. We should be there already in our experience. In other words, yell at yourself for once. You know what to do. Well... Do it!

Thank God for the mature believers whose life and experience have taught them how this whole thing works; their wisdom is excellent counsel.

I Can't Say That in Greek

scarcely... saved -1 Peter 4:18

P eter warned: If it is hard for the righteous to be saved, what will become of the ungodly and the sinner? (1 Peter 4:18) He wrote this, referencing Proverbs 11:31: If the righteous receive their due on earth, how much more the ungodly and the sinner! Peter quoted the Septuagint, the Greek translation of the Hebrew text. The problem is there is no Hebrew equivalent for the word *scarcely*. This means that whoever translated the original Hebrew into Greek did a little more than translate the verse. It appears, they interpreted it. What are we to make of this?

Does this mean that the Greek translation of the Old Testament is inspired? I would say no, no more than any translation.

But Peter quoted it.

Peter's quote is inspired. Definitely. But I would caution replacing the original with any translation. Translations are just that, translations. And sometimes what can be said clearly in one language cannot be said so clearly in another.

This conundrum has led some to prefer the *Peshitta*, the Aramaic version of the New Testament, assuming that this was closer to the language Jesus spoke, and therefore closer to the Hebrew. This would eliminate the problem of translating anything into Greek. The problem I have with this—and this is all I will say about it—is twofold: Firstly, the *Peshitta* is written in Babylonian Aramaic, not Palestinian Aramaic—it's not Jesus' dialect. Secondly, the oldest copies of the New Testament are in Greek, not Aramaic.

If you're interested—and you can get this from the web[1]—there are, I am told, 320 references to the Septuagint in the New Testament. Of those that are quoted, Psalms and Isaiah are the most popular, followed by Deuteronomy and Exodus. These four books show good strength of usage across the span of New Testament books. Eighty-two percent of all Old Testament quotations are from just six books: Genesis, Exodus, Leviticus, Deuteronomy, Psalms and Isaiah.[2]

"Less than half of the Old Testament quotations in the New Testament are from the Hebrew text," Dr Robertson informs us.[3] This should make the problem a bit less of a problem, because we can just trust the Greek for the interpretation of the quote.

⋆ ⋆ ⋆

One immediate benefit of these quotations is the added meaning they give to words that might otherwise be difficult to translate. Take the word *repent* as an example. We may think this is a simple idea—and there is nothing mysterious here—but Alcoholics Anonymous builds an entire lifestyle or coping mechanism—whatever they see it as—on the benefit of this one word. And the Greek meaning, at least as we understand it in the classics, could not possibly be sufficient to do this.

AA's founders were Bill Wilson and Dr. Bob Smith.[4] Mr. Wilson had a spiritual experience and became convinced in the existence of a God, a higher power, that could help him overcome his addiction to alcohol. Dr. Smith was part of the Oxford Group, a Christian movement. It is my contention that these men found the true secret of biblical repentance. Yes, there has to be more to it. Today's higher power, according to some, might be anything or anyone that keeps them from drinking. I think we should stick with God.

My interest in mentioning this is not controversial, nor have I gone to preaching. I discovered through a study of the Greek term for "repentance," without its Semitic roots, the word lacks the fuller meaning that becomes the secret to unlocking the treasures of God's grace.

Repent, and God responds passionately and mercifully. You will read this again in this book, because it is worth repeating that no matter what the crime, the record of it is expunged through repentance. Please, try not to, but if you commit any sin, any thing at all that would sever your communication with God, then cry out as did David, in sincere repentance to God to forgive, and He will. Psalm 51:8-12:

> Oh, give me back my joy again;
> you have broken me—
> now let me rejoice.
> Don't keep looking at my sins.
> Remove the stain of my guilt.
> Create in me a clean heart, O God.
> Renew a loyal spirit within me.
> Do not banish me from your presence,
> and don't take your Holy Spirit from me.
> Restore to me the joy of your salvation;
> and make me willing to obey you. (NLT)

Been there; done that. Have you?

True repentance restores relationship, and is capable of restoring the life that discovers this truth.

So, I came to the conclusion that the Greek language needed a little help in describing such an idea, which led me to Acts 28:27: ...turn, and I would heal... which comes from Isaiah 6:10: ...turn and be healed... Healing comes with turning. That is the Hebrew idea of repentance.

Learn the secret of turning from bad practices and sinful behavior, and God has His opportunity to heal. It sounds simplistic, but actually it is profound. Dr. Smith discovered this—I have no doubt—when he took the word of God at face value, and then proceeded to add the steps to make it happen. He found 12. You may see it differently, but when the New Testament writers spoke of repentance, they did not see it the same way as an Aristotle might have, as simply a regret, a wish they hadn't, or a changing of the mind.[5] It was a turning. It was life changing.

Professor Moulton comments on the Greek word for "repentance": "Its meaning deepens with Christianity, and in the NT it is more than 'repent,' and indicates a complete change of attitude, spiritual and moral, towards God."[6]

The word *turn* in the New Testament has the simple meaning "to convert."[7] Closer to the truth of the matter, this is an example of an ordinary term doing service for a far more important and spiritual concept. Put yourself in the place of Paul or Peter. How should the idea of true repentance, which incidentally is a divine gift (2 Timothy 2:25) be explained? In the letters to the seven churches, in the book of Revelation, repentance is the one and only cure for what ails the churches who have strayed from their appointed ministries. Repentance leads to a living relationship with God, and an open invitation to join Him in His heaven. Repentance is the narrow gate, in Matthew 7:14, that leads to life.

* * *

Another example would be Paul's use of the word *rise* to refer to the resurrection. The Greek simply could not have gone there by itself. They had no word for "resurrection." So, in I Thessalonians 4:16, Paul wrote, "the dead in Christ shall rise." There are in fact 57 words in our New Testament that were borrowed from Hebrew. There are 767 words in the Greek New Testament that J. H. Thayer calls "biblical"[8]

One of the 767 words listed by Thayer is found in Romans 2:11: For God does not show <u>favoritism</u>. This word, translated "favoritisim," was formed from the Old Testament phrase, "to lift the face." This is explained "in terms of the respectful oriental greeting in which one humbly turns one's face to the ground or sinks to the earth. If the person greeted thus raises the face of the man, this is a sign of recognition and esteem."[9]

Genesis 32:20 is part of the account of Jacob's reunion with his brother Esau, who Jacob had offended by robbing of his, Esau's, birthright. Before going out to meet Esau, Jacob had his servants precede him and plead his case with his brother for forgiveness. Jacob instructed his servant with these words: "'Your servant Jacob is coming behind us.'" For he thought, "I will pacify him with these gifts I am sending on ahead; later, when I see him, perhaps he will receive me."

"Perhaps he will receive me," in Hebrew literally reads, "perhaps he will lift my face."

In Romans 2:11, the word "favoritism" is actually the result of taking the Hebrew phrase, saying it in Greek, and then pushing the words together into one compound word. Romans 2:11, literally translated, says, "There is no face-taking with God."

This is just another example where the Hebrew played a major role in giving meaning to a Greek word.

* * *

A second benefit is the flip side: a New Testament writer explains the Hebrew for us. So for example, when Jesus referenced Isaiah 40:3-5, in Luke 3:4-6, we are given to understand that this refers to John the Baptist. We take this cross-referencing for granted, but that's only because Jesus quoted Isaiah. He didn't leave it to our ability to research the Old Testament and figure out the prophecies about His forerunner.

What if He had left it to us to figure out? What if the Old Testament references were not in the New Testament? What if the apostles didn't use a text when they preached? Could we read the Old Testament and see what they saw? I have my doubts. They had a calling as apostles, a relationship with Jesus, the teacher, and a calling to write the New Testament, all of which had a singular impact on their understanding, all of which we lack.

An obvious portion of truth that would otherwise challenge our understanding is Isaiah 53, which has been expounded in a number of New Testament books.

* * *

What do we make out of Jesus' words to Satan in the wilderness? Luke 4:8 reads: You shall worship THE LORD your God, and Him only you shall serve. (NKJV) In the Hebrew, He is referencing Deuteronomy 6:13: You shall fear THE LORD your God and serve Him, and shall take oaths in His name. (NKJV) And the Greek translated: "You shall fear the Lord your God, and Him only shall you serve and cleave to Him, and in His name only swear an oath." It is interesting to note that the Septuagint version includes the idea of carrying on a close relationship with the Lord, cleaving to Him. It should go without saying that Jesus had no reason to mention this to Satan. And the part about keeping an oath, well, Satan cannot tell the truth, so that's irrelevant, too. Of course, Jesus' point was that He would worship only the one true God, His father, but it is interesting to compare versions.

What about the word *serve* in this text? I am inclined to think the Hebrew word far more general in meaning than the Greek. In Hebrew, a servant is one who labors for another. He might be either a slave or employed in someone's service. It can be hard labor, or the service of a subject to his ruler. It can mean worshipping God. Maybe that last meaning fits here, because the Greek word limits its meaning—though not always—to service freely rendered. The Classical Greek word used here had once referred to service to men, now referring to service rendered to a higher power. For us, that's God. And that's how it is used everywhere in the Greek Old Testament.[10] The Greek translation of the Old Testament then helps to clarify what Jesus was saying. It speaks of service specifically to God. How good is that?

Thy Speech Bewrayeth Thee

...the way you talk gives you away -Matthew 26:73

The Galileans—Peter was one—had difficulty with the guttural sounds[1] in their native tongue, Aramaic. And their *sh*'s came out more like *t*'s. "The pronunciation of the people of Galilee," says Professor Lange, "was uncouth and indistinct; hence they were not allowed to read aloud in the Jewish synagogues."[2]

I can take a stab at an explanation of this one. The Hebrew for "man," *ish*, begins with one of these gutturals and ends with the *sh* sound. Peter probably butchered it when he said, "I know not the man."

Just a footnote here: according to Acts 2:14, Peter began his ministry—not in Galilee, but in Jerusalem—not just by what he said but the way he said it. The word *said* in this verse is actually not a word of everyday speech, but of dignified and elevated discourse. He spoke as an orator! Moses, it was alleged, had a speech problem, too, but they also hung on his every word. God still finds use for those of us who struggle with our words.

"Where are we going with this?" you ask.

The writers of the New Testament were Jewish, with the possible exception of Luke. So it would not be too surprising if they wrote—yes, in Greek—in a way that would reflect their Jewish way of talking. Such an idea is not far-fetched. Some idioms of speech, or phrases found in the New Testament, might be the product of Jewish thought. We already took a look, for example, at a word for "favoritism" in the previous chapter. The gospel story—I am told—was first told largely in Aramaic, a Semitic language.[3] Maybe so, but let's not jump overboard on this point. Our New Testament is in Greek.

How many New Testament words and terms are actually Old Testament language clothed in Greek words? We are told that only 150 words out of over 4,800 (not counting proper names) in the New Testament are peculiar to the New Testament and the Greek translation of the Old Testament.[4] What that means is that most words, 4,650 or so of them, are good Greek.

My dear wife found this chapter a bit difficult to follow when she reviewed it, so, I can understand a few scholarly types asking: What's your point?

My point is actually a good one. Because the New Testament is written in

Greek, we are more likely to ask Aristotle or Plato what a word in our New Testament means when we should be asking Moses or one of the Old Testament prophets. The New Testament is actually written in the vulgar or language of the common people but every now and then with an Old Testament twist to its meaning.

"The vocabulary of the [Greek translation of the Old Testament]," Dr. Robertson informs us, "is that of the market-place... [even though] the syntax [grammar] is much more under the influence of the Hebrew original".[5] He also told us, "The LXX [Septuagint] translators [the Greek translators of the Old Testament] had great difficulty in rendering the Hebrew tenses into Greek and were often whimsical about it."[6]

"One can read whole pages in places," says Prof. Robertson, "with little suggestion of Semitic influence beyond the general impress of the Jewish genius and point of view."[7]

Even so, some Hebrew thoughts, understandably so, made it into the New Testament through the Greek Old Testament. If you want to relate the Christ message to a world that speaks Greek, and you are using the Old Testament, the *Tanakh,* as your Bible, as your text and sermon material, you would refer to the Greek translation. The Greek Old Testament had a significant influence on the New Testament writers. In fact, the first complete Bible was the Greek Bible, and it was freely used for many centuries by the first Christians.[8]

A well-known example of this is the very name *Christ.* "It is an Old Testament name," Robertson documents. "The name Christ (anointed) is found in the [Greek Old Testament] and so the very terms Christian and Christianity arose out of the language employed by the Alexandrian interpreters [who translated the Septuagint in Alexandria, Egypt]."[9]

What, to illustrate, should we make of the Septuagint translation of Amos 4:13? The Hebrew says, "He who forms the mountains creates the wind and reveals his thoughts to man... THE LORD God Almighty is his name." The Septuagint translates: "For behold, I am he that strengthens the thunder, and creates the wind, and proclaims to men his _Christ_... THE LORD God Almighty is his name."

When we bring the Hebrew Bible into the Greek language, in spite of all the challenges in getting the ideas across, we bring it to the world. "The Bible whose God is Yahweh," remarked Dr. Deismann, "is the Bible of one people [the Israelites], the Bible whose God is *kurios* [Greek for "Lord"] is the Bible of the world."[10]

Secondly, there is much to learn from the Greek translation of the Old Testament, even if we understandably do not consider it to be on a level of inspiration with the original Hebrew. Professor Deismann remarked, "A single hour lovingly devoted to the text of the Septuagint will further our... knowledge of the Pauline Epistles more than a whole day spent over a commentary."[11]

So when we read the New Testament, how should we be translating God's thoughts to us? How big of a role do the Greek words in the Greek Old Testament play? Add to this the fact that one must not assume that a New Testament word necessarily has the same sense that it has either in the Greek Old Testament or the *Koine,* the Greek language spoken at the time.[12] So when I read the New Testament, it might be a translation of "good" Greek, or it might not.

Spaghetti? Impossible to unravel? Who unravels spaghetti? It's for eating! But add a hunger to know the Bible, and heat it with a passion to learn, and yum. Don't you agree?

Perhaps by this time you are feeling a bit ignorant? Good, because now I have someone to empathize with me. I am not bothered by my lack of knowledge. I know my salvation is real, and I can wait on the rest. The whole idea behind Bible study is not to learn it all, but to be learning it and applying it to life. And I don't take inventory. I don't know if someone else is smarter than me. One would think the college professors are, and I would be quick to agree, if they as I love our Lord. Just because they might know a foreign language, though, a little Greek, Hebrew, Aramaic, or even Latin, that doesn't mean they know the Bible. If they love our Lord and have knowledge of these languages, they would be enviable—were envy not a sin.

It might help you to know that this is a "subject of keen controversy... whether the N. T. Greek is wholly in the koine [Greek] or whether there is an appreciable Semitic coloring in addition."[13] So what we think we know, we might not really know.

Take the word "repentance" as an example. (I talk about this important biblical concept elsewhere in this book.) It is insufficient to only ask Aristotle what the word means. Repentance is an Old Testament concept! Without going into quotable detail, some atheists reject Christianity because it promotes pleasure without consequence through the mechanics of penance or repentance. While it costs a Tibetan monk every comfort for his faith and many Muslims are most literally prepared to die for their faith, many Christians take the easy way out by enjoying any and all pleasure they can afford and if they step into immorality or cross some ethical boundary stepping with insensitive belligerence over other less fortunate they can simply assuage their guilt by repenting. Because atheists don't buy into the Old Testament message they accept the New Testament Greek word for repentance as Aristotle might understand it. *Metanoia*, literally means a "change of mind". And some Christians are good at rethinking life's options without serious commitment to biblical principle. Repentance, it is true, as a term is not a change of lifestyle *IN GREEK*, but in the Bible thanks to the Old Testament twist it does carry the idea of a change of lifestyle through Grace. It does embody commitment.

* * *

A couple of study words might make this chapter complete. Usually, when we think about talking like a Jew, but in Greek, "Semitism," we think of Luke. Luke uses Semitisms uncommon elsewhere in the New Testament. "There seems little evidence that he [Luke] knew Hebrew."[14] He knew Greek, though, to be sure.

As he spake by the mouth of his holy prophets... Luke 1:70. "By the mouth" is a phrase Luke got from reading the Old Testament. He also liked to say, "And it came to pass..." which he also got from the Old Testament. In fact, he said "and" quite a few times, for a man who know better Greek than that.

For us, here and now, this isn't too informative, but in another book this might suggest something exciting to learn. A taste of an idea. Take a look at Luke 5, and the account of Jesus sharing the Word of God with a crowd of people who seem, in the account, to push Him into the lake.

The King James says in Luke 5:1-3, reflecting the Greek: And it came to pass, that, as the people pressed upon him to hear the Word of God, he stood by the lake of Gennesaret, And saw two ships standing by the lake: but the fishermen were gone out of them, and were washing their net. And he entered into one of the ships...

Now read the NIV: One day as Jesus was standing by the Lake of Gennesaret, with the people crowding around him and listening to the Word of God, he saw at the water's edge two boats, left there by the fishermen, who were washing their nets. He got into one of the boats...

Notice the "and's" in the King James. That's a little bit of Jewish blood—a little Hebrew idiom—in the text, running through it and making it live.

"As the people pressed Him..." I don't think they were simply crowding in—no disrespect intended to the NIV. They were about to push Him into the lake! Now, all those "and's" tie the narrative together. The fishing boats were probably docked there by Providence, as a way out of this dilemma. He stood off shore in one of the boats, now free from the necessity of going for a swim, and He continued to teach from there.

Luke's use of Semitisms bring his narrative to life with picturesque detail, at least, if you're Jewish.

* * *

The Greek word *réma* (pronounced "'ri.ma") means "word." There are seven *rémata* in this sentence. (You can count them there on the page.) But after the Greek Old Testament, this word took on the meaning "thing."[15] A good example is 2 Corinthians 12:4. Referencing a heavenly vision, Paul said: He heard inexpressible things, things that man is not permitted to tell. That was from the NIV. The King James says, heard unspeakable words. If you think about it, the NIV is more accurate, because it isn't the exact words that were untranslatable, but the actual vision, which in any language could not be described.

2 Corinthians 13:1 says: Every matter [not every "word"] must be estab-lished by the testimony of two or three witnesses. This way, we need not have a Philadelphia law firm draw up the account.

Sometimes the word *réma* means "a word," as in Hebrews 11:3, which says that the worlds were made by the Word of God. He literally spoke them into existence. I believe it.

* * *

2 Corinthians 1:22 reads: Who hath also sealed us, and given the earnest of the Spirit in our hearts. (KJV) The word *earnest* catches our attention, because it is not a Greek word in the Greek. It is on loan from Genesis 38:17: And he said, I will send thee a kid from the flock. And she said, Wilt thou give me a pledge, till thou send it? (KJV) There, it is translated "a pledge." That's the same word also in 2 Corinthians 5:5 and Ephesians 1:14, where the King James calls it an "earnest." I wouldn't have known what an "earnest" was here, had not Webster's dictionary included a third entry for this word:

> Middle English *ernes, ernest,* from Anglo-French *arres,*
> *erres,* plural of *erre* earnest, from Latin *arra,* short for
> *arrabo,* from Greek *arrhabōn,* of Semitic origin; akin to
> Hebrew 'ērābhōn pledge
> Date: 13th century
> **1** : something of value given by a buyer to a seller to
> bind a bargain
> **2** : a token of what is to come : pledge

An interesting reference to this word occurs in a receipt of payment written somewhere around the 2nd or 3rd century. It is secular, but it gives us the Greek word. "Regarding Lampon the mouse-catcher I paid him for you as earnest-money [Greek *arrabon*] 8 drachmae in order that he may catch the mice while they are with young."[17] Earnest money is a part given in advance of what will be given fully afterwards.[18]

This word has a similar meaning to "firstfruits of the Spirit," in Romans

8:23. We have some now; we get the rest later in heaven. How do we know this? The little bit now is a down-payment—bad word, since we don't earn salvation—or a guarantee or pledge of God's grace. Ephesians 2:6-7: And God raised us up with Christ and seated us with him in the heavenly realms in Christ Jesus [our salvation and our relationship with God now in this life], in order that in the coming ages he might show the incomparable riches of his grace, expressed in his kindness to us in Christ Jesus.

Polycarp in his epistle tells us that Christ's death (and resurrection) guarantees our acquittal at the last judgement. How is God's grace in this life a guarantee of the grace to come? It is a legal idea. Gesenius calls it a mercantile term.[19] Same difference.

I am glad Paul found this word in Genesis, but to be honest, I didn't need it to believe that I serve a God who finishes what He starts. And since He is eternal, I think, anything He gives us has to be *arrabon*.

I Can't Believe You Said That!

partakers of the Divine Nature -2 Peter 1:4

I am amazed at times to read something which I considered should have been above and beyond the scope and knowledge of the person who wrote it. Peter is an example of a writer, in 2 Peter 1, who penned details of what I would call the development of the godly life. I have studied the language there, and thought to myself that his use of terms, and the order in which he used them, was profoundly ingenious. If I am right—and the burden of this chapter is to show as much—then we have another glimpse into the divine inspiration of the text, and therefore of Scripture.

I am saying that I don't think Peter could have come up with some of what he said totally on his own. He was a fisherman—not a dumb fisherman, because fishermen are not dumb—but as such, he was more known for his bravery and knowledge of the sea than his psychological insight.

In any event, I hope that your curiosity is stirred a bit to investigate. We might even give Scripture a chance to defend itself against some debaters of the present age, who think the text is nothing but religious jargon and historical insignificance.

For the record, the Bible needs to defend itself; that is, God must defend Himself. I will not. I am not an apologist. I am only a little boy at heart, who has never lost his fascination with Bible words and thoughts. I almost bought a new Bible recently, just for the privilege of sniffing the new leather cover, and the pages, which bring back such fond and recurring memories of my continuing interest in this sacred book.

I am a little crazy that way, but it might do good to mention again that I am open to learn. I do not want to approach a study of Scripture with preconceived religious notions. I hope you agree. And this makes Peter's use of words even more interesting.

I guess I have to interpret what I think he said, and yes, this leaves room for discussion. But if a discussion ensues between you and me through these comments, I have accomplished what I set out to do.

You tell me what Peter meant. You must study Scripture for yourself and not depend only on what preachers preach.

Since I have no interest in turning this into a sermon, I will cut to the text, the first eleven verses, and hopefully link the words together as one idea worth considering. Words of immediate interest are underlined.

Simon Peter, a servant and apostle of Jesus Christ, To those who <u>through</u> the righteousness of our God and Savior <u>Jesus Christ</u> have received a <u>faith</u> as precious as ours: grace and peace be yours in abundance through the knowledge of God and of Jesus our Lord. His divine power has <u>given</u> us <u>everything</u> we need <u>for</u> life and <u>godliness</u> through our knowledge of him who called us by his own glory and goodness. Through these he has given us his very great and precious <u>promises,</u> so that through them you may participate in the divine nature and <u>escape</u> the corruption in the world caused by <u>evil desires</u>. For this very reason, make every effort to <u>add</u> to your faith <u>goodness</u>; and to goodness, <u>knowledge</u>; and to knowledge, <u>self-control</u>; and to self-control, <u>perseverance</u>; and to perseverance, <u>godliness</u>; and to godliness, <u>brotherly kindness</u>; and to brotherly kindness, <u>love</u>. For if you possess these qualities in increasing measure, they will <u>keep</u> you from being in<u>effective</u> and unproductive in your knowledge of our Lord Jesus Christ. But if anyone does not have them, he is nearsighted and blind, and has forgotten that he has been cleansed from his past sins. Therefore, my brothers, be all the more eager to make your calling and election sure. For if you do these things, you will never fall,and you will receive a rich welcome into the eternal kingdom of our Lord and Savior Jesus Christ.

Peter begins by reminding us that the faith, or trust, we have in God was a gift, which came through what Christ did on Calvary. No one conjures up a belief in Christ as Savior, like the cowardly lion in the *Wizard of Oz* holding his tail and trying to psyche himself out and reassure any listening ears, saying, "I do believe, I do, I do believe!"

Believers are believers naturally. It is impossible for them not to believe. No incantations or chants are required, and if they are, I would question the source of the faith.

The faith, specifically, is a trust in God to keep His promise to equip us with whatever we need to live a godly life, to live above sin. Peter doesn't define the term "sin" here, but elsewhere in Scripture, it is specifically detailed, and unfortunately Christians have been a bit misinformed as to what is and what isn't sin. I addressed that issue in an earlier chapter. But that is not Peter's problem here. He is looking positively on this thing known as living a Christian life.

Someone said that the best way to recognize a counterfeit is to become familiar with the real thing. I think this is where Peter is coming from here. Faith is necessary in developing goodness, according to his soteriology—that is, his view of salvation. Goodness is moral excellence or, I like to say, living within your current knowledge of truth. If you know something is right to do, then do it, live it, to the best of your ability. No one is so naïve as to think we will be perfect at it, but we will see some success in the attempt, because of His promise.

To this goodness we can begin to add knowledge. Such an idea is so simple, it's profound. Learn by doing! This works best with computer programming and auto repair and—I imagine—every other profession or discipline. It works equally well with studying Scripture. Like the old Baptist preacher said, the Scriptures are a guide for life and conduct as well as faith. If you can't do it or live it, what value does it have? Perhaps this is why Christians are prone to get off into Bible topics that are pure philosophy or prophecy, and have no current relevance to their lives. Did I say "them"? Us!

We are often thinking that unless I live it perfectly, I best not promote it or preach it. This philosophy doesn't encourage us, nor does it teach us Scripture. Like children learning to speak or walk, we need to keep trying, keep fumbling, keep making mistakes, keep falling down and bumbling, if need be, until we get it right.

Now we can talk about self-control. I mentioned this word elsewhere, in an earlier chapter, but here, we need to see the link with knowledge. Once we know what to do, we need to add the discipline that says "I will" and to put it into practice. The knowledge of truth must become principals for living.

And from here we advance to persevering in the discipline. Saying "No" to some temptation once or twice is not the same as getting completely by that temptation. Saying "No!" once and for all is persevering. In a positive sense, living the truth we know now has become a way of life.

This from a fisherman!

This, Peter said, leads to godliness, or according to the dictionary, a respect for God, piety. In the language of the Greek writings, this meant "being religious," but I believe with Peter it is a synonym for Paul's word *holiness*. We have precluded, therefore, that he meant we should dedicate ourselves to church attendance or some particular form of worship. Rather, Peter sees godliness in him who practices the principals of the Bible, and the instructions given in its wisdom. This person is pious.

And it is this person who can appreciate fellowship with people of like mind. Brotherly kindness, which to me is a synonym for Christian love among believers, which is fellowship, cannot be realized through mechanically organizing banquets and scheduling church events. It may or may not occur in the women's circles and board meetings.

Fellowship is a biblical term that first shows up at the birth of the church in Acts 2. Fellowship is not just a social gathering, but when people who want to live the life, and support each other in living that life, get together——regardless of the social reason or function—that brings about true fellowship. Brotherly kindness, or the affection believers are capable of showing toward each other, then comes out, and develops in that atmosphere.

The ultimate benefit of all of this is Christian love. This word, *love,* is difficult to wrap our minds around, but I think here Peter reminded us that the ability to care unselfishly, without wanting rewards or recognition, that is the outgrowth of living the Christian life, first in the context of our support team—other believers. We get things backwards when we say that it is easier to get along with people who are not Christian rather than with Christians. I know the feeling, but it isn't exactly true. What we are doing in that case is trying to hide away in a crowd of people who do not know us and cannot begin to figure out what really makes us tick. We feel safe, as long as the real issue of our pain or discomfort doesn't arise.

I think I'm right about this.

But the true dynamic in this text might be how it spirals upward and then loops back around, from love to faith, and brings the believer to a higher level of achievement in these areas.

Gal 5:6: The only thing that counts is faith expressing itself through love.

If this is a possible view—and I think likely—it provides us with an eight-step program for spiritual development. Peter in this portion of Scripture gives us a look at where our priorities must lie, in our pursuit of religion. He called it urgent. The translation tells us to "be all the more eager" (verse 10), which can only mean that there is a process here worth reviewing.

Christians who want to claim they are spiritual must reconsider the criteria by which such a claim can be made. It appears, it has little to do with how many songs we have sung, or how much money we have given to charity—unless these are expressions of this faith-to-love cycle.

Granted, this one text doesn't say it all. We need to focus on each word in the eight-step program, from faith to love, and study the details. But the overview these verses provide is a striking reminder of how our spiritual growth should be proceeding.

The psychology behind it is revealing as well. If, for example, self-control is an issue for you, this text suggests that the problem might be the foundational truths of faith, goodness, and knowledge are lacking. You can't build on water.

We can work our way back through the list. Do we have a problem with knowledge, as the word is understood in this context? We are not concerned with our grade on a theology test, but how well we know the Savior's approach to things. If this is a problem, it could be that we have a problem with goodness, or just living out our faith on some elementary level. This is an eight step program. Each following step has to be built on the previous one. That's the dynamic here. That's what makes this whole topic surprising from the pen of a fisherman like Peter.

If you and I can take seriously Peter's sense of urgency in these verses, we will discover that participating in the divine nature, as he worded it, is more than just a doctrine. If we can start with our simple faith—and faith is simple trust, a simple decision to give God's word a chance—and then add a serious study of His word, since it offers the closest and most scrutinizing look at the Savior, and then attempt just once, in some small way, to use His example in our experience, we will be well on the way to being a participant.

When you're discouraged, it's easy—because sin is so appealing—to forget the promise of God that this will work if you work it. It is hard sometimes to string two "no's" together in reply to temptation and go for a third. We look down the long road of our life, and we call it impossible to live that long, in that way. But this Scripture would encourage us to simply try for today, and if we fail, start again tomorrow.

When fellowship enters this picture, it gets easier, because this is our support group, and ultimately the thrill of being a visible and living testimony to the fulfillment of God's promise, and the sense of ministry that comes from supporting someone else on this same journey, it all begins to tie this whole text together.

I guess Peter had to be a fisherman to catch this truth—a fisher of men.

Let Me Underline That

my brother had not died. -John 11:21,32

One of the more difficult things—if I can call it a "thing"—to get clear is how serious you are about something, how important your point of view is to you, and what exactly that point of view is. Not only is it easy to be misunderstood, but also sometimes people do not hear the exclamation point at the end of your sentences.

The Bible is replete with truths that are written as clearly and as emphatically as God could have written them. Their underlining message is not, however, the talk of the Christian community. We have trouble trying to figure out what is important to God, and what isn't so important. As the disciples were warned about Pharisaic leaven, we are wondering if we should have included an additional loaf of bread in our picnic basket. And often enough, after we have filtered God's words through our limited understanding—and what is important to us, or what we hope to hear—the emphasis of the message is altered, if not the message itself.

On top of all of this, we have needs on all levels of life that are screaming, "Feed me!" Consequently, our own emotions drown out whatever God might be yelling in our ear. The ability to listen is all but lost, and the art of communicating, well, these days it has to be offered in college courses. Our informal education, while growing up, was all about how to convince others that *our* situation is the more serious, and why they need to back off and just give us what we want.

Oh, some peoples' pain can be beyond the listener's ability to know how to react. The classic example to me is a husband beside his wife who is in labor. He best keep his mouth shut and just hold her hand. What he wants to do, probably, is find a doctor who will give her a shot or something, and let him go into the waiting area and watch the ball game.

No wonder, when God starts sharing the painfulness of His offended Holiness, that sometimes we stand there like children, caught in the act without a defense, not having a clue what to say. We want to blame someone else, like Adam accusing Eve, but there is no one else around. No wonder, we might want to tell God, "What's the big deal? Suck it up! I'm not the only one who's done this, you know. Besides, I don't know what you're so upset about. It isn't the end of the world!"

Or is it?

* * *

How can we listen to God tell us how He feels?

A good example to look at is God's outspoken jealousy over Israel's worship of foreign gods. Israel never seemed to catch on, until in Babylon their sorrow in missing Jerusalem took away all joy, according to Psalm 137. Now, they get it and it is the *Shema* in Deuteronomy 6:4: Hear, O Israel: THE LORD is our God, THE LORD alone. (NJPSV) Every Jew knows that by heart.

God's pain would have been evident to any man who had gone through something similar, if his wife had been unfaithful. In Numbers 5, a man was given recourse when his wife—alleged to have committed adultery—was brought to trial. If found innocent, there was no counter-suit. It was God's way of dealing with the man's suspicions and his overwhelming jealousy, which could be fatal if not addressed.

God's agony must have reached a peak when He instructed Hosea the prophet—against His own principles, mind you—to marry a prostitute. God knew what Gomer would do to Hosea, emotionally speaking, and now God would have one man who knew what He, God, was feeling!

I have not counted the numerous times in the histories and writings of the prophets, where God reminded Israel of His feelings. He even made it clear —at least to some—that His very name was Jealousy, according to Exodus 34:14. And we even missed that one in listing God's names in the theology books.

I told my grandmother, after reading the ten commandments (Exodus 20), that God was jealous. And Grandma nearly jumped down my throat. She scolded me, and instructed me never to say that again, because jealousy, she reminded me, is a sin.

Go figure.

Well, in the Scriptures, jealousy is a form of zeal, and it's often the result of a brokenhearted love or romance. That's not sinful, but one has to take care how he reacts. In God's case, nothing He subsequently did was sinful. Quite the opposite. It was an expression of His Holiness. People who think that God should never allow pain or hurt in this life forget that God's Holiness, or the standard of His being, who He is and what makes Him "Him," cannot be ignored even in the name of mercy. Whereas a jurist must pronounce sentence on the guilty according to the mandates of state law, God's actions are necessarily dictated by the principals which define who He is. That's His law.

He is at times like a parent who won't allow sin to be carried on in His home, even though it tears Him up on the inside. And in God's case, it tore a hole in His side and punctured His hands and feet.

You get the point, but what is amazing is that the simplest emphasis, or the most visible dripping tear, we can ignore, and life goes on. I have always wondered how the nightmare of an eternal hell, described in detail in Revelation—and the Savior emphasized these more than he did the blessings of heaven—how this mention of unutterable anguish could bring *amen's* and *hallelujah's* from Christians, while they belittle their own testimony with infighting and church-splitting.

What has happened to the emphasis on hell, and for that matter, on a jealous God?

Emphasis is one part of a three-fold approach for language. Any language is designed by use and culture to provide a simple, clear, and emphatic dialog over common ideas. One language cannot say what another can say and the biblical emphasis of grace took the Greek to say it best. So says the preacher.

* * *

I want to take a closer look at something Mary and Martha, Lazarus' sisters, both said to Jesus, on the occasion of Lazarus' death. Both said the same thing, at different times, but each with the words in a different order, with a different emphasis. Both said the same thing, but both did not mean the same thing. Their personalities and needs surfaced in what they said, and we should be grateful that they said it to the Master, who knows how to listen.

It was a tender moment, when Jesus comforted His closest friends, while tears silently trickled down His own cheeks. In this simple story, Jesus listened to His friends, while they poured out their grief. Both Mary and Martha were perplexed by a four-day delay, and were unable in their own understanding to make any sense out of what had just happened a funeral ago, which took their brother Lazarus away.

Martha theologized, If you had been here, my brother would not have died. (John 11:21) And Mary through her tears likewise lamented, Lord, if you had been here, my brother would not have died. (John 11:32) Both statements appear identical, but they were not the same originally. Martha's words flowed naturally, but Mary actually said something a little different.

I found out there is something to be said about the order of words. In Latin, I am told, the rule of thumb is to put the verb at the end of the sentence. This is similar to German, were the sentence might end in an auxiliary verb, like *have* or *is*. Grandma—the same as I mentioned above—gave me the sentence, "Turn the dog loose, and let him run the alley out." I got it. Did you?

In Greek, the rough and ready rule is the reverse of the order in English. "I can do all things," in Greek is "All things I can do."

Let's say we want to capture the emphasis in the Greek of Matthew 23:9: You have one Father, who is in heaven. (RSV) That translation is pretty close to the original word-order in the Greek. But in order to capture the emphasis of the original, in English, we need to say, "For you, there is only one father —the heavenly Father."

Romans 5:6 reads: You see, at just the right time, when we were still powerless, Christ died for the ungodly. In the original, however, the word-order puts the emphasis on the beginning of the sentence: "For yet Christ— our being weak yet—in due time, he died for the ungodly." No one would die for someone else—well, perhaps for a good man, maybe. But for you and me, sick with sin? Forget it!

Yet Christ did.

So you can see that word order sometimes does mean emphasis and that in turn flavors the meaning of the phrase.

Similarly, the same words spoken by both Martha and Mary, but in differing orders, do offer us insight into the two sisters.

An earlier visit from Jesus to their home shows Martha the socialite, while Mary was somewhat of a private and withdrawn person, who simply loved to see Him. Luke 10:38 records: As Jesus and his disciples were on their way, he came to a village where a woman named Martha opened her home to him. She had a sister called Mary, who sat at the Lord's feet listening to what he said. But Martha was distracted by all the preparations that had to be made.

Now, after Lazarus their brother had died, the first stroke of character that distinguishes Mary from Martha, Dr. Lange points out, was when Mary went to Jesus and fell down at His feet.[1] Before this, Mary had been grieving alone, while her friends and family, unable to comfort her, simply kept watch for an opportunity to be of some help. They followed her, assuming she was heading for the grave site, to grieve there, as was the custom.

Martha, meanwhile, had already met up with the Saviour, and had carried on a theological—more accurately, an eschatological—discussion with Him about the resurrection to come. She no doubt took comfort in her belief that He, Jesus, was the Christ, the Son of God, and that she would see her brother again at the resurrection of the just, at the end of time.

Some people can gain reassurance from what they believe, and I too find a strengthening hope in this truth. But was it Mary's as well?

Martha took this message of hope to her sister. Martha was now armed with the promise of Jesus that Lazarus would live again, and Mary needed to know this. John's account tells us that Martha went to her and whispered in her ear, "The Master is here! And He is asking for you!" (John 11:28) This is when Mary got up and left, to the concern of all who saw her. But she wasn't on her way to the tomb, but to see Jesus.

I am not qualified to profile the two sisters, but on the surface, we can observe that Martha is a detailed person, who likes to see everything in its place. Life makes sense when everything, in her understanding, is tidy, when it's what and where it should be. Her brother's death was out of place in her mind, since Jesus could have prevented it, but the final resurrection cleans things up nicely for her. This is not just a theology for Martha, but a hope, and she can now go on with her life, awaiting her reunion with her brother.

Mary is not Martha. Mary is directed more by her heart than her mind. She was prone to letting how she felt direct her, so on His previous visit, she had enjoyed just sitting at Jesus' feet, even though there had been a table to set, and soup to stir, and burgers to turn in the frying pan, and so forth. Now, she just can't handle the death of her brother, not on an intellectual level that might have informed her that life has to go on. Instead, she withdrew, alone, into her own pain, until Martha took the initiative to encourage her to go and see Jesus, who was calling for her.

This simplified look inside the heart of these two ladies doesn't begin to explain the complexity of their feelings and thoughts, of course not. And we cannot presume to know anything, especially if we have not been through it ourselves. But Jesus knew. He could pick up on the differences between them —as He knows how different we all are from each other—and He responded, and responds now, in a way that tells us that He is listening. He hears our thoughts and our feelings. He knows the human heart, and He knows you and me as He knew Martha and Mary.

So Jesus answered Martha by reassuring her that her brother would soon awaken. Even though her theology got in the way of her understanding what he meant, it would suffice for now for her to know that Jesus did have things in hand.

Mary, on the other hand— This is the Mary who would pour expensive perfume over Jesus feet, much to the disapproval of a few. This is the Mary whose heart, not her head, would tell her to do it. I guess that Martha, the practical one, probably paid the bills in this household. This was the Mary who locked herself away in her mind, and would probably never become part of a support group for the grief-stricken. She probably would have kept it all locked inside, never knowing what that could mean later to her faith or her well-being.

And when she found Jesus, where Martha had left Him, she fell to the ground where he was standing, in tears, and she wailed, "Lord, if you had been here, he would not have died— My brother!"

Jesus said nothing to her.

He didn't talk eschatology with her. He did not reassure her of the resurrection. He did not even tell her that she would soon see her brother alive again.

He simply looked at her and allowed His tears to join hers on the ground where they stood. After a brief pause, He asked, "Where is he?"

And you know the rest of the story.

He has a remarkable ability to heal the heart, even without a word.

Our Lord can make sense out of what we say, and when Mary spoke from a crushed heart, He saw that her grief had overwhelmed her. It was as if the words between "Lord" and "my brother" were unnecessary filler.

Lord... My brother, my brother...

You and I might fail when it comes to such in-depth listening. I think it requires sensitivity and insight that may be beyond us. Here, too, Jesus is the Master. He listens. He hears. And John said, simply, in 1 John 5:15, And if we know that he hears us—whatever we ask—we know that we have what we asked of him.

He knows where to put the emphasis.

A Particle of Truth

Let us now go... -Luke 2:15

As we have pointed out elsewhere—and it is common knowledge —that a word in one language may have no clear translation in another. As in other languages, there are words in both Old Testament Hebrew and New Testament Greek that are particles or exclamatory remarks. These are understood by those who speak the language but are most likely not translatable.

Wow! Yipes! Ai yai yaiii! Wokachow!

Some of these particles are worth studying. If we capture their meaning, we should own them as if they were English. Translating such words usually does not promote the excitement and deep emotion they express.

* * *

In the following verse, for example, two words appear that never make it into the translation: *dé* (pronouced "di") and *te* (pronounced "te").

Acts 13:2: While they were worshiping the Lord and fasting, the Holy Spirit said, "Set apart *dé* for me *te* Barnabas and Saul for the work to which I have called them." The dictionary calls these "enclitic particles," and the second one *te* is "copulative."

Oh. That explains it, then.

Not!

The word *dé* is translated "now" in Luke 2:15. Here, a translation does offer us something. The NIV says: The shepherds said to one another, "Let's go to Bethlehem and see this thing that has happened, which the Lord has told us about." This isn't as expressive as the NASB: Let us go <u>straight</u> to Bethlehem then... Or the NKJV: Let us <u>now</u> go...

The word "now" betrays a little shepherd excitement. "Let's go" sounds nice, but maybe we can wait for shift change.

Or maybe we can take turns.

Or maybe we'll go together... And *now!*

I love the enthusiasm and absolute urgency, the need to know as soon as possible for themselves about the Savior's birth. Some things you don't want to read about in the paper tomorrow, because you can't sleep not knowing.

This interpretation supports their activity after their intro to Jesus, too.

Verse 16: They spread the word concerning what had been told them about this child.

The dictionary offers us a little clarity when it comes to Acts 13:2. It says that when *te* is used with *and*, as we have here, (*te* Barnabas *and* Saul), the wording represents "things connected or... which are akin... united by some inner bond."[1] The dictionary entry goes on to say that "the particles... give no intimation respecting the relative value of the two... the member with the *and* [Saul] is more emphatic."

So when the Holy Spirit called for Paul and Barnabas, he called them as a team, with Paul as team leader.

And as for the word *dé*, it can be taken as introducing something "settled, laid down indeed and in truth... now therefore... verily..."[2] So the Spirit is being emphatic, or in my opinion expressing some excitement that this moment of missionary work has come. It is a moment with great historical significance in the life of the Church.

* * *

"Hosanna," they cried at Jesus' triumphant Jerusalem entrance. You know the story, for example, in Matthew 21:9. In the Greek translation of Psalm 118:25, the Old Testament phrase is "Save *dé!*" This is the word *dé* explained above. The Hebrew, however, says "Save-*na!*"

Na doesn't mean "no." Gesenius in his dictionary refers to it as "a particle of incitement and also of request, entreaty, *I pray thee.* [The German says]: *doch!*"[3]

Na is like the Hebrew word for "please."

Another example: Nehemiah 1:5 starts out: Then I said: "O LORD, God of heaven..." The NIV leaves out the interjection of entreaty, included in the KJV: And said, I beseech thee, O LORD God of heaven... What adds to our interest here is that the *na*, "I beseech thee," is prefixed with *a-*, making it *anna*. I think we don't need a translation on this particle. We sort of know what "ah" means, as in "Ah! No kiddin'?"

So the Hebrew says *anna!* I think we just learned a new Hebrew word. Correction: I think we have had this particle in our vocabulary from a young age but probably forgot. Tell the children we are going to the amusement park, and then change your mind.

Anna! We want to go!

Okay, the Hebrew has a slightly different meaning, but we're close.

Take a peek at the fear Joseph's brothers experienced after Jacob's death. Beforehand, they had sold Joseph into slavery, and now that Joseph was the most powerful man in Egypt, second only to Pharaoh, they figured that their father was the only man still keeping them alive. So they beg forgiveness from Joseph, assuming their lives are in danger. They realize the value of both *anna* and *na*. They instruct their spokesperson, in Genesis 50:17: So shall ye say unto Joseph, Forgive, I pray thee now [*anna*], the trespass of thy brethren, and their sin; for they did unto thee evil: and now, we pray thee [*na*], forgive the trespass of the servants of the God of thy father. And Joseph wept when they spake unto him. (KJV)

The translators supplied the "I" and "we." In the NIV, the "we" is missing, which is okay. Only the *na* is translated: "'This is what you are to say to Joseph: I ask you to forgive your brothers the sins and the wrongs they committed in treating you so badly.' Now please forgive the sins of the servants of the God of your father." When their message came to him, Joseph wept.

Never underestimate the power of *anna* in prayer—even just a *na* is enough to get the attention of God's great heart. Glance at Abraham's intercessory prayer for his nephew. How we translate Abraham's burden for Lot isn't as noteworthy as the depth of his love for his nephew. It emboldened him to breach this issue in conversation with—if I can get lofty here—the God who made this world and the God who can take it out. Sodom is about to die, but not before Abraham has one, last, passionate moment asking God, face to face, to spare Lot.

Now that he has God's ear, the forefather of Israel does not come to the point. He argues for a reprieve for the entire town, ultimately for the sake of 10 people there worth rescuing. Would that be Lot's clan, in Abraham's mind? Anyway, he cried out, "*na*," to the Lord.

Notice how this is translated in different versions of our Bible in Genesis 18:27. Abraham is clearly emotional.

The New King James reads, Then Abraham answered and said, "Indeed now, I who am but dust and ashes have taken it upon myself to speak to the Lord."

The New International has: Then Abraham spoke up again: "Now that I have been so bold as to speak to the Lord, though I am nothing but dust and ashes..."

The New American Standard says: Now behold, I have ventured to speak to the Lord, although I am but dust and ashes.

And Young's Literal Translation,which I most favor for its literalness: Lo, I pray thee, I have willed to speak unto the Lord, and I—dust and ashes...

❖❖❖

There is no magic in this phrase. David's prayer of repentance was spot on in Psalm 51, and he never uses *na*. More to the point is God's ability to read passion in our praying, and to recognize a cry for help, and not a "you

91

owe me" or "you promised and better not lie to me" or "I got faith so you have to do it" attitude.

We cannot presume to know how God will respond to our prayers. Our interest should be in the moment, how are we going to approach Him. Words don't matter; heart does. We probably don't have a clue how to word our inquiry. We probably don't even know where it hurts, only that it does. I went to the dentist with a toothache and told the assistant which tooth I thought was hurting. The dentist examined my teeth, and root-canaled a different tooth. I'm glad he didn't do the tooth I had pointed out to him.

Does God do that? You tell Him where it hurts, and He goes somewhere else, and then does something like a root canal on your life? Well, the pain is gone and I still have the tooth.

We approach God "boldly," says the writer to the Hebrews (Hebrews 4:16). *Boldly* means "with all words," or "frankly." It is one place where our freedom of speech will never be challenged.

It isn't what we say that necessarily moves the heart of God, unless we get the wording just right. And for the record, don't be rude! Even Psalm 51 seems to say more to David than to God. He has learned a valuable lesson about holiness and righteousness, and he hears himself say it. So we are not minimizing what is said, but we don't want to maximize it either. That is, we don't want to suggest that words without heart have any value. Because they don't.

Even without the *na* in David's repentance, I can hear it anyway. A cry for mercy gets God's attention every time, and repentance moves Him to rescue us. According to David, in Ps 51:17: A broken and a contrite heart He will not despise.

Of course there is more to praying than this, but my recommendation is, if it is in our heart to say it, na and anna are indications of our level of excitement or heart's cry and incitement to stir and urge God to move on our behalf.

* * *

What are we trying to say, here? There is a lot of feeling in these contexts, which easily escapes the translations. That's what particles are all about.

This reminds me of a friend's excitement on one occasion, in which his emotions reached that inaccessible peak, where language cannot climb. His joy began to overflow the ability of his words to describe how he felt. As the saying goes, "I am drinking from the saucer, 'cause my cup has overflowed!"

So all he could do was to yell out, "Hot dog!" Over and over again. "Hot dog! Hot dog! Hot dog!"

Translate that.

And... And What?

And -Joel 2:30
The Son of God -Daniel 3:25

A third grader wrote a report of his vacation which read this way: "We went to the beach, and we went in the water, and the end."

I like it, especially the use of the word "and" to connect the story together as one piece. This is quite biblical. And I'm fascinated by the power of one word, when it adds important additional meaning to the verse, and therefore to the preacher's message.

Someone by the name of Charles Middleton wrote a 360-plus-page book on the word *the* in Greek. The book is out of print, and all God's people said, "Amen!" But *the* like *and* can bear a bit of responsibility to clarify the meaning of Scripture. Perhaps one's theology is not threatened by this revelation—if I might use the term here—but we could still gain insight into an important emphasis or clarity that could bring Scripture alive for us. Bible writers, and the characters whose lives are sketched by them, are real people, not fictional characters. And we should enjoy the glimpse into what they said or did. And when it's God who is spoken of? That should be especially meaningful. So *the* and *and* are words worth looking at.

* * *

An English statesman by the name of Granville Sharp researched New Testament Scripture and came up with a rule now called "the Granville Sharp Rule," which relates the Greek word *kai* (pronounced "ke"), meaning "and," and the word *o,* which loosely means "the." He maintained that in certain cases, *kai* could mean "even," and he used this translation to show the deity of Christ.

Titus 2:13 is an example where Paul talks about our great God and [even] Saviour, Jesus Christ. One little word can carry a lot of meaning.

* * *

In Daniel 3:25 a fourth person appeared in the flames that the three Hebrew Children were tossed into. They had refused to deify the King of Babylon, so he had them thrown into the fire. The King James Version identified the fourth person as the son of God, but the NIV reads it as "a son of the gods." The Greek translation goes with the Hebrew and says "a son of God."

93

What about the title for Jesus. According to Christian theology, in Matthew 4:6, he is called "the son of the God." And this agrees with Peter's testimony in Luke 4:41. The crowd and Jewish leadership at Jesus' trial claimed that He referred to Himself as "a son of God." Lastly, 1 John 5:10 recognizes that Jesus is "the son of the God."

My point is that our title for Jesus as the son of God is not grammatically correct. You either use the word *the* for both *son* and *God,* or you say neither, and that's not fair to our belief. The reason for this is because of the mere logic behind such a statement.

If the son is a definite boy that you are referring to, then the dad has to be as definite. You cannot be referring to the particular son of any dad. That makes no sense. Now, you can refer to any son of a particular father, or you could say "a son of the God," but that is not what the theology or the Bible's inspiration wanted to say. Jesus is not seen as any old son of the one and only God. He is the son of God, that is, the incarnate one.

We can offer the same discussion for the phrase "son of man" in Daniel 7:23, and throughout Ezekiel. It could most literally be translated "a son of a man." But the reference is not to his genealogy, but to his humanity, whether we are talking about the prophet or the Savior. Revelation 1:13 is one of many New Testament examples, where the translators supply the word *the* for clarification. *The* is not there in the original. We already know the significance of this title with Jesus. It refers to His humanity. What makes this meaningful is that there would be no reason to say this unless He was and is also deity, or the son of God.

With regard to Ezekiel, 94 times God called him "son of man," not referring to Ezekiel's dad, but to his humanity. Over and over again, God reminded Ezekiel that He, God, knew that Ezekiel was only human and would be asked to do some superhuman stuff. God actually referred to Ezekiel's ministry to the Jewish leadership during the captivity as a headbutting experience. The prophet's name meant "whom God hardens," and God told him that Ezekiel's forehead would be diamond against the flint of any who opposed him. God was in effect telling him to hang in there. It is nice to know that in certain difficult circumstances when we think this or that is beyond us, God reminds us that He knows we are human. That is never an oversight with God but part of the plan.

When referring to Jesus as the son of God, some theologies make a big deal of a missing word *the* in front of the word *God,* as if Jesus were the son of a God, or one of many. Anybody who knows the theology of Deuteronomy 6:4, which God pounded into the Jewish consciousness until it was buried deep inside their thoughts and their theology, also knows that there is really only one God. So the word *the* is not necessary. But the word *the* fits Jesus' title, son.

Was it Jesus who was seen taking a stroll in the fire? Maybe. I leave that with you. For now, take note of the difficulty God has to overcome in sharing His thoughts with us. We are still his disciples, His students, wondering, because some of what we read in Scripture, as John described it, "... is ... hard ... who can hear it?" (John 6:60)

"Will ye also go away?" Jesus asked in verse 67.

I appreciate Peter's response to Jesus' concern about their faithfulness in verses 68 and 69, and how he clears up this whole issue of *the* or *a* son of *the* or *a* God:

Then Simon Peter answered him, Lord, to whom shall we go? thou hast the words of eternal life. And we believe and are sure that thou art that Christ, the Son of the living God.

* * *

Now the word *and* is equally as dynamic. It often indicates in the Hebrew a continuation or further development of something that happened or was spoken about just before. The simplest form of this is the phrase "and he said."

Take for example Genesis 3:1: Now the serpent was more subtle than any beast of the field which THE LORD God had made. And he said unto the woman... (KJV) It should really be translated, "and he [the serpent] *proceeded* to say..." Then it would be clearer that Satan's deceptive craftiness is doing the talking.

And all the people answered together, and said, All that THE LORD hath spoken we will do. (Exodus 19:8, KJV) This might be better translated, "The people answered, saying..."

I like Psalm 18:1 which we start with I love you, O LORD, my strength. We like to take everything before this as a chapter title or annotation. The problem is, the words "and he said" in that title:

He sang to THE LORD the words of this song when THE LORD delivered him from the hand of all his enemies and from the hand of Saul. He said, I love you, O LORD, my strength.

This makes it clear that David's song of love for God came as the testimony of his rescue from Saul and his many enemies. His spoken love is the refrain or chorus for the song of His life.

There is a story to tell about the word *love* as well, but not here.

Psalm 34:7 reads: The angel of the Lord encamps around those who fear him, and he delivers them. That's why they, the angels, are there. That is what they are doing, pitching their tents about the children of God. They are the armies of heaven, moving with God's people, setting and breaking camp as God directs His children to move about, and becoming God's rearguard as well as His lookouts.

If we see this verse saying that the angels are there, say, as spiritual reporters, to simply relay information to and from God, if any spiritual skirmish they might chance to get involved in is incidental to their main task, we don't see or understand the word *and*.

Isaiah 9:6 is a familiar verse: To us a son is given: and the government will be on his shoulders. And he <u>will</u> be called... I agree with Professor S. R. Driver, whose grammar book is offering us these jots and tittles. The word *will* is misplaced, because it disconnects what the word *and* connects. The government *is* on His shoulders, and His name *has been* called Wonderful... His sonship makes Him the ruler. His name was not changed to Wonderful. He has always been, as the Son of God, Wonderful.

Driver calls the word *will*, that is, putting Christ's lordship and the wonder of His person into the future, an "unwonted transition... a gross error... an entire misapprehension of the Hebrew point of view."[1] Not "he will be," but "He is and has been" all of the above. Sounds a bit like Revelation 4:8: ...who was, is and is to come...

* * *

This brought me to Joel 2:18: <u>Then</u> THE LORD will be jealous for his land and take pity on his people. Notice the word *then*. In the original, this is our word *and*. There are a lot of "and's" in this chapter, but many of them do not carry the force of nuance and meaning this one has. That's why the translators used the word *then* in translation.

How can one know which *and* is worth a closer look? Generally, the translation alerts us, but where it doesn't, a little study might suggest added insight. You may feel like this is looking for a needle in a haystack, but isn't all research that way? Isn't it thrilling to learn something in a verse which you missed the first hundred times you read it? I anticipate a rich learning experience when I meet the Savior. I will sit quietly in the last row on some grassy hillside, while He expounds His truth to us like in the good old days in Palestine.

For now, in verse 18, here's the explanation I want to proffer. The first seventeen verses rehearse the divine warning to God's people to honor the covenant and return to Him. God does not threaten; He warns. He prophesied of a pending nightmare that not even the producers of *Friday the Thirteenth* could dream up. Unless they repent and return, catastrophic misfortune is inevitable.

I don't know how that fits with your theology but there is a happy ending coming in verse 28. For now, verse 17 itself amounts to a tearful prayer of repentance offered God by the priesthood in Israel on behalf of a desperate Jewish nation. After such an outpouring of grief filled with pleas for God's involvement, verse 18: <u>Then</u> God will be jealous for His land...

The entire text hinges on this word *then*. It is the fulcrum upon which everyone's eternity rocks. It is the turning point in the life of an individual or a nation when they repent and the storm ceases, replaced by soft breezes of mercy.

I recently read the Bible through in the NIV, and this simple message was so evident in its pages. Regardless of how unspeakably horrifying the crime, God always responds favorably to repentance, with grace. We wouldn't think to be that way. Some crimes deserve no mercy—ever. Some people, even in the minds of believers, have earned the flames of hell and deserve whatever the wrath of God can dish out. But that is not the mind of a God who took on all the forces of evil on Golgotha to rescue you and me from this wrath. If this lesson doesn't come through to us in the pages of the *Tanakh*, the Old Testament, we need to reread it again and again, until we at least begin to see it. It is the lesson of Old Israel's history that God stands ever--ready to forgive the repentant. It is the amazing lesson of this word *then*.

You can study the rest of God's merciful and gracious response to a priestly prayer for forgiveness in the verse to follow, but I draw your attention to verses 28 and 30:

And afterward, I will pour out my Spirit on all people. Your sons and daughters will prophesy, your old men will dream dreams, your young men will see visions. Even on my servants, both men and women, I will pour out my Spirit in those days. [And] I will show wonders in the heavens and on the earth, blood and fire and billows of smoke. The sun will be turned to dark- ness and the moon to blood before the coming of the great and dreadful day of the Lord. And everyone who calls on the name of the Lord will be saved; for on Mount Zion and in Jerusalem there will be deliverance, as the Lord has said, among the survivors whom the Lord calls.

Maybe we should ask Peter, from Acts 2:17 -21:

In the last days, God says, I will pour out my Spirit on all people. Your sons and daughters will prophesy, your young men will see visions, your old men will dream dreams. Even on my servants, both men and women, I will pour out my Spirit in those days, and they will prophesy. I will show wonders in the heaven above and signs on the earth below, blood and fire and billows of smoke. The sun will be turned to darkness and the moon to blood before the coming of the great and glorious day of the Lord. And everyone who calls on the name of the Lord will be saved.

Peter understood the Day of Pentecost to be somehow a part of the total prophecy, but perhaps separated in time. Could the events recorded in Acts 2 be a part of the restoration of verse Joel 2:25? "The years the locust ate," does this reference only a period of Jewish history recorded already in Chronicles? Or one of the earlier prophets? Or is this a general overview of all hardship Israel had to endure from the period of the kings up to Peter's day? Plainly asked, could Peter be telling us that the outpouring of God's Spirit on Pentecost was the fulfillment of the promise of restoration, prophesied by Joel?

How connected is Joel 2:18-27 with the prophecy Peter used as his Pentecost Day text? They are connected somehow because of the word *and.*

Then we can race ahead in time to verse 30, when the prophecy suggests a book-of-Revelation event. These verses, too, are somehow all part of one piece.

It is interesting to note that Peter ended his quote—at least according to the account in Acts—in the middle of Joel 2:32. He didn't finish the verse that says, "for on Mount Zion and in Jerusalem there will be deliverance, as the Lord has said, among the survivors whom the Lord calls."

Might you be interested in looking into this? Or does the word *and* still seem like such a small word? I'm sorry for the twinge of sarcasm. Every word is a kind of jot or tittle that deserves my attention. I think God, the author, was ingenious enough to put the words together in exactly the way He wanted them, and that I do not need to say that only the thoughts or ideas are inspired, but I can research those ideas through the words and the language—what little I know of them.

Here's what I think the word *and* is saying. The road appears shorter when flying over it at 6 miles up rather than walking it. So is a prophetic picture which spans centuries of time from the time of Joel to our time. The restoration or revival Joel envisioned was the subsequent blessing of repentance—as is always the case. We must learn this theological note. Repentance always precedes and is a requirement for revival and restoration.

God promised for a restored Israel, which Paul reminded us through his new covenant ministry, includes nations of non-Jews, a Spirit outpouring, a deluge of His grace, coupled with empowerment to spread the message of this same grace to subsequent generations of believers.

That's a mouthful, but the last *and* that couples the end-time with the revelation of the end-time, about a bloody moon and a darkened sun, suggests to me that this truth once introduced to God's people is unchanging until His return. The outpouring of His Spirit does not cease until Christ's return.

The message on the Day of Pentecost was a message for all time remaining. The outpoured Spirit of God was for generation after generation of believer, until such an outpouring could be replaced with the simple, real, and visible presence of the eternal God in our midst—the return of Christ.

Can you see it? One prophecy. One complete account connected by *and*.

I doubt I will ever look at the word *and* the same way again. I doubt that I can glance over it as if it were not written there on the page while I search out the action words. I must at least pause in my reading, just for an instant and say with David, *Selah.*

In Psalm 41:11, when David remembered his defeated enemies, who had sought to destroy him in his weakened condition, he credited God with holding unto him tightly *and* helping him to stand on his spiritual and emotional feet. In my integrity you uphold me <u>and</u> set me in your presence forever.

The *and* in this verse adds reason to God's powerful grip. It wasn't to restrict the friend of God, much less, by such a grasp to cause him any discomfort. It was to keep him on his feet.

December 21, 2012

...and then shall the end come... -Matthew 24:14

As many know—and this information is readily available on the Internet—the Mayan Indians of Central America over 5,000 years ago devised a calendar system that today is considered the most accurate of all calendars. Their calculations maintained that a new era will begin on December 21, 2012. Interestingly enough there are even astrological assumptions and meteorological probabilities that make this sound more and more possible to some. When we put this together with a global economic crisis, and start comparing current events to biblical prophecy, we begin to wonder if the return of Christ isn't just around the corner.

No Christian questions the soon return of Christ, but when we ask the question "When?" we go too far, according to Jesus. He not only told His disciples at His ascension that it was not for them to know, but the grammar lacks necessary support in answering such an inquiry. If we are determined to get around our Savior's clear instruction in Acts 1, we discover that we are suddenly sinking in a quagmire of "myths and endless genealogies," as Paul put it to young Timothy in 1 Timothy 1:4-7: These promote controversies rather than God's work—which is by faith.

"Oh not so!" you may argue.

We have a right and even an obligation to investigate and interpret prophecy to become better informed witnesses. There is no myth in the Revelation account, and certainly no one here is using lineage or the right of secession—genealogies—as a claim to authority or interpretation. Prophecy is nothing less than history still to happen, and it is connected to current events as one continuous historical thread. We only want to understand how this might relate to us and our children, and that's legitimate. Well said and not disputed. But the word *when* is what is questionable, since neither the Hebrew or the Greek of the Bible clearly represents this idea.

How so?

* * *

Before I answer that, understand that what I want to do here is to defuse an old controversy about the time of Christ's return. Will it be before or after, or maybe during, a seven year period of absolute global chaos? Will believers in

Christ see any of this? Will the church hang around at least for the beginning of what is call "The Great Tribulation"?

This controversy might already be dead and buried, and if so, I have no interest in some future ministry digging it up. But the question must still linger in the minds of God's people, especially when their own lives are suddenly chaotic: they are out of a job; they have to foreclose on the home of their dreams; someone they know or even love suffers severe trauma.

You see my drift here. Our favorite Scripture—and this is as it should be —becomes Luke 21:28: Stand up and lift up your heads, because your redemption is drawing near. I get excited, too, over this verse. It actually says is—our redemption is *drawing* near. Not that Christ was returning at the time of writing but—remember, Greek—the word wants us to see the Lord descending or put in our terms, His return is imminent. I think we should be looking up in our hearts—not literally, else you will have trouble reading this.

But the question before us here is "When?" Or in the words of the prophet Habakkuk, "How long?"

* * *

Well, there's the tittle! That is where the language of the Bible is failing me because—and, probably, no one else will be crazy enough to suggest this to you—the emphasis in the language of the New Testament wants us to ask a different set of questions. When we read the New Testament—say, the Book of Revelation—we need to ask: "Is it seen as being over? Are we reading about events in progress or completed?" or "What is it?" or "What character- izes this period at the end? What kind of man walks the earth on the eve of its destruction? "

Such questions are intended to identify the end times or the tribulation that is to come. We want to define this phrase "Great Tribulation," not say when it will happen. These are two separate inquiries. Such questions that describe the events that anticipate our Lord's return are alright. The question "When?" is not asked and therefore not answered in the New Testament, and that means we should not be asking it, either.

Huh? We can get a rough idea of the order of events leading up to the end, but we cannot know exactly when it will all go down. Some events may overlap. Others may take a long time happening before the next thing takes place.

The old theological argument that purposes to answer the question "When will our Lord return?" in reference to the last 7 years of recorded time —before it starts; right in the middle of it; when it is over—is asking the Bible for an answer it was not written to offer. In plain English, God didn't care to go there.

He cares for us to see the movie of events perhaps in fleeting images or pictures that provide a view, perhaps a bit hazy, of the condition of this world when time runs out. It is a picture of unrepentant evil, of a world against everything God stands for, a world that has reasoned away the absolute principles of the laws of God that define holiness.

Take a look at 2 Thessalonians 2:1-12 (NLT):

Now, dear brothers and sisters, let us clarify some things about the coming of our Lord Jesus Christ and how we will be gathered to meet him. Don't be so easily shaken or alarmed by those who say that the day of the Lord has already begun [to the effect that the day of the Lord has come, i.e., we are living yet in that day]. Don't believe them, even if they claim to have had a spiritual vision, a revelation, or a letter supposedly from us. Don't be fooled by what they say. For that day will not come until there is a great rebellion against God and the man of lawlessness is revealed—the one who brings destruction. He will exalt himself and defy everything that people call god and every object of worship. He will even sit in the temple of God, claiming that he himself is God.

Don't you remember that I told you about all this when I was with you? And you know what is holding him back, for he can be revealed only when his time comes. For this lawlessness is already at work secretly, and it will remain secret until the one who is holding it back steps out of the way. Then the man of lawlessness will be revealed, but the Lord Jesus will kill him with the breath of his mouth and destroy him by the splendor of his coming.

This man will come to do the work of Satan with counterfeit power and signs and miracles. He will use every kind of evil deception to fool those on their way to destruction, because they refuse to love and accept the truth that would save them. So God will cause them to be greatly deceived, and they will believe these lies. Then they will be condemned for enjoying evil rather than believing the truth.

What I glean from this portion of Scripture is that there is a mysterious evil that was already at work in Paul's day. It is a general spirit in mankind that intends to support another world leader other than our Lord. It is lawless in the sense that it has no regard for God's law. In my argument, it is a social order that negates the one God envisioned in Eden.

Inevitably a battle ensues between the two kingdoms, Christ's and Antichrist's. Guess who wins?

We can ask when or as the first disciples phrase it, "Will you at this time restore again the kingdom to Israel?" Christ won't tell us.

* * *

What I have been asking you to do is read the action words differently than you are used to reading them in English. Instead of asking "Is it happening now?" ask "Is it seen as still going on?" Instead of saying, "It happened already." Say, "It is described as being completed." Instead of thinking, "It has always been that way." Think, "This is what it continues to be."

Oh my head! What am I attempting to say? Put simply, the Revelation is a movie of events and conditions that describe the end of time. But we do not know when the movie happens. It is even difficult to know if the events are continuous or overlap or if there are time gaps in between some of them. I think I said that already! All we can glean from end-time prophecy is the ultimate condition of man and his self-destruction.

Mark in his gospel narrated the events of our Savior's ministry as if they were happening now. In Mark 11:27, "they came to Jerusalem" actually reads, "they are coming to Jerusalem." He relates the activity, the movie, the progress of Jesus' journey through Palestine.

Similarly, something still to take place is seen vividly as if it were taking place at the time it is being told. Mark 9:31: The Son of man is delivered into the hands of men. Actually at the time Jesus said it, if He had said it in English, He might have said, "The Son of man shall be delivered..." Instead, though, he spoke of it as a vivid and impending event.

Acts 15:21 might appear to be saying Moses... has in every city them that preach him... but we can and should extend this sermon material backward into the past. "Moses... *has had* in every city them that *preached* him..." The sermons that contained references to Moses and his writings are endless, continuing to the time Peter once again mentioned his name.

One of my favorites is Luke 3:22: You are My beloved Son; in You I am well pleased. The Greek actually uses a past tense here: "in You I *was* well pleased." In school, we were taught to view this type of action in its simplest use as something that has completely happened. But how can that work here? It doesn't mean complete, done, over with, as if to say that the father's excitement over His son's willing obedience was a thing of the past. Now He's no longer happy about Jesus? I can't go there, and neither does the Bible.

How are we to read this? Should we just cop out, or give up and make it a present sense? It appears that is what the translators did. It has drawn no small interest from scholars and understandably so.

A parishioner told me once my sermons gave her headaches. I probably forced her to think. Perhaps, but it has never been my intention—it should go without saying—to get bogged down in a philosophical or theological quagmire of details, or attempt to prove how smart I am when I'm not that smart.

I am probably not so intelligent, just hungry to learn.

What we need to understand is that it is stupid to think we are smart. It is the curse of a little knowledge that can make us dangerous, when arguing our point against another Christian's. I wish I could convince other believers that they are just as dumb as I, because I don't know enough to enjoy winning theological debates with other Christians or supporting church infighting over textual minutiae. I had to say that before I led your thoughts into the next paragraph because it is a clear example of how little we do know and how unwise it is to argue our intelligence.

E. D. Burton—and he is smart—devoted a little space to this verse, Luke 3:22, in his grammar book.[1] I'll try to summarize his remarks. The use of a seeming past tense "I was well pleased" coming from God when, we know that He is well pleased with Jesus and always will be, requires a grammatical explanation. The word "pleased" could be used in an historical sense. God was pleased with Christ for being baptized. But God says this again on the Mount of Transfiguration, as recorded in Matthew 17:5, and this explanation simply doesn't work there.

It could be a general statement about Jesus' existence with the father before His incarnation. He has always been well pleased with Jesus. Burton's problem here is the absence of a phrase like "before the foundation of the world," which would have cleared this whole thing up for us.

Maybe it is like our present-perfect tense, "God has been pleased." He had and does take great joy in His son. This would be referring to Jesus' time on earth up to and including the time of speaking, either at His baptism or on the Mount of Transfiguration. But, again, it would have been nice to have read here something like "up to this time." That's the usual way of writing such an idea.

Maybe it should be translated, "I became well pleased... and am accordingly well pleased..." There are a few Old Testament passages that suggest this possibility. Psalm 102:14, for example: For thy servants take pleasure in her stones, and favor the dust thereof. "Take pleasure" is the same word and tense as in Luke 3:22. The problem here is that—well—we are getting perhaps a bit desperate since other Scriptures, Old and New Testament, that use this word in this form can be explained as denoting past time. They can be explained without resorting to so unusual a use of this form as we seem inevitably obliged to use to understand God's comment at Jesus' baptism or on the Mount.

We can understand God to be referring to some indefinite past time, when He first became overjoyed and excited about His son, or His mission. The translation should read, "I have become well pleased..." But this is only a vivid way of saying "I am well pleased." It appears that two pages later in this book, and the translators got it right after all? Burton says, "The English version is... substantially correct..."[2] What this is saying is that God's current or present pleasure is suggested from His "always was there" joy in His Son. Isaiah 42:1 agrees: Behold! My Servant whom I uphold, My Elect One in whom My soul delights! [same form as Luke 3:22] I have put My Spirit upon Him; He will bring forth justice to the Gentiles. And Matthew all but quotes Isaiah in his gospel (Matthew 12:18): Behold my servant, whom I have chosen; my beloved, in whom my soul is well pleased.

These two verses, and in the Hebrew for Isaiah 42:1, as in Luke 3:22 and Matthew 17:5, all these verses are written in a past time or completed form. Burton calls these a rhetorical figure on the way to become grammatical idiom.[3]

There is also something known as the dramatic use of the verb. Luke 16:4 says, "I knew what I shall do," and understandably means "I know what I shall do." This is said to be a vivid state of mind just reached. Perhaps, that is what happened at the river's edge and on the mount. The father's emotions toward His son peaked in some sense. It was a vivid moment, frozen in time for God, and He cried out in His excitement, "I am so pleased with my son!" The English translation is correct.

* * *

Before you reach for the aspirin bottle, let me reiterate. True scholarship takes great pains to share with open honesty what can be learned from Scripture. Join me in a resolve never again to take part in a religious zeal that denies this innocent hunger to know. Stay open and teachable. A favorite verse of mine which some students had put on a plaque, as a gift to me, is Isaiah 50:4, and the NIV has it right (We are not the teachers but the students), The Sovereign LORD has given me an instructed tongue, to know the word that sustains the weary. He wakens me morning by morning, wakens my ear to listen like one being taught.

* * *

Getting back to the verbs in 2 Thessalonians 2:1-12, can you see why remaining teachable is a good idea? I need to avoid the urge to preach this text because it is full of relevancy. Is the world going to end soon? Are you frightened by the thought? Paul said, "Please, don't be!" There must first come an apostasy and someone known as the man of lawlessness needs to be identified.

Who is he?

You don't know?

Than he hasn't been revealed yet. There is nothing to worry about.

But when? When will he be revealed?

In his time! In his time!

I am more interested in verse 7. There is a working mystery of lawlessness. Working might be translated, becoming energized. I maintain that there is an undertow of godlessness or social change that is gaining strength. It is gradually obtaining a global popularity, a universal recognition and acceptance, a social legitimacy that means inevitably that when it surfaces, it rises out of the sea of ideas as current thought. It will be a familiar lifestyle and not recognized for what it really is, a tsunami of social destruction.

Social change is slow and methodical and may not be the product of any one man's or even one generation's thoughts. It is like being wrapped with threads which can at first be broken and its victim freed, but which eventually by being strengthened by adding thread upon thread becomes too strong and no one can get loose of its hold.

I think that is what is happening. We have been prophesying about single events and trying to tie them to a "when." We have been preaching about wars and earthquakes and slowly the thread count rises in our society unseen by even the preacher.

We have been wanting to write a timeline, a chronology of prophetic events instead of observing social change. It is so gradual like the hour hand of the clock that we tire of staring at it. It appears not to move and we are convinced that nothing has changed from the beginning of recorded history. The market will recover. The pendulum of social change will swing back again—someday. Nothing new.

There is the tale about placing a frog in a bowl of water and bringing the water slowly to a boil cooking the frog because the temperature change was too gradual for the frog to realize the danger. This story has been scientifically challenged and discredited. It has been used by everyone along the continuum of political ideologies to suggest urgency and involvement before it is too late. I won't use this illustration here because it has become somewhat of an overused metaphor and is laughed at by skeptics who have more and more credence in our world. The warnings of Scripture are not boiling frogs but real issues that should be heeded.

I think we are wrong if we say nothing has changed. Some of the verbs in Paul's instruction to the Thessalonians are in a tense showing progress. I will leave the rest of this idea to the pastors.

Sign Here, Please

If any man sins... -1 John 2:1

Who wrote the epistle to the Hebrews? Scholarship has gone round and round on this one and I have to admit that when I read those letters known to be written by Paul and then read Hebrews, I wasn't so sure either. Then I read a part of the epistle of Clement and wondered, maybe he wrote Hebrews.

You see, you begin to think that you have picked up on a writer's style of writing, which I call his signature. You are more and more convinced that according to that signature such and such a book was written by the author whose style you think you recognize.

Scholars can argue this type of analysis. They are biblical handwriting experts of sorts—the textual critics—but you and I are far more restricted by what we know or rather don't know about the Bible languages. I am not a handwriting analyst, but I find interesting some phrases and words that I—not unexpectedly—read in one author instead of another.

* * *

I thought that it made sense to read Peter warning about meddling in other people's affairs. I Peter 4:15: But let none of you suffer as a murderer, a thief, an evildoer, or as a busybody in other people's matters. He invented the word "busybody" to say it and if you know anything about Peter, you can see the connection. Peter showed perhaps an uncommon curiosity in John's well-being when he, Peter, was told that in old age he would have to be assisted getting around. "What shall this man do?", he wanted to know looking at John. What is that to you? Jesus quizzed the nosey Peter in John 21:21.

Footnote: This conversation was on the eve of Jesus' ascension which leads some to erroneously think that John the beloved apostle would not die but be here when Christ returns.

Peter had another weakness which I can relate to. He didn't like pain. He didn't want to suffer without good cause. This led him to disassociate with some gentile believers at Antioch on one visit because he was called to minister to his fellow countrymen and it made political sense to avoid an unnecessary photo op with non-Jewish Christians.

107

In those early days there was a slight difference in dogmas and what was and wasn't important to religiously observe. Uncircumcised gentile believers probably ate pork—to boot! Galatians 2:11 and 12 tells us: Now when Peter had come to Antioch, I [Paul] withstood him to his face, because he was to be blamed; for before certain men came from James, he would eat with the Gentiles; but when they came, he withdrew and separated himself, fearing those who were of the circumcision.

Peter—I think I observe—was prone to avoid suffering, if possible. When, however, at the end of life it directly related to his witness, he willingly—again I think, willingly—went to his cross. Tradition says he hung upside down because Jesus died on a cross and Peter did not think he was worthy of such honor.

Peter said in 1 Peter 3:14: But even if you should suffer for righteousness' sake, you are blessed. The word *should* indicates the possibility but not probability of suffering. Only Peter used this form or way of talking in connection with suffering. I smile thinking, "Yeah, that's Pete!"

* * *

When I read "little children" in a letter, I see an elderly saint. That's John the beloved apostle who lived—we are told—into his 90's. But what is of more immediate interest to me are the words *and if* starting the second chapter of his first epistle: I John 2:1 My little children, these things I write to you, so that you may not sin. And if anyone sins, we have an Advocate with the Father, Jesus Christ the righteous.

It actually means, "If any of you might perchance—maybe should—ever sin..." I stretched that out a bit to show the gentle language of this beloved apostle. He avoided the accusation of any critic that he was reprimanding God's people for sin. He was not accusing them although he could have. Any one of us could be scolded for sinning and probably at any given moment we would deserve it, but there is a problem with this condemning approach.

An accusing tone usually brings a defensive attitude in the accused. The preacher may say, "I am bringing conviction!" The problem here is that only God can pull this off where conviction leads to repentance.

Beside John wasn't noticing or referencing any particular sin that he observed. His comment was general. Christians need to be encouraged to use introspection and observe their own actions and motives. They don't need a preacher turned psychologist to tell them what they—no doubt—already know.

John actually had great news in verse 12. Your sins are already forgiven! There should be no "but" to follow this that accuses or condemns.

And sin for believers is remote. It was also John who pointed out that repeated sinning in any one area is a bad sign. In chapter three he adds, Whoever has been born of God does not sin... He does not repeatedly, habitually and naturally sin. I am leaving that one for the preacher, that is, how John can assert that Christians don't sin over and over again. The only thing I will say about this Johannine comment is that a true believer will be virtually tormented by conviction and a heart crying for mercy even if they temporarily resist this inner voice to let it go and repent. Christians are capable of struggling with sin over decades! I think.

John is the elderly grandfather figure who has boiled his Christian message down to love. It is usually the youth who full of investigative curiosity and a keen interest in debate might complicate the simple message of faith. Old men dream of what was and can be; young men are visionaries, ready to change the world! There is nothing wrong here.

David said in Psalm 37:25: I have been young, and now am old... Study the Psalms and see what the old man discovered. He discovered the simplicity of faith. While young, the explanation for life and experience is found in a theology, for theology is best studied by the young, who are capable of imagining that all things are explainable and one's knowledge of Truth can be complete enough to give answer to the questions of life. When old, life becomes a Psalm, where wisdom means learning only to wait on God, to trust in His ability and wisdom to know what to do and when; and to cling to a faith that says He will.

It is no surprise to me to hear the gentle voice of the apostle of love. It is John.

* * *

Now, I may have gone out of my way here to see something that may not be there—a spiritual mirage in a writer's desert. In other words, I wanted one more example to finish this chapter.

Do you like honesty?

Put this one out there for your pastor to expound on. I am interested in the phrase "to suffer with" which appears was something Paul would say. Even when Peter had opportunity as we already mentioned, he didn't talk about suffering in the same way. The phrase—found in Paul's writing and not Peter's—means to suffer evils along with someone else and that someone else for Paul was Christ.

In Romans 8:16,17 we read: The Spirit Himself bears witness with our spirit that we are children of God, and if children, then heirs—heirs of God and joint heirs with Christ, if indeed we suffer with Him, that we may also be glorified together.

Suffering persecution seemed to be no big deal to Paul. He seemed to expect it unlike Peter who probably hoped God would providentially minimize that source of pain for him. Romans 8:36: For Your sake we are killed all day long; We are accounted as sheep for the slaughter... He also told the Philippians in 1:29: For to you it has been granted on behalf of Christ, not only to believe in Him, but also to suffer for His sake...

Peter did remind us in 1 Peter 3:18 to weep with those who weep. But this is showing sympathy or maybe empathy and not actually joining them in the furnace. Paul accepts what Peter has to say, in 1 Corinthians 12:26: And if one member suffers, all the members suffer with it; or if one member is honored, all the members rejoice with it. And to the Romans in 12:15, he adds: Rejoice with those who rejoice, and weep with those who weep.

But Paul's consciousness of suffering and in particular Christ's suffering made him want to join in. Suffering "with" meant getting to know and that was his interest. Philippians 3:10 reads, ...that I may know Him and the power of His resurrection, and the fellowship of His sufferings, being conformed to His death...

This is the man who dusted himself off after nearly being stoned to death and returned to Lystra to continue his ministry among the people who just dragged him out of that town. It doesn't sound like Peter. But it is Paul.

* * *

There is a comment or two a want to make about Ezekiel. Reading his prophecy reminded me of Moses' writings or the first five books of the Bible, the Torah or the Pentateuch. This lead me to think that this prophet spent considerable time studying and learning the Torah. It was probably a love of his. I understand that he was in line for the priesthood but with the captivity and the destruction of the temple, he was unemployed. He was a good candidate for the pastorate of the captivity.

Some of the most difficult books of the Bible are not difficult because of the language but the content. Perhaps, Ezekiel's prophecy of the valley of dry bones and the thoughts surrounding this scene are impossible to figure out until it happens—perhaps not. And the vision he had at the start was awesome! But language wise Ezekiel was a humble man simply longing to follow the law of God. Ezekiel thought and spoke the language of Scripture.

It might be worth asking, "Is our heart so in tune with the message that it escapes our pen and lips as well?" I had a secretary once that needed to have a package measured for mailing. I worked the ruler while she wrote down the dimensions of the box.

She asked me, "What's the length?

I told her.

She then inquired, "What's the width?"

I told her.
"And the height?" She wanted to know.
I gave it to her.
And then she asked, to my surprise, "And what's the breadth?"

Threads

...one flesh. -Genesis 2:24

As in any work in which the author needs to develop an idea, God develops certain themes in our Bible. The most obvious example of this is the progressive revelation of God through the names for Him we meet in its pages. We start with "God" in the first verse and end up with "Jesus" in the last. Along the way, He is given other names which further reveal something about His character or His attributes or who He is in relation to us.

A progressive revelation ties the books of the Bible together into one book and gives someone like me further evidence of its Divine authorship. Several writers working independently and with independent thought and interests could never have offered us so visible a common thread of truth running through the entire work. Not only is the theme well represented along the path of biblical thought but it is progressive; it is in the process of being developed or revealed in steps or stages. This fact alone is the Divine signature that authenticates this work as God's. I call this a thread.

It is also a dissertation, God's dissertation. Regarding dissertations, I spoke once with a professor from a university local to our residence at the time. He was on the committee to review dissertations for PhD candidates from this university. He told me that one of his primary interests in any work is continuity of thought or theme. Students who go off on tangents as they write or ramble along on the page are likely to be disapproved because the theme is the important thought or thread that must run through the entire document. The theme is what the candidate attempts to explain, exemplify and prove.

Well, that's the word of God, a dissertation proving man's need of a Savior and God's solution to this problem. So, it makes sense to find certain ideas in support of this singular theme being themselves introduced and developed in its pages.

* * *

One of the biblical ideas that first caught my attention—perhaps, as a pastor —was God's introduction to Adam of the aptly-named "henotic" relationship. *Henotic* comes from the Greek word for "one." Genesis 2:24 reads: For this reason a man will leave his father and mother and be united to his wife, and they will become one flesh. God offered this explanation of the marriage relationship to Adam, I would maintain, as an instruction and a promise. Often enough there needs to be a balance between God's part, the promise: they will become one flesh and man's part, the instruction: "leave ... father and mother."

I found it reasonable that God introduced the henotic relationship to Adam even though he, Adam, had no parents. God was introducing society, social order, not just to Adam but all mankind through this simple and direct statement.

This, I think, is the God idea: "It is not good that man should be alone," is how He began. God intended to provide Adam with companionship, but more than that, God was addressing some level of loneliness that not even a good hound dog could fill. We might say God made Eve to help Adam populate the globe. Yet, that would accuse God of a deception since He should have so stated that His intention was simply children. He hadn't. Procreation is not the subject here. Oneness is. Eve is to be a companion like none other. No part of God's creation can take her place. Yes, later, as her name denotes, she would become the mother of all living people. For now, God's point is that she and Adam are to become one.

"Husbands, love your wives as Christ loved the church", was the way Paul put it. Paul's instruction goes from "leave" to "love." This a clear movement of a man's affection from his mom to his Mrs. If a man even begins to understand what this verse is saying, his bride has found a piece of heaven. She has become the center of his world. And all the wives said...

Going on: It sounds like a punishment when Eve in the Garden of Eden after eating forbidden fruit, was told, Your desire shall be for your husband, And he shall rule over you. The "desire" part is good and should be understood as her contribution to this love relationship. It provides a mutual response to his love. Sounds simplistic? No, romantic!

The God idea—as I refer to it—is profoundly ingenious.

The man who has taken the leadership in his relationship to love his wife, is a true leader. He does not argue his needs, defend his interests, or dwell on how neglected he is. His interests are centered on his Eve, and if I could be bold and say it, her interests now, by the sheer power of his love are on him.

This is a true love relationship. Let me define it. A love relationship becomes always and only between two a mutual awareness that "I love and am loved." Young love has a marked advantage here in having such a relationship in its innocent acceptance of future challenges; its spontaneous embrace of another; its passion for life.

Some of us are sadly damaged having been in broken relationships, but Eden represents God's dream, God's ideal relationship for man.

Yes. Adam and Eve blew it and theologically we share the blame. I guess it's human to struggle in relationship and sometimes to do things that estrange us from the people we actually do love.

And he shall rule over you. God's words spoken to Eve after the "Fall." This "rule over you" part is not God's original nor His ultimate design for marriage. When God made them man and woman, Eve was bone of Adam's bone and flesh of his flesh. They were intended to be one and the same and yet their individuality should never be challenged or lost in this growing intimacy.

The story of Adam and Eve depicts the start of romance, the beginning of intimacy, the initiation of relationship that was intended to complete the picture of the Garden of Eden, which I freely translate, the Paradise of Pleasure. God envisioned marriage as a Henotic relationship or two people in some spiritual, social, or psychological sense blending their desires and interests to a greater and greater degree into a life they have in common.

* * *

The two should become one in the divine plan and that means closeness, sharing secrets no one else knows; discovering each other: Each other's strengths and weaknesses; passions and fears and needs. Now, that's the God idea when He invented the marriage relationship. It is so God! So much so, it could represent Christ and His church in Paul's mind.

Somehow I can't see this any other way than a monogamous life-long relationship between a man and a woman. If I am offensive in saying so, I regret it only because I am someone who wants everybody to like me, but I cannot set aside the point I want to make here that this henotic relationship envisioned in Eden by God for man is a thread of truth because it by divine design is a vital part of the domestic framework of heaven. It is woven into the social fabric of God's kingdom through the relationship between Christ and His church.

If He had an ulterior motive in mentioning it to Adam other than its immediate application to Adam and Eve's experience, it had to be Christ and His church that was on His mind when He drew this blueprint for happiness. Ephesians 5:31 reads: For this reason a man will leave his father and mother and be united to his wife, and the two will become one flesh. This is a profound mystery—but I am talking about Christ and the church.

Remove a thread and the whole truth comes unraveled. If that happens, the message is not the message and God's reason for writing it is lost. If we plan to redefine the henotic relationship or determine it to be unimportant in the divine plan; if Eden represented nothing eternal and was only the beginning of things—nothing more, than the marriage relationship can be reconsidered, redefined, and reinvented.

In a letter dated April 18, 1940 to Mary Neylan, a former pupil, C. S. Lewis responded to her perceptions regarding marriage. She questioned the church's teachings on the subject. She thought outdated: The Bible's view of a woman's relationship with a man, male headship, "being in love" and the meaning of the wedding ceremony. That was in 1940.

We have come a long way since then tweaking the definition of the marriage relationship, editing the ceremony, and reconsidering our interpretation of Scriptures on this subject. If we go so far as toss the henotic relationship of marriage away, we have lost also the Christ-church relationship. We are not ultimately tampering with the plan of God. That's not possible. We are in effect closing the book and deciding not to read or study its message.

There are a number of theological points of interest that we can take or leave and do that even with God's blessing but not the threads... Please, not the threads! Never the truths that deal with Salvation and define our developing relationship with a God that wants to have that relationship with us.

So, why do I think that Adam and Eve's oneness in Eden deserves such recognition other than Paul's use of this relationship to define ours with Christ? Well, that's enough right there but the other indicator to me—strangely enough—is the absence of this idea until we arrive at Christ's death. Jesus explained the absence of this truth through the Old Testament Kingdom period as the result of "hard heartedness." Matthew 19:8 says Jesus replied, Moses permitted you to divorce your wives because your hearts were hard. But it was not this way from the beginning.

"From the beginning..." And then the henotic relationship is re-introduced through the Gospels, as for example in Matthew 19:5. My antennae go up when a Bible thought is introduced, then disappears, and then shows up again, this time to stay and then an apostle finds a spiritual application that relates to the plan of God.

A thread.

* * *

Take the Garden of Eden itself which disappears from the record after the first couple leave it until the prophets remind us that God doesn't chuck His plans but only postpones their fulfillment until the right time. It shows up again in the last book, Revelation 2:7, where the tree of life again is seen only this time we get to enjoy its fruit.

In Isaiah 51:3, the prophet gives comfort to Israel by sharing God's promise that He, God, will make her wilderness like Eden. Ezekiel agrees in his prophecy, chapter 36 verse 35, the land that was desolate has become like the garden of Eden. It is also on God's mind in Joel 2:3.

This qualifies the Garden to be a thread or something on God's agenda to ultimately be replanted. It is the tree of life that more specifically dominates His thoughts.

This is a simple but profound piece of insight into the Heart of a God of infinite patience and love. Adam and Eve—all of us represented by them—exiting the garden without a taste of that tree's fruit did not nor could it discourage our God from wanting His Garden back. Through Christ, He would find another way to share that fruit with us!

* * *

Looking at another example: What did Noah experience or "find" in Genesis 6:8? The KJV reads: Noah found grace in the eyes of THE LORD. The NIV says: Noah found favor in the eyes of THE LORD. Was it grace or favor? I was taught that these are not the same thing. Grace is not earned. but favor is.

Right?

Wrong?

Will someone help me out here?

The action or verb form of this word, "to show grace," or "favor," in our Old Testament speaks of "the kind turning of one person to another as expressed in an act of assistance... the process whereby one who has something turns in grace to another who has nothing... a heartfelt movement of the one who acts to the one acted upon."[1] Proverbs 14:31 is an example, whoever is kind to the needy honors God.

Said another way, the verb "to show grace" actually comes out meaning "to show mercy." This is important to observe because showing mercy and showing favor are two quite different things. We know that from how we use the words. In 56 occurrences in the Old Testament of the idea of showing favor/mercy 41 refer to the Lord as showing it and 26 of these are in the Psalms.

Favor...mercy...grace; what is the difference? The meaning of grace, as we understand it, as a free gift of God, is best seen in Exodus 33:19 where God chooses to show mercy for His own reasons even if those reasons are not clear to us: And THE LORD said, "...I will have <u>mercy</u> on whom I will have <u>mercy</u>, and I will have compassion on whom I will have compassion." I underlined the translation of our word.[2]

This sounds like we wrapped it up and there is nothing more to add. One word/favor/mercy/grace does triple duty. But to my personal confusion I am reading three different things here. The noun "grace" means "favor," but the verb means "to show mercy." And neither of these answer for our known definition of "grace" as a free and undeserved gift of God. My added concern is over the use of the word applied to someone other than our Lord. I think He alone is the author and administrator of grace. That's why we also refer to it as divine grace!

Unlike the word "compassion" in our Bible, which always refers to God's love, this word, "grace/favor," can be the offering of anyone who wants to help another—not only God.

Genesis 42:21 is an example where Joseph's brothers fess up when they are reunited with him, We saw how distressed he was when he pleaded with us for his life, but we would not listen. "Pleaded" is our word "to seek mercy" and it was requested in the language of the day from 11 men—not God— who said, "No!" Also, in Genesis 32:5 Jacob seeks favor—not grace—- from Esau. It is an attempt at warming Esau up to forgive him. Jacob sent on ahead donkeys and camels and herds of animals as a gift to his brother Esau.

* * *

It gets better. In Jeremiah 16:13 God says, I will not shew you favor. Here, the word "favor" is a slightly different spelling than the word used about Noah.

Two words for favor or grace! I'm not confused enough!

Let me take a peek ahead so you have an idea of where I am going and it is here: Grace is not an easy idea to wrap our thoughts around. God couldn't just say it and we would understand it. It is an idea that needed to be worked, introduced and then made visible through God's interaction with men and finally in the single event on Golgotha. Grace is the overarching theme of Scripture; it is the heart of God, the plan of God, and the act of God to provide for our salvation, and that cannot be easily communicated by just grabbing some term from our vocabulary and saying, "There it is."

Getting back, to some scholars two words for favor/grace means something. It tells them that the word grace/favor used about Noah focuses less on the giver and more on the gift itself. This is disturbing in a pastoral sense since it must remind every pastor of the parishioner who grabs the blessing and leaves forgetting where they got it and from whom. It is like the parent who simply leaves the cookie jar out in the open on the table for the children to raid at will until all the cookies are gone and the kids haven't a clue how the cookies got in the jar in the first place. The gift is detached from the giver and there are no "thank yous" for the thoughtfulness. Favor says "gift" but grace cries "giver."

To show grace or favor also means in the Old Testament what it could mean in our language, "to show oneself friendly." Exodus 3:21 And I will make the Egyptians favorably disposed toward this people, so that when you leave you will not go empty-handed. This says, that Israel found grace in the

117

sight of the Egyptians. God made Israel look attractive, the kind of people you want to befriend.

Grace or favor here is gracefulness. Israel and Egyptians. friends? They certainly appeared graceful or friendly—thanks to God. I wonder if Israel figured that out.

You can see this meaning in Genesis 39:21 but here, Joseph—I maintain—knew it was God's doing: THE LORD was with him; he showed him kindness and granted him favor in the eyes of the prison warden. The point is that this word favor doesn't carry the New Testament idea of God's grace.

This might get a little philosophical but scholarship prompts the question: How does one find grace or favor? "There is a veil of mystery over this process."[3] God decided to make Noah more attractive? More friendly? I simply don't get it! I am told that Noah became attractive to God.[4] The same is said of Moses in Exodus 33:12. Moses said to the LORD, "You have been telling me, 'Lead these people,' but you have not let me know whom you will send with me. You have said, 'I know you by name and you have found favor with me.'"

And then there is Numbers 11:15, where Moses is talking to God and saying, "Kill me, if I have found favor in your eyes." That's an oxymoron—or just a moron—because favor does not include the act of killing, not in our minds—unless the phrase is to be translated, "Do me the favor and kill me."

Again: This is not at all the message of God's grace. The Old Testament word as applied to Noah just doesn't cut it.

Now here is the quote of the day about the Old Testament word favor/grace: "How little of the full weight of the grace of God remains in the term... may be judged from the fact that in the Psalms with their full use of the verb [to show mercy] the word [grace/favor] does not occur at all in the context of petition [i.e. prayer]."[5] In Psalms 45:2—which has nothing to do with talking to God—it is actually given the meaning, "charm," i.e. captivating powers of speech. In Proverbs 3:22 it means "adornment." My point is that the Old Testament word for "grace" doesn't mean "grace"!

Charming! But do you get the impression that we are talking more about favor here given to someone who is gracious or beautiful. Do you get the impression that we are not talking about God's grace or a free gift here?

I do. The verb "to show grace or mercy"—to summarize so far—means to confer good on someone in need but the Old Testament word grace/favor is detached from this verb and somehow refers to a qualification of the one receiving such grace, i.e. they find it because of how charming or beautiful—whatever!—they are.

I know. Things got a bit muddied when we investigated the real meaning of the word and we can conclude that it does mean "favor" and not "grace." ...Until Zechariah!

* * *

It isn't until we hear this word on Zechariah's lips (12:10) that—and I will cut to the quick here—God begins to give this word a New Testament nuance or meaning: And I will pour out on the house of David and the inhabitants of Jerusalem a spirit of grace and supplication. They will look on me, the one they have pierced, and they will mourn for him as one mourns for an only child, and grieve bitterly for him as one grieves for a firstborn son.

Scholarship calls this a "gap,"[6] between Noah and Zechariah, that had to be filled by another word, the word "mercy" in the Hebrew. So, if God wanted to talk about unmerited favor or doing something for man which was undeserved, since the Old Testament word for "grace" didn't work, He had to talk about "mercy."

Stay with me on this. This word for mercy, I read, "is complex, so that uniform rendering [translating it with one English word like our word mercy] is almost impossible"[7]

I love it! We are informed through the best investigative work scholarship can provide that the heart of God hasn't been figured out yet! Oh, the depth of the riches of the wisdom and knowledge of God! How unsearchable his judgments, and his paths beyond tracing out! Romans 11:33.

At the same time God needed to raise the issue of grace even if like one commentary defined it—I paraphrase—to measure the grace of God—to describe it—is like marking out the boundaries of a lake only to discover that you have come to the immeasurable sea! Grace is a New Testament word and understanding what it is has to be observed by experiencing God Himself in relationship. There is no English equivalent.

In the languages of the Scriptures we can appeal to more than the word alone. We can look at the grammar more closely but that's another book. Here we admit that "grace" in the New Testament did take on a meaning closer to the heart of God and more descriptive of His absolute and uncondi-tional love. It includes forgiveness. We could have assumed that. We know this, however, because one Greek word for forgiveness comes from the word "grace" as in 2 Corinthians 2:10. You can look that one up.

So here again as we noted earlier about oneness, a New Testament idea tied directly to the main theme of Scripture—and no one can dispute that "grace" is tied to this theme—is introduced in the Old Testament first, Zechariah 12:10.

It is fascinating to hear a Paul or Peter reference the *Tanakh*, the Old Testa-ment which was their Bible, and, through a little Greek and a lot of revelation and inspiration, see the message of God's grace where a good Jew—and I say this with the greatest respect, a good Jew—could not see it! Isaiah 53 is the classic example we are all aware of.

The grace of God is real, real to us at least who have experienced the otherwise unexplainable touch of God upon our lives. One teacher of mine used to say, "I don't know how I know, but I know!"

Professor Taylor Lewis wrote, "[One] may know that a thing is, that it must be, though not how it is. So here, a moral necessity compels us to hold that there is such a region of the divine emotional, most intensely real,—more real, if we may make degrees, than knowledge or intellectuality—the very ground, in fact, of the divine personal being."[8]

Ephesians 2:5-7: It is by grace you have been saved. And God raised us up with Christ and seated us with him in the heavenly realms in Christ Jesus, in order that in the coming ages he might show the incomparable riches of his grace, expressed in his kindness to us in Christ Jesus.

This is clearly another thread in the comforter—interesting word—that covers a multitude of sins. It had to be on God's heart and mind throughout the history of man from Eden and earlier, no doubt, even if sharing it with us took a Calvary experience for Him in the person of His Son.

* * *

Look at the word "trust". Isaiah in 26:3 says to the Lord, The steadfast of mind You will keep in perfect peace,Because he trusts in You. We understand the concept of trusting in the Lord and because of the lessons of faith have no trouble with this verse. But the idea of trust as spoken here is actually an unusual one to say the least. It is another thread.

I read an interesting thing about our word, *trust*. This word is preserved in Hebrew and Aramaic. The meaning of the word with the same spelling in Arabic has a completely different meaning. It can hardly be traced with certainty in other semitic languages.[9] What am I saying? "Trust" is a Bible term!

I also found out that the modern Aramaic or Hebrew word for promise comes from this word, trust. That makes sense but if my research is correct, the Old Testament Hebrew has no word for "promise." The promises of God are simply His sayings! The word promise is a more implicit way of saying that God does not lie. Numbers 23:19, but we knew that already. We do find the word "promise" in our New Testament. Wow! Glad about that!

Trust in the Old Testament means "to feel secure, be unconcerned."[10] Perhaps this explains the difficult verse Psalm 22:10: Yet You are He who brought me forth from the womb; You made me trust when upon my mother's breasts. No one thinks in terms of an infant trusting. That's a pretty lofty idea for a one month old. Scholarship has gone in a number of directions with this one, but , just an idea, what if we attribute to a nursing child a lack of anxiety, a disinterest in life around them—no worries or fear—while they focus on mamma. Perhaps, psychologically, kids get a good head start against fear and anxiety if they nurse.

I'm sorry but even now putting my arms around my wife and getting close has a calming effect on me. It puts me to sleep when I sit on the couch with her in my arms even though I have been especially plagued by the failures of the day. The human touch has a healing effect. Does it not? Well, Psalm 22:9, do what you will with it.

Here's the rub. The general meaning of the word "trust" in the Old Testament has a negative ring to it, i.e. false security. Even the translators of the Greek Old Testament saw it this way. Generally, trusting the Lord was translated by the word "hope."

I could hang out in the *Theological Dictionary of the Old Testament* which is footnoted in this section and write umpteen examples of this false security, but I won't. I offer one that sums it all up. Proverbs 11:28, He who trusts in his riches will fall.

Okay, one more. Isaiah 31:1: Woe to those who go down to Egypt for help And rely on horses, And trust in chariots because they are many And in horsemen because they are very strong, But they do not look to the Holy One of Israel, nor seek THE LORD!

I get it! Security in the culture of Old Israel was tied to good times and a sense of being safe. Micah 4:4: ...everyone sitting under his own fig tree and vine unafraid. If you are rich and there is no war, you are secure. Win the lottery if you want to be worry free? And avoid the draft.

God was the unseen and unknown variable in their world. To use a Pauline phrase, they were not "in heavenly places" but tied to the earthly. As you read the Old Testament history, it is not hard to conclude this and thus the word "security" gets a bad rap. At some point the prophets and poets needed to rescue this term from its cultural prison. First—I really don't know if this is first, but it is logically near the beginning—Proverbs 25:19, Like a bad tooth... Is confidence in a faithless man. I can relate ever since my root canal. I was over two hours in the dentist's chair underneath a jack hammer and a garden hose, a few chisels and—I was afraid to ask.

Solomon is saying, "Stop trusting in man!" If we can break free from false trust, since trust is an essential part of well-being, we can then turn to God. I hate it, though, when I have a physical problem the doctor cannot solve. Trusting man is easy if he/she is expert in their field. And there isn't a preacher—or very few—who would deny you the right to seek professional help when you need it. The problem is leaving God out! The problem is a lack of spontaneity in prayer over all our concerns. We talk to everyone but Him about some things, and that isn't right. Jeremiah pronounces a pox on us if we do. Jeremiah 17:5.

Oh, for the record, it is okay for a man to build a trust relationship with his wife, Proverbs 31:11; with biblical principle, Proverbs 11:15; and our fellow soldiers, Judges 20:36. We won't jump overboard here.

Two well-known Scriptures can bring this point home. You probably have these hanging on a living room wall. Proverbs 3:5 and Psalm 37:3,5: Trust in the LORD with all your heart... [you finish it]. Trust in THE LORD,... Delight yourself also in THE LORD, And He shall give you the desires of your heart. Commit your way to THE LORD, trust also in Him, And He shall bring it to pass.

Don't know what "it" is. The verse simply says that He will move into action. Remember, if we really trust Him we won't have preconceived conclusions about how things should come out. My pastor's wife once said, He will do it because it refers to desires we now share with God because we have been getting close to Him through trust.

The debate goes on as to how the word security or trust developed in the Old Testament. Some think it started with Solomon offering the idea of turning our trust from man to God, from wealth to wisdom. Then Isaiah grabbed the baton and ran with it in 30:15, In returning and rest you shall be saved; In quietness and confidence shall be your strength. In any event I think it is historically accurate to say that the lesson of trust for a nation, Israel, was learned line upon line, step by step. It seems to follow the same path as the lesson of faith learned by all of our Lord's disciples, including you and me.

Man may be disappointed by man, but he can know there is security in God's care.[11] That's a New Testament idea under Christ, 1 Peter 5:7. But it started somewhere between a Psalm and a prophetic promise. Said in a most basic way: Salvation is built on trust, faith, in God. He couldn't wait to share it; so, He introduced the subject by shifting the emphasis of security in Israeli thought from things unto Himself.

This is a thread worth studying, a lesson worth learning.

Psychological Insight

...the measure of faith -Romans 12:3

An elder once told me I was using psychology in my sermons instead of Bible. I couldn't interpret his comment since the Bible is—I believe Francis Shaeffer referred to it as—one of the most comprehensive resources on psychological insight ever written.

There is the *Allelous* principle, for one. *Allelous* is Greek for "one another". All we have to do is look up the references for this phrase in relation to the Christian Community and we will see all kinds of good psychology at work. It is God's brand and it works. "Love one another; forgive one another; pray for one another; submit to one another; bear one another's burdens..." You get the point. And this is just an introduction to some good heavenly behavior!

Here is the psychology part: It honors every believer and gives each one a significance within Christianity. It fulfills every commandment. It provides spiritual and emotional healing—a kind of support group for Christians wanting encouragement as Christians. It effectively deals with crushing grief and sorrow. These are for starters. God's not so dumb when it comes to our needs.

* * *

There is, however, the problem of separating all the voices that offer solutions to our problems or who think they know best what we need.

We also live in a scientific age where even the social sciences are offering counsel which no pastor would discredit probably for fear of retribution. At least if we are intent on referring God's people to seek emotional or psychological help, pick a Christian doctor if there is a good one around!

I tell the account of a young lady who told her psychiatrist that she talked to God and she didn't deny that God in some way "talked back." He diagnosed this as a psychotic break from reality. I sat there and listened while he puffed on his cigar and admitted her into the ward. She did have emotional problems that exceeded my immediate ability to address; so, I did need help in helping a friend but—psychotic—that's a bit out there! Well, be wise in choosing your doctors.

* * *

New Testament teaching does provide a nine fold manifestation of the Spirit in I Corinthians 12:7 thru 10—a manifestation of love—that has a great deal of psychological insight into—at least—our spiritual needs. And since the spiritual is connected to the emotional and the physical, these ministries go a long way in helping us live out our lives with some degree of happiness and fulfillment.

If you want the tittle associated with these verses, it is the word "another." There are two words for "another", one means another of the same kind and the other means—you guessed it—another of a different kind. I was given the illustration of ties, bow ties and neck ties or long ties. If I hand you a bow tie and then a long tie, the long tie is another of a different kind. But if I hand you a bow tie and another bow tie, I have handed you another of the same kind. Get it?

The gifts are separated this way as well. There is wisdom and another of the same kind, knowledge. Then another of a different kind, faith, and 4 more of the same kind as faith: healing, miracles, and prophecy and discernment. Then the last two, tongues and their interpretation are a different kind again.

So, here is how I lay this out. Each gift provides a necessary resource—a psychological one—that applies to some aspect of our lives because we have certain needs. I offer possible examples. You be the judge.

God gives wisdom as a source of counsel to be applied to how we live and decisions we need to make—forks in the road—because we need guidance.

See how it works!

Oh. Acts 13:1 thru 3. Someone was God's means of providing Paul and Silas with direction.

> Now in the church that was at Antioch there were certain prophets and teachers: Barnabas, Simeon who was called Niger, Lucius of Cyrene, Manaen who had been brought up with Herod the tetrarch, and Saul. As they ministered to the Lord and fasted, the Holy Spirit said, "Now separate to Me Barnabas and Saul for the work to which I have called them." Then, having fasted and prayed, and laid hands on them, they sent them away.

God gives knowledge as a source of insight which is applied to our understanding because we need to be taught. I think Acts 18:24 thru 26 might be an example. It is self-explanatory.

> Now a certain Jew named Apollos, born at Alexandria, an
> eloquent man and mighty in the Scriptures, came to
> Ephesus. This man had been instructed in the way of the
> Lord; and being fervent in spirit, he spoke and taught

accurately the things of the Lord, though he knew only
the baptism of John. So he began to speak boldly in the
synagogue. When Aquila and Priscilla heard him, they
took him aside and explained to him the way of God
more accurately.

God gives faith to do something or to be committed to some task to its
end. This is a source of confirmation applied to service for the Lord because
of a need for reassurance. Take Acts 18: 9 thru 11 as an example.

Now the Lord spoke to Paul in the night by a vision, "Do not be afraid,
but speak, and do not keep silent; for I am with you, and no one will attack
you to hurt you; for I have many people in this city." And he continued there
a year and six months, teaching the Word of God among them.

God provides healings as a source of healing—the plural is probably all
types—applied to our frailty because we need restoration from time to time.
This truth almost needs no example but I offer one, Acts 3: 1 thru 7

Now Peter and John went up together to the temple at
the hour of prayer, the ninth hour. And a certain man
lame from his mother's womb was carried, whom they
laid daily at the gate of the temple which is called Beau‒
tiful, to ask alms from those who entered the temple;
who, seeing Peter and John about to go into the temple,
asked for alms. And fixing his eyes on him, with John,
Peter said, "Look at us." So he gave them his attention,
expecting to receive something from them. Then Peter
said, "Silver and gold I do not have, but what I do have I
give you: In the name of Jesus Christ of Nazareth, rise up
and walk." And he took him by the right hand and lifted
him up, and immediately his feet and ankle bones
received strength.

And then there are miracles which God performs as an open door or
opportunity. God knows there will be opposition and we will need a miracle
or two along the way. We ultimately find fulfillment and significance in
God's plan for us. O.K. This one doesn't sound psychological but think about
it—fulfillment! Look at Acts 19: 11 thru 20.

Now God worked unusual miracles by the hands of Paul,
so that even handkerchiefs or aprons were brought from
his body to the sick, and the diseases left them and the
evil spirits went out of them. Then some of the itinerant
Jewish exorcists took it upon themselves to call the name
of the Lord Jesus over those who had evil spirits, saying,

"We exorcise you by the Jesus whom Paul preaches." Also there were seven sons of Sceva, a Jewish chief priest, who did so. And the evil spirit answered and said, "Jesus I know, and Paul I know; but who are you?" Then the man in whom the evil spirit was leaped on them, overpowered them, and prevailed against them, so that they fled out of that house naked and wounded. This became known both to all Jews and Greeks dwelling in Ephesus; and fear fell on them all, and the name of the Lord Jesus was magnified. And many who had believed came confessing and telling their deeds. Also, many of those who had practiced magic brought their books together and burned them in the sight of all. And they counted up the value of them, and it totaled fifty thousand pieces of silver. So the word of the Lord grew mightily and prevailed.

Prophecy provides a source of inspiration applied to the heart or the will because we need to be motivated. Acts 15: 32 is an example.

Now Judas and Silas, themselves being prophets also, exhorted and strengthened the brethren with many words.

Discernment makes sense as a source of direction applied to leadership because—whether we admit it or not—we need to be led. Acts 5:1 thru 5 is a sad account but it makes the point:

But a certain man named Ananias, with Sapphira his wife, sold a possession. And he kept back part of the proceeds, his wife also being aware of it, and brought a certain part and laid it at the apostles' feet. But Peter said, "Ananias, why has Satan filled your heart to lie to the Holy Spirit and keep back part of the price of the land for yourself? While it remained, was it not your own? And after it was sold, was it not in your own control? Why have you conceived this thing in your heart? You have not lied to men but to God." Then Ananias, hearing these words, fell down and breathed his last. So great fear came upon all those who heard these things.

Last but not least—or is it—two gifts together, tongues and interpretation, as a source of encouragement applied to our feelings or emotions because we need emotional support or as C.S. Lewis—I believe—said it once "to hear the band playing while we march." Acts 10 44 thru 48 is the traditional portion of Scripture referenced.

While Peter was still speaking these words, the Holy
Spirit fell upon all those who heard the word. And those
of the circumcision who believed were astonished, as
many as came with Peter, because the gift of the Holy
Spirit had been poured out on the Gentiles also. For they
heard them speak with tongues and magnify God.

Then Peter answered, "Can anyone forbid water,
that these should not be baptized who have received the
Holy Spirit just as we have?" And he commanded them
to be baptized in the name of the Lord. Then they asked
him to stay a few days.

We cannot simply maintain that these gifts are to enhance our ritual or
our Sunday worship. The New Testament is predictably silent on this subject.
These gifts whether we believe they are still needed or not were applied to
the ministry of the early church in its infancy.

Many maintain we still need them.

* * *

There are also seven ministries outlined in Romans 12: 3 thru 16 which speak
volumes to God's wisdom in organizing His church. Is there any psychological insight here? You decide.

For I say, through the grace given to me, to everyone
who is among you, not to think of himself more highly
than he ought to think, but to think soberly, as God has
dealt to each one a measure of faith. For as we have
many members in one body, but all the members do not
have the same function, so we, being many, are one body
in Christ, and individually members of one another.
Having then gifts differing according to the grace that is
given to us, let us use them: if prophecy, let us prophesy
in proportion to our faith; or ministry, let us use it in our
ministering; he who teaches, in teaching; he who
exhorts, in exhortation; he who gives, with liberality; he
who leads, with diligence; he who shows mercy, with
cheerfulness. Let love be without hypocrisy. Abhor what
is evil. Cling to what is good. Be kindly affectionate to
one another with brotherly love, in honor giving prefer–
ence to one another; not lagging in diligence, fervent in
spirit, serving the Lord; rejoicing in hope, patient in tribu–
lation, continuing steadfastly in prayer; distributing to
the needs of the saints, given to hospitality. Bless those

who persecute you; bless and do not curse. Rejoice with
those who rejoice, and weep with those who weep. Be of
the same mind toward one another. Do not set your
mind on high things, but associate with the humble. Do
not be wise in your own opinion.

The seven are Rulers or leaders, ministers, givers, the merciful, prophets, teachers, and exhorters. These are an amazing stroke of Divine genius.

* * *

Rulers are motivated by vision, able to see the finished product and utilize resources. They are challenged and willing to endure stress and hardship. Verse 8 says they are diligent. They are called to organize the distribution of resources to care for the needs of the Christian Community. They are the administrations in I Corinthians 12:28 and they lead by being patient in tribulation according to verse 12.

Administrators have typically been placed at the top of the food chain. We even elevate them above pastors unless the administrator is the pastor., which is how quite a few churches see it. Administrators or rulers organize things but not according to their own design but according to the biblical pattern laid down in Romans 12. When we say they are motivated by vision, we say a mouthful because Romans 12 does not seem so visionary in the context of today's church world.

Vision today is directly tied to being able to see something, measure results, see progress, like a building project or a fund raising endeavor. When vision is simply organizing believers to work ministry, it isn't immediately measurable. We can not chart it so easily like saying n number were saved or we passed out n number of tracts or phase one of our building is complete. But Romans 12 is God's vision and the administrator is only a keeper of that vision. God has the statistics and will probably put them up on some Power-Point cloud for us someday in eternity to see.

* * *

Ministers or deacons are blessed with physical stamina, a sense of urgency, and a great desire to serve others. They are called to visit the sick and tend to their needs; to be occupied especially with the care of the poor. I Corinthians 12:28 calls them "helps." They take the leadership according to verse 13 in being given to hospitality.

These are not pastors, per se. The real difficulty is identifying biblically what the pastor's main responsibilities are. Setting that aside, deacons visit the sick. They serve. They make excellent waiters and waitresses.

* * *

Givers are just that. They support God's ministry with finances. They are wholehearted and spontaneous but also wise investors and sensitive to financial need. Verse 8 describes them as liberal and they lead according to verse 13 in distributing to the needs of the saints.

Some financial needs approach real money! We live in a legal world that short-circuits the burden and interest of benevolent individuals from responding to need. We like to have tax deductions. We are frightened from legal entanglements or future commitments. So, we collect offerings anonymously with a tax write off but that isn't what givers do. They are more immediate in their response, less programmed, more interested in meeting the need than worrying about a hundred other possible side effects of their gift.

Giving isn't based here on tithing according to Romans 12 but on ministry and calling.

Did I say, "Don't tithe."

Of course not!

And givers do not attach requirements to their gifts like naming a bench after them. Real need is their concern not a collection to repair the steeple. That's a rough comment but only intended to emphasize that financial needs biblically are attached to people not buildings.

* * *

The merciful are gifted with sensitivity, understanding, and the ability to perceive real need. Verse 8 says they do it with cheerfulness. They are called to lessen another's pain, hurt, or distress. They might employ the gift of healing spoken of in I Corinthians 12:28. Or they may just fluff your pillow in your sick bed. They must make good nurses. They know how to weep with those who weep. Perhaps, not in a literal sense because such a subjective approach to ministry wears one out quickly. They can sympathize, however, and perhaps we might say, they have empathic understanding.

* * *

These meet material and physical needs but to meet spiritual and emotion needs God provides three other ministries.

Prophets, for one, are frank, emphatic, bold, and—yes—intolerant. Verse 6 describes them as persons of faith. They are called to affirm, motivate and call to accountability. I Corinthians 12:29 also lists them. They lead by being fervent in spirit serving the Lord. A prophet sees the distant peak of holiness, not the valley between, and stirs us to reach it.

* * *

Then there are the teachers—I think I can relate—who are detailed, objective, and noted for strict adherence to the Scripture. They are also listed in I Corinthians 12:29. They are obviously called to teach the Word of God and also to create a greater interest in and hunger for its message. They also apply the Word to real life situations. Sounds psychological! They take the leadership in having the same mind toward one another. There's that one another phrase again.

The ultimate goal of teaching is sharing common knowledge not discovering something new. Their gift is teaching or finding the way to communicate common truth to different minds and hearts. Not an easy task since everyone's experience is different and we each have a different brain cell count probably. Unlike the prophet, teachers do see the valley and show you how to traverse it. Then they give you the secret of the climb that follows.

* * *

And last but by no means the least are the exhorters who have a positive and simple message—often with music—because they are called to uplift the heart, encourage, bring hope, instill faith and offer positive reassurance and not the odds on recovery. There seems to be no depth in their message because it is often part of a simple chorus or musical refrain . But don't be led to believe that this vital ministry is of little value. Exhorters lead in rejoicing in hope.

Exhorters make good song leaders if they are left to minister in their own way. Their timely comments though so simple as to be make them appear almost naïve are not the result of a lack of biblical depth but the dynamic of uplifting the hearts of the weary and discouraged. They play the march and encourage us to step to the music.

* * *

How refreshing, how absolutely exciting—I fail to find the words here—if we could limit ourselves to the ministry where God wants us and not meddle or have to apply ourselves in areas we don't belong and don't want to be in.

Perhaps this is not the place to say it but over the course of church history many other ministries have been added and given importance. There has been no rule against expanding the church government model provided in Scriptures; so, church constitutions have been drafted, fund raising has been perfected, social functions added to name a few. The electronic age has given us sounds systems, synthesized music, PowerPoint and overhead presentations and computers and this has required additional personnel, as well.

No one is wanting to minimize the importance of web-page development or using the media more effectively to reach the community with the Gospel. These are important. I had this book printed! But in the endless meetings to perfect these modern ministries, we may have unintentionally neglected one or more of the basic seven offered when the church began.

We can argue that Jesus would have used all modern means to reach His world with the message and the only debatable point would be to ask whether or not He is doing that now, today. What isn't debatable is that Paul, were he ministering in today's world, would be involved in the services to the Christian Community which he recommended from the beginning to the Romans. How could we deny this?

We need sound technicians, good musicians, ushers for offerings, nursery workers, janitors, trustees for legal reasons, and at times administrators that know how to raise money and follow building codes, etc. but we also need prophets and teachers and those who can show mercy to name three of seven.

Perhaps, today's ministry needs a little more psychological consciousness —to coin a phrase. We don't mean social programs and we can't recommend disregarding the professional services available for helping people. Again, some of those professionals are believers and serve God's people admirably. What we are saying is what one denomination I once served in used to say. God's Word is profitable for faith and conduct. Conduct, living the message of Truth, exemplifying the fruit of the Spirit in our lives, taking part in biblical ministry.

You can also collect offerings or adjust the acoustics in the Sanctuary. Knock yourself out! But our relationship with others in our home and in our church are where real ministry is at!

Psychology?

You bet!!

Sorry if my posturing sounds defensive. If I understand my elder and I give him the benefit of any doubt here, he wanted to be sure that all our psychological insight was purely biblical. So I guess scream therapy is out? If Christians just get a bit closer to the message of I Corinthians 13, the love chapter, we'll have it. We will be applying a purely biblical psychology.

Soteriology

...great is the mystery of Godliness... -1 Timothy 3:16

Soteriology is the study of salvation. A certain bishop, renowned for his studies in the Greek tenses, is said to have been asked by a certain person whose zeal exceeded his discretion whether he was 'saved.' The bishop...replied, 'It all depends whether you mean ...[I am saved, I was saved,] or [I have been saved]... I trust I am saved, I know I was saved once for all by the death of Christ, I hope ...[I shall have been saved], delivered from all dangers of falling by being received into Heaven'[1]

This story is probably just that, a story designed to point out the different ways of viewing salvation. Whether the story depicts perspectives on Christ's work correctly or biblically is for the theologian and the preacher to decide. If you want to take a stab at it, look up Acts 2:47 and 1 Corinthians 1:18: (being saved); 2 Timothy 1:9 (was saved) and Ephesians 2:5 (have been saved)

In Acts the Lord was continually adding to the church those being saved. The present tense shows that one person after another after another is accepting membership in God's church, citizenship in His kingdom through accepting Jesus Christ as Savior. In Timothy, Paul uses a form that indicates that salvation is a total and—I think—instant thing not progressive. There is no such thing as half saved, if you get my drift. And Ephesians is a favorite verse because it indicates salvation as a condition of the soul—we say "new nature" that is unchanging. Some say it is permanent; maybe, but the tense need not go that far—my opinion.

* * *

We are talking about the plan of Salvation? This is the red thread that runs through the entire text of the Bible and links everything together as one continuous work of Divine authorship. Yet, how are we to understand some of the terms applied to this subject? If you have been reading along in this book you can hopefully pick up on the difficulty there is in understanding what God meant, Terms like "propitiation" and a "mercy seat" to name two might have a clear "Webster" definition but is that theologically correct?

We cannot always depend on Greek—at least not the philosopher's use of terms that describe God's salvation plan. Greek thought could not explain the heart of God! The plan of Salvation we maintained earlier in this book was a logical impossibility to the Greek way of thinking. Even the resurrection was a babbler's ramble, according to the Athenians.

Perhaps, the Greeks could strike a baseline for us, a general meaning which we could extend into our faith. But to quote D.F. Paine:

"... soteriological terms ... will have been common currency in the early church, in quasi-technical senses, drawn from and based on the [Greek Old Testament]; therefore, no early Christian is likely to have used them in a purely Hellenistic [Greek] sense... "[2]

* * *

Have you read *Peace Child* by Don Richardson? You should! Don Richardson was a Christian missionary to the Sawi tribe of the then Netherlands New Guinea, now part of Indonesia. The Sawi people had no Bible and no knowledge at all of God's salvation plan. They had no phrase for "the only begotten son." Their religion condoned revenge killing. They practiced cannibalism as a way of life. So I ask, "How does one explain Christ's death and resurrection to the Sawis—yes, for whom Christ did die?" How can you talk to them using words that make no sense to them; words you need to invent and introduce into their language to start with? Read *Peace Child*.

The Sawis had a practice of reconciling with a native clan by giving an infant to the very family group that cannibalized them. One clan would bind with another by giving a new born to be raised by the other. This was a peace child and the adoption ceremony put an end to the killing between them. Richardson taught them that God had sent His peace child and his name was Jesus.

* * *

The following account reaches back in time but it is intended to support our awareness of the difficulty the first missionaries, viz. Apostles, had in bringing the Gospel message to their world. R. C. Trench relates,

"Moffat in his Missionary Labors and Scenes in South Africa gives us a very remarkable example of the disappearing of one of the most significant words from the language of a tribe sinking ever deeper in savagery; and with the disappearing of the word, of course the disappearing as well of the great spiritual ...truth whereof that word was at once the vehicle and the guardian. The Bechuanas, a Caffre tribe, employed formerly the word 'Morimo,' to designate 'Him that is above,' or 'Him that is in Heaven," and attached to the word the notion of a supreme Divine Being... Thus is it the ever repeated complaint of the Missionary that the very terms are well nigh or wholly wanting in the dialect of the savage whereby to impart to him heavenly truths, or indeed even the nobler emotions of the human heart."[3]

Professor Trench gives the example of the "residence of Van Diemen's Island, that in the native language... there are four words to express the taking of human life... while at the same time... any word for 'love' is wanting..."[4]

Missionary work transcends culture. Christian missionaries are not called to bring so-called civilization to so-called heathen nations. "Uncivilized" is a politico-cultural or social term that is not part of the Bible message even though we might think so.

The task of the missionaries and evangelists is to explain Christ —His incarnation, His death and resurrection—to people whose language may not even have words they can use for that purpose. This is where the early Christian missionaries and the Apostles found themselves.

Paul, to show you how difficult this was, tried to talk about a resurrection to the Athenians who believed in something called metempsychosis, a kind of reincarnation. Reincarnation was logical to the Greek mind since they saw things as being in a continuous state or being repeated. It might even make sense to us since we have not improved on their logic. Birth and death make some sense to us because these happen repeatedly to our observation, even if we haven't a clue how birth actually works to bring into being another life and why there is such a thing as death.

Reincarnation is not God's idea. Our lives are on a time line extending from birth into eternity. There is no repeat performance for us in a resurrection, only an eternity of more discovery into the inexhaustible resource of Divine grace. In was inevitable that Classical Greek would have no word for "resurrection." Paul explained it by using the Greek word "to awaken from sleep." That's why in I Thessalonians 4:15 Paul referred to those who died in Christ as being "them which are asleep."

* * *

So, if the plan of Salvation uses a Divine logic and some of the details are a bit foggy or fuzzy, remember this was a mystery cloaked in the rituals of an Old Testament religion until Paul.

We need to start by believing the historical record, that Jesus was real and He did die on a Roman cross and He did rise from the dead. If we have that much, we can ask, Why?

If we can believe that this somehow had something to do with punishment for breaking God's law—such a faith makes Isaiah 53 easier to interpret —and that Jesus on the cross took that punishment for us or instead of us and if we understand that punishment was eternal, that is, if we had to be so punished, we would have been forever barred from the presence of God—if we can accept this even if we do not get the logic behind it—we have saving faith—we have the plan in the heart if not in the head.

Now the only other truth here to accept is our own resurrection at time's end. This point to me is logical if the plan is acceptable. Why would God do something with a temporary result? He is an eternal God! That's what "God" has always meant! He is eternal or everlasting. I do not recollect that fact ever challenged.

Psalm 41:13: Praise be to the Lord, the God of Israel, from everlasting to everlasting. Psalm 90:2: Before the mountains were born or you brought forth the earth and the world, from everlasting to everlasting you are God. Romans 1:20: For since the creation of the world God's invisible qualities—his eternal power and divine nature—have been clearly seen...

Let's glance back at the previous chapters and make a few additional comments relating to our salvation. These might be disconnected jottings instead of jots, tidbits instead of tittles, because these are additional thoughts on salvation collected from the chapters already covered, lengthy footnotes of sorts, that I thought deserved some notice. Perhaps the following comments might help explain things better.

* * *

What is in a Name?

I started to read a book by a Julius Wellhausen, The Prolegomena to the History of Ancient Israel.

What's a prolegomena?

It's an Introduction.

I couldn't finish it, I was so enraged! Now I understand that his theory—also called the Documentary hypothesis and co-authored by a Karl Heinrich Graf—basically claims that the first five books of the Bible were not written by Moses but by four editors using different names for God. One used the name Jehovah and was called the Yahwist, a second editor called God Elohim and became known as the Elohist, and then Wellhausen and Graf maintained someone else wrote Leviticus, he is the priestly writer and someone else wrote Deuteronomy. These are known as J,E,P, and D respectively.

This theory maintains that the Torah was composed of selections woven together from several, at times inconsistent, sources, each originally a complete and independent document. (Wiki this info if you want.)

Well, don't come unglued over this. Some Old Testament authors affirm Mosaic authorship, as do numerous New Testament writers and the early church fathers.[5]

Who are you going to believe!

I can appreciate the work of the textual critic—Textual Criticism—to figure out who wrote what and when. But challenging the authorship of the Torah is the work of Higher Criticism, I think originally developed as a discipline to deal with alleged contradictions in the Old Testament writings.

⋆ ⋆ ⋆

When I read the Torah in the Hebrew, however, I saw a progressive revelation of God through His name. Take for example the word God, Elohim, and His name Jehovah. I came to the conclusion that the name Jehovah was given to Moses at the burning bush when he, Moses, asked who it was that was sending him back into Egypt. (Actually this sacred name for God, Jehovah, Jahweh, Yahweh, the rabbis do not like to pronounce, so, they say "master" instead.)

The Bible starts out with Elohim, the word God, itself. Elohim is in the plural, Gods, because—as the rabbis believe—it speaks of His many attributes. By this name Elohim He created everything! Christians say it is plural for the Trinity. I am happy either way.

If my view is correct, Abraham did not know God by His name, Jehovah. Jehovah-Jireh. the name for God we put on Abraham's lips when he intended to sacrifice his son, Isaac, was not the name he knew God by. Abraham never called God, Jehovah. Abraham said "Elohim-Jireh", God will provide. Actually, the Hebrew says in Genesis 22:8 "Elohim will see to it!" (In verse 14 Abraham named the place "The *Lord* will provide" which leads some to discredit my general hypothesis that, according to Exodus 6:2-3, God also said to Moses, "I am the Lord. I appeared to Abraham, to Isaac and to Jacob as God Almighty, but by my name the Lord I <u>did not</u> make myself known to them. This is addressed in the appendix: *Is the Bible Inspired?*

Who did Abraham see standing in the doorway of his tent at Mamre? I get goose-pimply when I read in Genesis 18:1 that it was Yahweh or Jehovah that came to see Abraham about Sodom and Gomorrah. But Moses is telling the story. Moses—yes, Moses—could have said Elohim came to see Abraham but Moses said Jehovah!

What is so important about the name? Moses sees clearly that this is the same God that was at the bush! The same God that later would deliver Israel is about to rescue Lot.

Jehovah, for Israel, is the name of deliverance not punishment. It is an instant and constant reminder to them that God will do what He has to do and be Who He has to be in order to deliver them as He promised Abraham.

Am I going too far in saying God is also a very personal God—not just the Almighty God! I believe the message of the Old Testament and its history is the divine relationship God had or didn't have with His people. God got very personal with Moses when He shared that name with him! The name Elohim simply means God and even the nations about Israel recognized and used that word for God. But Moses and God actually met face to face as friends. Theirs was a relationship not a religion.

If He is just all powerful and seeking man's worhsip, we view God's involvement with Israel not as an act of love but somehow as an act of pure power to instill fear in would-be worshippers. If we know anything about our God, Jehovah, in the record of Old Testament history and prophecy, we cannot see Him in the mythical sense of seeking sacrifice and obedience as an act of appeasement. The sacrifices are a <u>type</u> of Christ's death. God's contacts with His people through prophet or priest are intended to communicate His interest in a relationship not rote servitude. Isa 1:13 makes no sense in the context of myth and the religion of appeasement. Stop bringing meaningless offerings! Your incense is detestable to me. New Moons, Sabbaths and convocations—I cannot bear your evil assemblies. Appeasement always needs sacrifice in the stories of mythology; but in the plan of God, sacrifice is truly sacred and represents the coming Calvary event. Israel in Isaiah's day profaned it.

Relationship is important to God. Is this not also true of Jesus who is God incarnate and the ultimate fulfillment of all those sacrifices? John 15:15: I no longer call you servants, because a servant does not know his master's busi- ness. Instead, I have called you friends, for everything that I learned from my Father I have made known to you.

Relationship is what God has always been about. In fact, in the warmth of His distant memories in Hosea 11:3 and 4 , looking back—I remember when! —, He cried, "I led Israel by the arm, taught them to walk! I loved them!" That's not Elohim talking. That's Jehovah! Same God, different name.

And then in Hosea's prophesy God takes another turn for the best. Hosea 2:16 He says Israel will no longer say of Him baali, my master, but ishi, my husband. Women who have been objectified as private property instead of loved as persons and as wives know what this is saying. The difference here is that the Lord never wanted to be viewed as their owner, their master. That was a relationship Israel got from heathen religion—I maintain. Is there just a hint of the marriage of the Lamb in this kind of talk!

* * *

I must admit that anyone who wants to could debate my logic but never my faith! Sorry, Mr. Critic. I am useless to you. But I have a mild interest now in reading the Prolegomena—maybe.

Step back from the picture "a ways"—as we used to say. Or let's get a 50,000 foot high view, that is to say, from a distance. We see God cast in three roles. In order: First, Creator in Genesis, then Judge, Abraham's "Judge of the earth" (Genesis 18:25) and the God Who spoke through the prophets, and finally Savior, the New Testament message. The theologians will fill in the terrain as you come closer and closer to where you live. It is when we fail to appreciate this three-fold revelation of God that the message of Scripture is lost in endless criticism and debate.

God has to be our creator. Any relationship with God must be built on the premise of "likeness of image". This is what makes metaphors like Father/son and Christ/bride work. Because we are in His image we can relate to Him and carry on relationship in salvation. No Creator, no image, no Father/son, Christ/bride, no relationship, no salvation.

If we deny that He is the Judge; if we deny His judgeship, we ultimately have to discredit the absolute principles of His Word and His holiness. We discredit holiness as a working proposition. No Judge, no Divine law, no holiness, inevitably, no further need for God—at least not the real one.

If ultimately we deny the image of God that we are made in and deny any standard of holiness, we are left without a salvation. Think of it. Why should God if after all of this reasoning we still maintain He exists—why should He —want to die on a cross. What's the point since no law has been broken and no true relationship can be established between Him and us.

What's in a name? A revelation of Divine interaction with man. Denying or discrediting this revelation, rearranging the details as if arbitrary points of personal theology by unnamed redactors can come dangerously close to losing the message altogether. The message of God and His love that can save our souls!

* * *

Apples and Oranges? How does the fruit of the Spirit relate to the subject of salvation? Nothing can be more exemplary of the Christian way of life than God's love described in terms of an exciting expectation for God to do something meaningful in one's life and for others; a desire to be always and only a peacemaker and to stay forgiving and reconciled to all believers; the ability to stay plugged-in with people even if they seem difficult and personalities clash big-time; longing to be used of God; loving God's Word; trustworthy, sensitive and caring, always wanting to be part of the solution and never the problem; and an example of how to overcome temptation.

We can view these nine traits as descriptive of the Christian life. If someone claims salvation and these characteristics are not visible in their relationships—well—we could question their relationship with God. But let's not judge.

* * *

Is the Savior still being *awakened out of a sound sleep*? I speak figuratively. Is He called on in our panic because we cannot get control of our circumstances? God knows what we have been trying in vain without Him!

I, for one, am grateful for lessons in faith. When the disciples found themselves on a stormy sea of Galilee, they found themselves in God's classroom learning to trust. Faith is learned. Trust comes with a developing relationship. Saving faith is our starting point but from there God must show us how to become spiritually focused—not trusting in our own abilities but His; calm and at peace in fearfully dangerous situations; trusting a divine logic to make sense out of meaningless tragedy; ready to jump knowing He will somehow catch us. We need to develop a spiritual sense that sees God in situations that are beclouded by sorrow and pain. We need to be able to look into the heat of any furnace stoked white hot by the rage of those that—for political or social or religious reasons—want to throw us in and—we—remain resolved as ever through it all to stay faithful to God. What did Hananiah, Mishael and Azariah—yes, that was there Hebrew names—say?

Daniel 3:17 and 18: If we are thrown into the blazing furnace, the God we serve is able to save us from it, and he will rescue us from your hand, O king. But even if he does not, we want you to know, O king, that we will not serve your gods or worship the image of gold you have set up.

* * *

Impossible! Matthew 19:26: Jesus looked at them and said, "With man this is impossible, but with God all things are possible." What a statement! We are prone to fill in the "all things" part with our favorite requests and a few personal blessings but that isn't what Jesus was saying. What is possible is the ability of God's grace to save anyone! Anywhere! At any time! In Africa! In the dark ages! And even in Boston!

The plan of salvation was a stroke of genius! We may not fully appreciate how a "mercy seat" and propitiation work into it, but they do! I have a confession to make, first. If I cannot explain something to an 8 year old, I can't explain it to me and that is a problem. So, truth has to get simple for me to understand it. I got this book, Nelson's Expository Dictionary of the Old Testament and he says that the mercy seat was the lid of the Ark of the Covenant. It was a slab of gold and there were two Cherabim, golden images of angels, standing one on each side of this ark and facing each other. Nelson says, "This slab of gold represented the throne of God and symbolized His real presence in the worship shrine [The Holy of Holies]"[6] Then we are told that the Septuagint or Greek Old Testament refers to this as a "propitiary"[7] Actually propitiary seems to be the place of propitiation. It is a religious term that came to mean atonement. So the mercy seat is the place of Atonement. I don't like the word "propitiation"! It's too big! I'm only eight! Remember!

We are told in plainer English that on the Day of Atonement, Yom Kippur, the High priest would go into the Holy of Holies and sprinkle the blood of a young bull—the Bible says, before the Mercy Seat, Leviticus 16:14. I don't know if the blood got on it or only on the floor in front of it. In any event, this ceremony was said to appease God and their sins were expiated. They live to see another year.

Appease means to calm or pacify or conciliate. It seems like this act mitigated God's anger. That's the word propitiate. Expiate probably refers to extinguishing the guilt of sin. I see these as theological terms designed to explain what happened when the High priest sprinkled the blood in the Holy of Holies.

I must admit; there seems to be many directions to go in here, theologically. Obviously, the sacrifice for Israel's sins did give them another year to live as a nation. But I tend to ask a lot of questions that may or may not have answers.

Was God actually going to wipe them out in rage if He wasn't "appeased" by this offering? It sounds like heathen sacrifice and that lacks meaning for me. I think God had to be appeased but only by the suffering of Christ. He would wait! Acts 17:30. In the past God overlooked such ignorance, but now he commands all people everywhere to repent.

Isaiah 53:11 says something interesting here. He will see the result of the suffering of his soul and be satisfied... Satisfied? Is this appeased? Does this make Jesus' death—Christian interpretation—the actual event that the blood sprinkling in the Holy of Holies symbolized? He is the—I'll say it—propitiation for our sins? Satisfied in the Hebrew means to have one's fill. It was as if God saw Jesus suffering and said , "Enough! It is enough!" And then Jesus said, "It is finished" and died.

Another question comes to mind: Why has all this ceremony and ritual centered on a lid? Can I be bold enough to suggest something? A lid covers and therefore hides from sight the contents of whatever it is the lid is on. This lid hid the Law from God's sight. The Law was on the tablets in the Ark. It is purely symbolic because God does have X-ray vision but He could have been symbolizing the idea of forgiveness not harping about the Law which Israel broke and demanding immediate retribution.

Symbols make up rituals which make up religious truths worth learning. Israel needed to know that sin offends God and something had to be done, Even though Israel wouldn't know what the symbols really meant, the broken Law some day would be fulfilled in Christ.

Peter (I Peter 4:8) also spoke of love covering a multitude of sins. Hmm!

And it wasn't just a lid. It was a mercy seat.

Who sat there?

God! He positioned Himself between the Cherabim while the High priest sprinkled the blood. Interesting! Mercy! Not a jurist bench! Not a king's throne—per se. A mercy seat. I had a teacher who told us students that grace is God's way of rescuing us from dangers imposed by other's and by circumstances but mercy is God's way of rescuing us from ourselves.

Maybe Romans 3:25 and 26 says it all.

God presented him as a sacrifice of atonement, through faith in his blood. He did this to demonstrate his justice, because in his forbearance he had left the sins committed beforehand unpunished—he did it to demonstrate his justice at the present time, so as to be just and the one who justifies those who have faith in Jesus.

* * *

Perfect! Jesus' death fulfilled all the ceremony associated with the Old Testament religion introduced to Israel by Moses. All sacrifices pointed to Calvary. You don't need a sermon from me on this point; so, I won't preach it. But I am curious about the myriad of details left unexplained!

Details?

Uh huh. Yes. Exodus 25:40 says, See that you make {them} after the pattern for them, which was shown to you on the mountain.

What's a "pattern"?

Model. Likeness.

O.K. If we allow for God doing some practical stuff like overlaying the Tabernacle with badger skins because they were water-proof (Numbers 4:25) or putting hooks on the Altar for carrying, we still have details that must symbolize something about Calvary but were not applied in New Testament teaching. I still want to know! Why patterns of almonds on the candlestick? (Exodus 25:23)

I compiled a dictionary of terms from Exodus 25 through 30 from "agate" to the word "wreathen" or "interwoven" in Exodus 28:14. Twenty six pages which includes gems like the carbuncle or emerald which we know is green in color and perfumes like galbanum used, perhaps, more for its sweet fragrance than its medicinal benefits. There were horns on the altar and I am sure the cubit as a measurement meant something. Did God choose it because it was a common unit and easy to explain? Why then is the shekel of the Sanctuary—well, "of the Sanctuary"? (Exodus 30:13). It was—like—a sacred metric!

Enough for now. I don't have answers but I want you to ask God when we get there so we can find out. You can do it! I'm right behind you.

* * *

When Christians get into trouble because of their witness, who is to blame? Paul's challenge in sharing the Gospel with religious folk makes more and more sense to me the more I study religion. I don't want to open up old wounds or—God forbid—make new ones, but as you know—think about it —brilliant theological minds live in all religious camps.

Within Christianity alone there are scholars across the denominational spectrum. These are smart people who see things differently even though all be believers and followers of Christ.

What do you make of that?

I know some of the logic and some of the interpretation behind some of the doctrinal differences and I have to say—makes sense! I'm like the rabbi— you heard this one—who told two men arguing different positions on some issue that they were both right. The rabbi's secretary corrected him by clarifying that they both can't be right.

"You now, you're right!" the rabbi agreed with his secretary.

Here is not the place to list these differences. That's another book which I probably would never write. I don't want to focus on the differences but what we have in common.

All Christians are agreed on the five basics which I have written about already in *Can You See God in This Picture?*—my first book. Let me summarize:

1. The verbal-plenary theory of Inspiration that says all Scripture is the inspired Word of God. I know the Catholic church has a few more books but oddly enough—not an issue.

2. The virgin birth of Christ. Mary was a virgin when she conceived the Savior. Again, our Catholic brethren say Mary was never intimate with Joseph her husband. Maybe so, but if so, poor Joseph. Oh, by the way some say that the reference to a virgin in Isaiah 7:14 is really the word "young maiden." The point is moot since in Israel and Old Testament culture, they were one and the same.

3. The Trinity or three persons in the Godhead but one God.

4. The Deity of Christ which is a primary truth that the above three support.

5. The vicarious atonement. Christ—God incarnate—died on Calvary for us —the message of Scripture!

* * *

Not everything we want to say about our salvation can be said clearly in the

Greek. A primary tenet of our faith is the two natures of Christ in one person. He was totally God and totally man or human. We do not need to detail this truth here, however. Within the Christian community this is commonly accepted being expounded as a tenet of faith at the Council of Chalcedon but —I understand—that the word "person" in this context is better expressed in Latin! The two natures but one persona[8]

There is much to our Faith that is just that ...taken by faith and not logic. I usually work backwards. I know Christ died for me and I think I have somewhat of an understanding why He had to. He took my eternal punishment so I wouldn't have to. But why did God require this? Why not just let bygones be bygones. I am sorry for being bad and I want to be good and go to Heaven. Grace could just accept me and forgive me and that would be that.

Not exactly because we have a two -fold problem. One, and the obvious one, just because I say I want to be good doesn't make it so. I need to change! I need to be different.

Well, can't God just change me and call it a day? He is God and He is the Creator. What part must Christ's death play in all of this?

The other problem has to do with satisfying the Holiness of God. I am reminded of a comment from a friend whose husband deeply upset her and then came with his apologies without any defense or argument or excuse. She remarked that she still needed time to dissipate her built up rage. She didn't want him to just say "sorry" and walk away!

This doesn't exactly illustrate God's feelings. Of course not. But there is something about His holiness, the standard that defines who He is and what is required to live in His house that demanded a satisfaction, a punishment for sin. More than this it required something be done to procure our obedient compliance to that standard—to become holy as He. We know the Scripture. I don't need to throw references on the page.

For God so loved the world that—to paraphrase—He came Himself to die. The word 'so' means 'such was the manner of His love'. It compelled Him; it drove Him; it simply required Him to come and do something to bring us back into communion with Him. And to bring about this communion without compromising His holiness -which compromise was and always will be impossible—He choose to die on Calvary. What does a parent do when they want their kids but not the drugs? God found a way through a new birth experience provided through His death and resurrection.

God has deep feelings, eternally standing norms that will not be ignored and somehow just saying "You're sorry? OK. We're good!" doesn't work. He, God the Father, deemed it necessary for our reconciliation that His Son die for us. Now, that's all I know!

The burden of the New Testament was to yell, "Grace!" God did not share all His thoughts with us or if He did, we still have much to learn. Perhaps, we have been belaboring other theological points of interest in our debates and discussions.

* * *

Jot this down. I like cheerios—I mean cheery "o's". I'll explain. I am glad the doctrine of salvation was explained in Greek because the Greek during New Testament times was very informative. The Bible through the Greek language provides some great insight into God's mind and the idea of justification.

In English, take the word *just*. We have justify and justification by sticking a 'tion' on the end. Or we can tweak the word a bit more by putting an 'ly' on just, justly. If we want to put an 'ness' on the end we use the word righteous, righteousness. Same word at least in the language of Scripture. Or we can talk about the person who does the justifying, the judge. There is also the word justice.

My point?

It's a good one. In the Bible the same thing happens, that is, a letter or an ending here or there adds meaning to a word and that meaning may bear an important significance to our theology. And in this case with the word *just*, it does! In New Testament Greek the word has what is called a thematic or connecting vowel, actually, the letter 'o'. If we did this in English, we might use the word justify-o-ing. My speller just put a red line under that word as if I misspelled it! How about in Latin: justifico. It looks better in Greek.

Anyways, words with an 'o' connecting the ending usually mean 'to make' whatever the verb says. 'To make a slave' or 'to enslave', 'to make blind' or just 'to blind'. That should mean that to justify should mean 'to make righteous' or 'to render someone such as he ought to be'

I hope you are still with me. I titled this chapter The study of Salvation; so, I thought the word *righteousness* or *justification* would serve well to illustrate my point about a jot or tittle, a word fragment, that is important to us.

So, we are saying that to justify literally means to make someone right? Is that what the letter 'o' in Greek is doing? The problem with making our word justify mean to make right is that "this meaning is extremely rare, if not altogether doubtful"[9]

That's when scholarship thought they should ask the writers of the Greek Old Testament and they referenced Psalm 73:13, Surely in vain have I kept my heart pure... "to keep pure" is in Greek "to make righteous."

I trust you haven't tuned out. Did David really mean to say "I purified my own heart"! I think not!

He actually said, "I have shown my heart upright."

So this idea of "showing" or "exhibiting" righteousness—rather than making righteous—began to be tossed about. Ezekiel 16:51 you... have made your sisters seem righteous by all these things you have done. Luke 7:35 wisdom is proved right by all her children.

There's more!

Then the scholars went to 'evince' righteous. Evinced? "To display clearly, constitute outward evidence." I got that from Merriam-Webster. I Timothy 3:16 And without controversy great is the mystery of godliness: God was manifest in the flesh, justified in the Spirit,... Clear evidence that God's plan of Salvation works even though it was unknown to us!

So, the commentators and the guys that write Greek dictionaries decided to look at another meaning for the 'o'. They discovered that the word "worthy" with an 'o' never means "to make worthy" but "to declare worthy." 2 Thessalonians 1:11 Wherefore also we pray always for you, that our God would count you worthy of [this] calling, and fulfill all the good pleasure of [his] goodness, and the work of faith with power. There are other words as well that have the 'o' to mean 'to declare'

So, to justify means 'to declare or pronounce righteous.' And that is so important to see. That's why I took the space to talk about cheery "o's". It is good news! Romans 3:28 For we maintain that a man is justified [declared righteous before he actually becomes righteous] by faith apart from observing the law. If we waited until we were totally in compliance with all of God's law—that's total holiness—if we needed to be righteous before God would reconcile with us ... you fill in the 'then' part. Then we are hopelessly lost! But by grace through faith are we saved, i.e. God made an emancipation declaration freeing us from the bondage of sin on Calvary and long before we even knew He did it and long before we could be called 'holy'!

Do you see it!

This is grace!!

Galatians 2:16 sums this up for us: now that a man is not [declared or pronounced] justified by observing the law, but by faith in Jesus Christ. So we, too, have put our faith in Christ Jesus that we may be [declared or pronounced] justified by faith in Christ and not by observing the law, because by observing the law no one will be [declared or pronounced] justified.

* * *

I'll Drink to That! That's a chapter title! Sin was and is the problem that sent Christ to Calvary; so, we shouldn't belittle the importance of what has burdened the great heart of God since Eden by defining it as drinking soda or wearing rings or a somewhat lengthy list of denomination specific descriptions of misbehavior that when avoided makes us better church goers but does not address the real issue of how we live in relation to God.

We have added a list of "do's" also to the "don't's" designed also to better our church experience as Christians and offer an added sense of security. Do's are good if they are Bible. But we need to be careful for God does provide freedom within limits.

Today's Christian weddings, for example, include dancing and a toast, usually champagne, both of which were taboo thirty years ago in fundamental circles. I even saw at a more recent wedding the pastor's wife on the dance floor! How cool is that!

* * *

Our Speech sometimes *betrays us* or identifies us as Christians but not because we are simply testifying to the love of Christ but because we are—pardon my being blunt—programmed to use or say certain phrases that have perhaps overextended their stay or outreached their usefulness in our world. "Born again" is a good biblical phrase but needs to be revisited since today's street walker is immune to its message. "Being saved" is another which needs to be rephrased. Say it in your words from your heart and people will listen.

* * *

I Can't Believe You Said That!

How unaware we are of the wisdom we are capable of expressing simply by telling the story of our life in Christ. Others don't have to believe us. All that matters is that we believe us!

When Paul says God has chosen the foolish things of this world to confound the wise, in 1 Corinthians 1:27, he didn't call us fools.

John on Patmos learned according to Revelation 12:11 that there is a victory awaiting the believer who relates his or her experience in Christ.

What we are saying is that what we have lived as believers, our awareness of God's hand on our lives—if we get the story straight—is more logical ultimately to any jury in any courtroom than the philosopher's locution.

Life speaks volumes of Truth; it shouts over and drowns out the weakly uttered and often meaningless noise that often comes from philosophical chatter that attempts to reason things out without living them out.

Perhaps the most instructive verse is Matthew 10:19 and 20. But when they arrest you [I don't particularly like reading this part but the rest is OK], do not worry about what to say or how to say it. At that time you will be given what to say, for it will not be you speaking, but the Spirit of your Father speaking through you.

Prepared speeches don't become us when what we have to say comes from the heart—and the heart of God at that. Eloquent speech and fancy

146

quotes and poetic license is unnecessary when we have a testimony that trumps them all!

* * *

Let me underline this thought. It isn't always what we say but how we say it or the spirit in which we say it. People are always going to take our words out of their context and reconnect them in a way to make you or me look either like someone who doesn't know what they are saying or someone who spoke out of turn. They can twist your words into pretzels of angry and foolish remarks.

And all I have to say is "So what!"

It is not easy to get the emphasis just right and sometimes with some people it is impossible. But you sometimes reach a point where speaking in love is more important than political correctness; caring enough to say something or get the dialog started than being just an observer of suffering; to think out loud even though you risk someone calling this your final thought; breaking the silence of isolation and wanting to reconcile instead of saying goodbye forever.

Love is its own emphasis. Somehow even children—no, especially children—seem to know what you meant when spoken in love. Getting the emphasis right is not so hard when the heart speaks and it speaks in love and not rage.

Getting the emphasis correct might require a little excitement; after all, joy is emphasis in motion—or is that emotion.

* * *

Hot dog!! Salvation is an exciting concept. We don't need to hold back just because our joy is an uncommon human emotion. Grant it, when we shout for joy, people who are not used to seeing it—much less experiencing it—must think we are a bit off. But joy is not a frightening thing; rage is. Love is not a frightening thing; hate is. No one to my knowledge has ever ran in panic from a ball game because the person next to them got excited over their team's scoring.

Expletives are good if they're positive. A relationship with Jesus is a good thing. Psalm 37:4, delighting one's self in the Lord means to take exquisite delight. It is coquettish behavior. In one wedding toast, the Bride's maid of honor gave me ammunition here by telling the guests—me included—that the bride would squeak loudly every time she would talk about her groom. It's a female thing! It's a lover's thing! Scholarship actually refers this word, delight, to the ogling and other coquettish jesters of women.

Don't deny yourself the right to laugh. If your experience in Christ is exciting and—fanaticism aside—you are simply enjoying yourself in that experience, don't deny it because someone might think you goofy. Be who you are.

* * *

And ... And What! Our relationship with Christ is in some regards a progressive thing. What relationship isn't? Each life is a collection of events, highlighted moments in which something special has happened—perhaps something miraculous—all connected by "and".

We don't see the links; we are not aware that somehow what had happened and what is happening are connected, but they are. We probably don't see how something God does for us relates to something we did for Him. Words like reciprocity and mutuality are not common when talking about God and us.

Connecting the dots can be impossible even if we have the numbers, dates, because we may not know them all. I, for one, cannot always look back from tragedy or heartache or suffering and claim to know why I endured it.

But God is an excellent dot connector. Many of them are from His pen anyways. Our lives are going somewhere. To believe that our lives are meaningless circles of events, often repeated and repeatable, often explainable as the all familiar patterns of human behavior or the results of synapses and brain function or pills and chemicals—this view—forgets that God is a God Who relates to us and Who teaches us and Who plans things for us. The last "and" is His return for us.

* * *

2012 give or take a year or so? When will the Lord return? Perhaps when our unity provides for us the type of witness that Jesus envisions for the church in His prayer in John 17:17 that all of them [us] may be one, Father, ... that the world may believe that you have sent me. Is this the kind of sermon this world needs to hear? Jesus seem to offer a timetable in Matthew 24:14. And this gospel of the kingdom will be preached in the whole world as a testimony to all nations, and then the end will come.

I don't anticipate this happening on December 21 a few years from now. Since our Lord's return is imminent, perhaps, the Good News is already promoted world-wide. Maybe it is happening through the satellite based media as we go about our daily routine.

My opinion is that the church will and is united along the basic message and simply by our unity—one common message of salvation spoken and lived—God is able to wrap things up and bring this present age to an end. I hear the name Jesus—it seems—these days more and more on TV and news programs; I see prayer at sport events along with the testimony of sports figures recognizing Christ when interviewed. Jesus gets at least as much credit as mother which is an interesting sign of the times!

My advice to all believers who desire to hasten our Lord's return is to go home and be with their families. I say, live your testimony there in your own living room and kitchen and if you are asked about your hope or your faith or your convictions—by anyone—just be honest and tell them truthfully what you practice and live and what you teach your own children.

Are church services in front of city hall a thing of the past? Are passing out tracts on main street a thing of the past? Are week long evangelistic services in our home church a thing of the past? Are door to door invitations to attend our services a thing of the past?

Don't know. Maybe! But the plan of God and His providential control of things aren't! The plan and the doctrine of salvation are not past. In fact, they are coming into focus the closer we come to the end of the current age.

* * *

Sign Here.... Be yourself. Verbally sign your own work with the language that you speak and not the polished rhetoric of yesterday's orator. I heard of a new convert to Christ who after asking God's blessing on a meal finished—not with an amen—but pausing he then said, "that's all, God." That had to warm the cockles of the Divine heart.

This is what makes prayers real—speaking from the heart. This is why I am reluctant sometimes to pray in public because I get personal with God. There is no flowery wording, no "supreme master of the universe" speech. I talk to God! At times, I do not like eavesdroppers.

I sometimes tend to use words or pronunciations that people find amusing or confusing. Sometimes, we do run the risk of being theologically challenged. God doesn't get bent out of shape over these peculiarities. He understands our language.

When it comes to witnessing or sharing your testimony, say it your way! I know, there are a few good tracts out there worth memorizing but I wouldn't. They might misrepresent what is important to you and those tracts might speak to another type of person than the one you are talking to. You relate best to the people in your world. Stay there!

How does God love me? Let me count the ways!

Did you get them all! You can add on later but don't limit yourself by another man's thoughts. Only stay the course. The message is Calvary.

* * *

Threads? Actually there is only one and that is the plan of Salvation which God worked out—I believe—long before Eden. How little I need say here of that because much has already been written about this simple but most dynamic fact.

What I wonder about is how any other message could be preached other than this on any pulpit that professes biblical teaching. Are we bored with the greatest story ever told? Have we learned all there is to know about Calvary?

Do we have a problem relating some scriptures to this overarching theme? Do we believe we see something else in the Scripture that supports our own ideas about life and church, right and wrong or whatever? Do we prefer to interpret prophecy by current events? Do we prefer arguing doctrine in the name of Bible study?

★ ★ ★

Psychological insight! I have been accused of seeing too much psychology in Scripture. People apparently got confused whether Saint Paul said it or Dr. Gesundheit. And if the doc said it, it isn't important because it isn't Bible—so they say. There is a ton of psychology in Scripture. Some of it the doc would not agree with. Behavioral psychology doesn't include God in their formula for coping but Paul made Him the center of our health!

Salvation is psychological because it touches the soul as it touches the life but I, for starters, must be careful not to document Scripture with comments from the doc. We need to be biblical and clear about that! All Scripture is God-breathed and is useful for teaching, rebuking, correcting and training in righteousness, so that the man of God may be thoroughly equipped for every good work, Paul wrote Timothy (2 Timothy 3:16 and 17). That's good psychology!

★ ★ ★

As we approach the end of time—for a believer this is a real coming event—my best guess is that Christianity will become increasingly unpopular. The church through division and infighting has been dormant. It has been a sleeping spiritual giant, inactive in terms of its united, single witness—its real purpose for being. But that is changing with more young churches starting up refusing to carry denominational labeling; the introduction of a common chorus book that believers across denominations enjoy singing; the general political alignment that lumps all evangelical believers under the umbrella of "the right wing." Add to this: Recent polling which suggest that the popularity associated with being a "Christian" is waning and moral social trends moving away from traditional biblical interpretation of the family and you begin to see a spiritual and cultural chasm opening up between believers in the biblical message of grace and the rest of the world. This is here while Christians in other nations of the world experience even worse conditions—in some instances persecution and even martyrdom.

The World Missionary Conference of Edinburgh held in 1910 was said to mark the transition into the twentieth century. The conference defined the mission of the Church in clear and evangelical terms paving the way for more dialogue along these same lines in future conferences. The minutes of that meeting contained a warning for the church which taken seriously carries us into the twenty-first century and beyond:

> Until there is a more general consecration on the part of
> the members of the Home Church, there can be no hope
> of such an expansion of the missionary enterprise as to
> result in making the knowledge of Jesus Christ readily
> accessible to every human being.[10]

A couple of changes can be made in this statement. The "Home" church no longer exists since even so-called "Christianized" nations need missionaries in today's world. Also through modern media and a shrinking world in which English as a language is recognized on a global stage—add to this a global market—the name "Jesus" is not so unknown anymore.

Then the conference summed up its conclusion.

> Whatever... can be done to make the...Church conform in
> spirit and in practice to the New Testament teachings and
> ideals will contribute in the most powerful manner to the
> realization of the great aim of...evangelization. A new and
> resolute awakening of the Church to the richness of its
> heritage in the Gospel and to the duty of an ardent,
> universal, and untiring effort to make disciples of all
> nations, is the clear message of God to the Church of
> today.[11]

The missionary council meeting in Jerusalem in 1928 went further to define "Go and make disciples of all nations."

> Our message is Jesus Christ. He is the revelation of what
> God is and of what man through Him may become. In
> Him we come face to face with the Ultimate Reality of the
> universe; He makes known to us God as our Father,
> perfect and infinite in love and in righteousness; for in
> Him we find God incarnate, the final, yet ever-unfolding,
> revelation of the God in whom we live and move and
> have our being... ...Jesus Christ...through His death and
> resurrection...has disclosed to us the Father, the Supreme
> Reality, as almighty Love, reconciling the world to
> Himself by the Cross...[12]

Now here's the rub and again the council says it best:

> If such is our message, the motive for its delivery should

be plain. The Gospel is the answer to the world's greatest
need. It is not our discovery or achievement; it rests on
what we recognize as an act of God... We believe that
men are made for Christ and cannot really live apart from
Him... Herein lies the Christian motive; it is simple. We
cannot live without Christ and we cannot bear to think of
men living without Him... Christ is our motive and Christ
is our end. We must give nothing less and we can give
nothing more."[13]

It is in this statement that evangelism and missionary enterprise went too far according to those whose trust is not solely in Christ for salvation or future hope. The Council, speaking of the good news of this Gospel, says it in one sentence: "Either it is true for all or it is not true at all."[14] This is where the earth between evangelical believers and the rest of the world begins to open. We claim one and only one way to future bliss and salvation and that way is Christ. All roads may lead to Rome but not to God's heaven.

* * *

Salvation is the only message or theme of Scripture. It is the red thread or, they say, the blood line that runs through every book. Follow the thread as you read Scripture. Point out the thread when you teach Scripture. Proclaim the thread when you preach Scripture. What else is there worth saying?

I Want to Speak in Tongues

...joy inexpressible ... -1 Peter 1:8

There are three words—all different—translated "unspeakable" in the authorized Version of our Bible which have caught my attention. Together with some comments by Professor Trench, whose study of words and language is renown—I said that before—I have decided to—no, more like, excited to—write—no, more like theorize—about the language of heaven.

2 Corinthians 9:15 Thanks [be] unto God for his unspeakable gift.

2 Corinthians 12:4 How that he was caught up into paradise, and heard unspeakable words, which it is not lawful for a man to utter.

1 Peter 1:8 ye rejoice with joy unspeakable and full of glory.

An unspeakable gift is indescribable.

Unspeakable words are words too sacred to be spoken.

Joy unspeakable is joy for which words are inadequate.

We may not realize how tied we are to our language for expressing ourselves. Or maybe we do realize it. If we have no word for an idea, that idea might live in our thoughts as pure images. Or our emotions may represent feelings we haven't identified; so, how do we describe them? Emotions play a key role in the expressiveness of who we are on the inside. They are the gas in the car that gives it energy to go. And it is often a challenge to determine exactly how we feel; for example, I say I am hurt but not bitter; joyful but not exactly happy; at peace but somewhat concerned. That's one reason why we pay counselors to help us find a word for what is churning on the inside. We use words like "love" and "like" at will in a sort of random display of affection. We like people and love cars or the color blue. It is as if some words have to do double duty for us depending on whether it is a wife we are talking about or our new four wheel drive.

It is interesting that in the Old Testament there is a special word for marrying your brother's widow (Deuteronomy 25:5, 7).

There is a word with great respect and affection that refers to your uncle on your dad's side, your dad's brother, viz, uncle (Esther 2:15). It eventually became a more general word of endearment as seen in the Song of Solomon where it means "my first love" (Canticles 1:13).

153

Orphans are fatherless—not motherless—children in the language of the Old Testament. And we can go on listing words and expressions that have great value in one language but may be meaningless or inexpressible in another.

This we know already, but what if that means that heaven has a language which is capable of describing glorious joy and unbounded love! What if in heaven there will be no word for sin, no concept of it at all and the language loses the vocabulary of broken relationship and death. That's my theory!

* * *

"How shamefully rich," says Professor Trench, "is the language of the vulgar everywhere in words and phrases which...live...on the lips of men, to set forth that which is unholy and impure.. And of these words, as no less of those which have to do with the kindred sins of reveling and excess, how many set the evil forth with an evident sympathy and approbation, as taking part with the sin against Him who has forbidden it... How much wit.., yea... imagination must have stood in the service of sin."[1]

There are no fewer than 9 words in Hebrew meaning "to kill." In Greek one word "to kill" is intensified, whatever that means. It is given the meanings, to extinguish, abolish, kill in any way whatever. I have to believe that heaven's vocabulary will have no word for this idea.

There was, R. C. Trench tells us " a tribe in New Holland [Australia, specifically, the aborigines or Papoos in Southern Australia circa 1800 ?], which has no word to signify God, but has one to designate a process by which an unborn child may be destroyed in the bosom of its mother."[2]

* * *

On the other hand, in Hebrew there is at least a dozen words that try to express "joy." They usually show strong emotion and a physical display such as leaping or twirling, jumping, shaking or giving off a shriek or tremulous sound, a shout or scream, a shaking of the voice—not articulate. You got it.

One of these words expressing strong feelings can represent any one of the four basic feelings: joy, fright, grief or anger. Same word! Even the sea is said to be afraid when its waves roar (Isaiah 51:15, It is the word "divideth" in the Authorized, "churns" in the NIV).

One word for fear is used to describe an earthquake.

All of this makes sense since what we are looking at is deep emotions heaved upon the vocal cords in wave after wave of intense feeling. I tried to get poetic there because there is no technical language in which to say it—none that I know.

* * *

Throughout I have been misusing—according to some—the word "passion."

154

It is somehow akin to the word "passive", to be acted upon and refers not primarily to someone of energy and strong will but someone—quite the opposite—suffering because of something done to him or her. So, we correctly speak of the "passion of Christ" or "Our Lord's passion" referring to His death on Calvary.

When it is used as a synonym for fervor or enthusiasm, it carries a negative undertone as an ungovernable emotion. Synonyms which seem available to me which imply warmth and energetic excitement I still find lacking unless I can group them together under one definition and then tweak the nuance a bit.

I need a term that belies intense emotion or feeling that is steady, actually enduring, not given to failing or fading, devoted but not fanatical, always focused, eager with a correct sense of urgency. I need a word that describes the very heart of God when it came to planning our salvation and then working that plan.

I need a word that—I believe—should describe our joyous interest in our new world, this new Jerusalem, when we rejoin with loved ones who have preceded us to glory; when we walk and talk and share and learn and discover with them things that have no earthly equivalent; when we see and smell and hear and feel and taste the newness of new life possessed of a brightness and fragrance and music and sensitivity and richness that requires resurrected bodies to experience.

I freely use the term "passion" referring to our driving hunger to know God's Word. If you wish to reread what you have already read and substitute fervor or zeal or enthusiasm for passion, well, consider what you would be reading.

We share a *fervor* to know the Word of God. This is an intense feeling, but if I err not, it would be more appropriate to refer to one's fervor while reading it—not studying it. Our interest in God's Word sometimes exhibits a quiet and peaceful adherence to its message. Sometimes how we feel is challenged by our own interest in His Word. God's Word has a way of healing emotions. A study of Truth is not governed by them.

We share a *zeal* to know the Word of God. Zeal sounds really good since it is an ardent pursuit. However, to me, it suggests an active pursuit of something in particular and in studying God's Word, it suggests an interest in having the Word prove some point or support some doctrine. We need a heart that embraces whatever God wants to share with us through Scripture not a mind seeking support in debate. Zeal, also, in the language of Scripture can also imply jealousy; so, one needs to be clear in using it.

We share an *enthusiasm* to know the Word of God. Enthusiasm is a great word! In actually means "in God" and shows an excitement that some say approaches an intensity which is Divine. It means "inspired" but also serves to describe religious fanaticism; so, I needed to rethink using this word.

Do I really need a new word? I call it passion!

* * *

"To study a people's language," says Professor Trench, "will be to study them, and to study them at best advantage; there, where they present themselves to us under fewest disguises, most nearly as they are."[3] Jesus said it another way: Matthew 12:37 For by your words you will be justified, and by your words you will be condemned.

Putting all this in the most positive of lights, the language of heaven or the language—I assume a common one for everybody—by which we will communicate our hearts and thoughts to one another and by which Christ will undoubtedly continue to reveal Himself and His Word to us will have to be able to describe and bear witness to Divine truths that were inexpressible in this life. Holiness must take on a meaning that reveals the Nature and the Glory of a God we could not look on before and live.

The veil placed over Moses' face—even though he was not aware of the change in his countenance but Israel was—because his whole being had been impacted physically as well as in spirit by what he saw on the Mount while face to face with God—this toning down of the impact of a meeting with God —will not only be no longer needed but the glow will be far greater and more intense—so much so, that heaven will need no sun to call it day.

How do we express that! How do we describe it!

I read words like, sanctification, holiness, glory, godliness, love and fail to appreciate their full meaning. I believe God only introduced these and other terms to us with meanings that no current language can effectively define. We still wear the veil.

We may not want to admit it, but—and at least I think so—there are still verses in our Bible where the meaning totally escapes us. We haven't a clue, for example, what Paul meant when he told women to let their hair grow—if in fact he did say that—because of the angels (1 Corinthians 11:10). I'm glad I'm a guy!

But the good news is that in God's presence, in eternity, all will be explainable. The simple fact is that then, in glory, we will have a language capable of such knowledge sharing and you and I will speak it! And that language will tear aside the veil. The glass we look through now—as Paul called it in 1 Corinthians 13:12—that is smudged with our half-understood interpretations and the weaknesses and drawbacks of our current language

—that glass—will get a wipe down with a divine Windex! We will behold His face! We will know!

* * *

Needing new words is not a new idea in describing the work of God.

You are familiar with Matthew 6:9: In this manner, therefore, pray: Our Father in heaven, Hallowed be Your name. "Hallowed" is a biblical word doing duty for the Old Testament word "to declare holy."

There is a family of words: to be made holy, to declare sacred, to separate or dedicate to God, consecration, purification, sanctification, holiness, moral purity—all—Bible terms never used before in the Greek language. This isn't the place to define them. That is subject matter for Soteriology. Here, the point is the need for a language and words with which to say something that —to be blunt—is a heavenly idea!

What fascinates me is the fact that the word for ceremonial cleansing or self-purification as well as the simple word holy are not new. "Holy" as a religious term signifying an object of awe has been around a long time. Is that what we mean when we sing, "Our God is an awesome God"? Holy was the term applied to "the most beautiful and sacred things ... not accessible to the public."[4] So the whole idea of separating something to God's use to make it holy is an old religious one.

Likewise, ceremonial purifying or washing, cleansing from unclean things, such as, touching something dead, was also a common idea that was used in the Greek religious world. It developed into the concept of moral purity or blamelessness.[5] Interestingly enough, cultic purification or bathing before sacrificing is not a New Testament concern. That we could have guessed.

Bible holiness is a lot more. In fact, it is something different! I freely view it as the total of all Divine moral and ethical attributes—God's stand-ard—that are quintessentially all that is God and all that is His heaven. Holi-ness is the very nature of God. Godliness is living life in harmony and lock-step with this Divine standard. The 10 commandments in essence describe God. "The history of the term [holiness in the Old Testament]...is... with reference to the name of God... the concept of holiness merges into that of divinity... God's holiness thus becomes an expression for His perfection of being which transcends everything creaturely"[6]

The idea of sanctifying one's self can only refer to God. Isaiah 5:16 says, But the LORD of hosts will be exalted in judgment, And the holy God will show Himself holy in righteousness. Self-sanctification is showing one's self holy. We needed to translate that phrase in a way that made sense to our understanding! God will reveal Himself —show Himself the Judge of all the earth (Genesis 18:25) whom we have prayerfully waited for—grandly draped in His jurist's robe seated on the Great Bench.

* * *

Inevitably with the writing of Scripture new words are needed. Definitions of old terms need changing. And some old terms like "ceremonial cleansing" no longer serve the Christian world of thought. I maintain the Bible revelation of God's holiness and the use of terms declaring us righteous or enabling us to live godly lives or separating us to a Divine plan for our lives—these terms, all of them—are only a partial understanding of what God has in mind for His people.

We need a new language.

* * *

And what about the relationship and terms that describe it? We have already underlined the new biblical term, love. In fact we all know it as agápê love. It introduces to us and our study the need for a new language and new terms to describe the relationship between you and me and between God and us. The relationship of Christ with His church, His bride, has been compared to Adam and Eve's before sin also underscoring the uniqueness of how we will ultimately relate in God's heaven.

The language of love here is not the romantic endearment of lovers in the park; this is the common language of two friends by which true communication and understanding—a common ground of interest—is reached. The difficulty lies in the fact that Christianity since its first days when fellowship was a brand new and exciting idea—Christianity—has been unable to achieve such a "all things in common" approach to relationship.

A common language means a common purpose at work, a common interest at play and a common faith at worship—what I have affectionately referred to as the *allelous* principle. *Allelous* is the Greek word for "one another" and it is only in the plural because—quite obviously—it takes more than one to make it work. We are to love one another; (John 15:17) and submit to one another (Ephesians 5:21); to serve one another. (Galatians 5:13)

It speaks of a mutual faith. (Romans 12:1) It decries a competitive spirit but conversely prefers the other over self. (Romans 12:10) It is the joints and sinews that hold the body together giving it united purpose—a kind of large and fine motor skill for God's people moving in unison in God's plan for His church. (1 Corinthians 12:25) And one of the biggees: Speaking the truth with kindness to one another (Ephesians 4:25 and 32) with forgiveness when necessary. And on and on the Scriptures enjoin us to peace and unity—and if necessary, reconciliation—but over the course of church history it hasn't happened that way. I don't need to tell you that.

Allelous means reciprocity and mutuality. It requires honest and open communication. It includes a spontaneous simplicity that cares first about the other person. It is the natural response of innocence and a "passion" to love.

Our problem is that despite the fact that these qualities are already in our vocabulary, they have been compromised by political correctness, a need to keep friendships, a fear of isolation, estrangement or divorce and the defensive posturing we are all prone to because of past hurts and broken relationships. Friends are hard to come by and most of them are nominal at best. Most hurts and fears we keep to ourselves and we live with unspoken sin that only God knows about.

It seems that on the day of Pentecost God did again what He had done in Eden. He introduced us to a perfect plan, a pristine environment free of selfish desire, united with one overwhelming interest in the Kingdom of God, alive with the hope of togetherness—alive with the ultimate, permanent, and perfect cure for loneliness. But then we partook again of the forbidden fruit of greed (Ananias and Sapphira). We slipped (Hebrews 2:1) ever so slowly and indiscernibly, like a small boat on a glassy lake drifting, floating downstream, away from the first principles of fellowship.

The church divided. We do not mean splitting like a living organism in the process of growth; that's good and part of the original plan of God. No, we are talking about division which came with all the painful realities that tore at the great hearts of the early apostles and brought warnings and admonitions in page after page of their letters to a church that had left its first love and whose light to their world might soon die out if God doesn't rescue it from itself.

I am part of that church, the church still alive, the church rescued by grace. But I think there is more to it than God wanting to save our present witness or provide a natural formula for church growth—as immediately important as these must continue to be to Him. God's designed for His people is to be one—and listen to these words from the Savior, Himself—even as ... You, Father, [are] in me, and I [am] in you, that they also may be one in us... (John 17:21)

What amazes me is that our Savior's prayer was to perfect our witness in this life and did not speak to the unity of Heaven in the life to come. That level of togetherness is unspoken.

Heaven will mean the return of innocence and openness. Heaven, I believe, will provide us with a language of the heart whereby we will freely and excitedly offer ourselves, how we feel, what we think, toward one another without the regret of misspeaking or the fear of rejection. I maintain —but how can I know this?—that in the absence of sin, there will be no "I wish I hadn't said that!" Christians will be getting to know each other, work together, play together, worship together and love on a level of intimacy—oneness—that has to take us far beyond our current vocabulary and language to even explain it let alone express it.

We will need a new language.

Epilogue

My sister speaks her mind, a trait she owns which I appreciate. Few people I have met in life are as genuine. Few people seem to know nothing about political correctness like she—knows nothing about political correctness or verbal protocol. But my sister's apparent ignorance of telling people what they want to hear, her innocent spontaneity in saying instead what she is feeling, makes her easy to talk to. She has a heart big enough to support any claim to honesty but she possesses a humility that doesn't care to.

Jesus said to let our nays be nay and yeas be yea. You must know that Scripture—Matthew 5:7—and anything else, our Lord reminded us comes from the evil one. I admit that sometimes I have been too careful in what I say. I have weighed my words and tried to avoid confrontation. She is simply not this way.

The problem is that you must be prepared for this level of transparency. You never know what she might say. And this brings me to my point. Many pastors ago and a few more yesteryears she confronted the leader of the church she was then attending and bluntly asked, blurting out, "Why aren't you teaching us the Bible?"

Ouch!

She wasn't being nasty. She wasn't leading an inquisition to challenge his right to his pulpit. My sister doesn't have the drive for such a thing. She can't have a hidden agenda—not and be so outrageously simplistic, so clean-glass clear in what she actually wants to say. She was simply asking in her own inimitable way if her pastor would teach her the Bible.

The Bible. Not a bad request!

But that is a very general subject. She wasn't seeking any particular teaching; she wasn't asking for emotional reinforcement over some pet doctrine. She didn't seek support for her view point on anything. She simply wanted to be taught. Being teachable, she was expressing an interest in learning something—a little something more—from the Bible. In her own way she was asking him to open the book and point and then explain what his finger fell on. As she observed things, a Sunday morning service wasn't doing it for her and she wanted a bit more.

Not everyone feels that way. Not everyone finds a Sunday Morning service a little less than filling. Some, and perhaps most, christians are totally satisfied with the portion of God's Word they hear in one service a week and no one—least of all my sister—would look on these believers as lacking a desire to know God's Word. Everyone's appetite is different.

In addition it is improper to accuse the person in the pulpit of not fulfilling their commitment to God's Truth because they kept the message short or didn't dive into a monologue of technical chatter in the name of learning. Sometimes we get more Truth in five minutes in one sermon than we might enjoy or find in hours of another. A pastor's "Gettysburg address" might stamp upon our memories a far more lasting impression than an Edward Everett's. Most school kids can quote Lincoln but does anyone—beside some dedicated historian—know what Mr. Everett said? It was over 10,000 words long!

Keep in mind that quality trumps quantity and quality does not mean the use of Greek words. Most pastor's tone down the rhetoric and the technical jargon without losing the emphasis and impact of Scripture. They talk the interpretation of the Greek and Hebrew without our even knowing it, because it isn't the Greek we need to learn. It is God's Word in our language that we must get into our heads.

* * *

Talking about "pastors". The Bible, however—and I think I am right about this—doesn't clearly define the role of a pastor in the church. Since the word pastor means shepherd—same word—we can conclude, I think, that among their duties is opening our minds and hearts to God's Word. They are—I believe—commissioned by God to feed us.

Feed the flock of God which is among you, Peter reminds someone—I Peter 5:2—and I think he was talking to pastor types. For detailed information I refer you to Pastor John Lathrop's work, Apostles, Prophets,Evangelists, Pastors and Teachers Then and Now, copyrighted 2008 by Zulon Press.

But for here and now, I am saying that pastors need to communicate God's Word and, frankly, giving us grammatical terms and unnecessary documentation doesn't do that for us. So we must be careful not to accuse God's servant of not fulfilling his or her calling to the people of God just because we didn't get a lesson in Greek!

We need more people like my sister, though, don't you think? Perhaps, there is a better way to say it with more politeness and a little more expressed respect for a person of the cloth, but it should be a harmless request for a pastor to hear that his or her people want more Bible.

Epilogue

And more pastors are encouraged by such a request because they, too, want to study the Scripture and share it. The Bible is their life or at least ought to be. It translates into a rush of enthusiasm if they can recognize the same hunger in the people they serve. Trust me on this one.

* * *

A final comment is in order here. Some Christians take offense at the thought that they missed something in reading the Scriptures. They feel cheated in thinking that you have to become a Greek scholar in order to learn the Bible and since they are not Greek scholars, they draw the conclusion that the preacher is saying that he is smart and they are biblically stupid.

The argument went: If the King James—translation of the Bible—was good enough for Peter and Paul, it is good enough for me, too. I suppose this idea embodied the offense and it was a defensive posture taken against too much scholarship. One pastor who incidentally had a PHD in Textual Criticism advised me not to be "one up" on the people.

Truth be told, knowing Greek is of small advantage in knowing the Bible since most of it was written in Hebrew and most pastors never learn Hebrew. And yes, most pastors are smart—by calling! It is their ministry to teach us God's Word; so, they can't be too stupid.

Also, learning a language is an ongoing exercise. If you stop researching and investigating the meanings of words and phrases and how they might have been used in the Bible, if you stop learning, wouldn't you lose your place among the scholars since they continue to out distance you in grammatical insight?

Put another way, I have found out that the more I learn, the more I need to learn or the more I know I don't know. I get more stupid, the more I study because I uncover veins of truth that run deep inside the Mountain of God's Word. Think about it. A study of God's Word is a study of God and dare anyone presume to know beyond doubt or further meditation anything spoken of Him or by Him.

Furthermore, it takes prayer and living the knowledge we do have if we want to learn more. Peter pointed out in his second epistle (1:5) that we should be passionate about adding knowledge or learned experience, to our virtue, that portion of Truth we are currently living. Makes sense? Use it or lose it! Live it if you would know it.

The believers that practice their faith are the true scholars of Truth. These are the people who can hopefully find some encouragement in these pages.

All a knowledge of a little Greek ever did for me is humble me into realizing how much I didn't know. Academic pride shows a lack of study and I hope our hunger to know God's Word drives us to our intellectual knees.

* * *

So where are we going here?

If you're interest didn't drop off somewhere after the introduction of this book, I am hoping you can take with you three simple things which perhaps I can call lessons which I hoped this work offered you.

1. I hope you have an increased awareness of your own need to learn more Bible. It is alright to say, "I don't know" if by this you are expressing an interest in learning. I trust that you—that we all—can become more aware of a teachable spirit within that hungers for more Truth.

Have you heard the term bibliolotry? I am not quite sure what it might mean, but it suggests that a belief in the inerrancy of Scripture and that every word is inspired is a worship of the Bible and not God. That would make me a bibliolater.

Bible worship? I think the idea was invented by someone who either challenged the Bible message as Christians see it or, perhaps, they thought guys like you and me go overboard with our inquiry into the content of Truth. I can hear Festus in Acts 26:24 say to Paul again, "You are out of your mind, Paul! ...Your great learning is driving you insane."

I have not great learning only a great interest and I trust so do you. Don't let the ingenuity of a dissenter deter you. Just because they are good at inventing terms doesn't make them right. We worship the God of the Bible, the Savior, written about in its pages and the Bible is our means of learning more and better how to serve Him. Beside, I, for one, maintain, there is no difference between the written Word and the living Word, Jesus. Study the one, you study the other.

2. I hope that reading this work has underscored in your understanding the total futility of arguing with other believers over some interpretation of Scripture. Be content to know that they know no more than you even if they think otherwise. Let God teach them also and don't play teacher's pet and ask to grade their papers. Offer them a heartfelt embrace into fellowship and let the rest go.

There had been—I hope it is over—simply too much heated discussion over the meaning of this verse or that verse—and this by God's people who mean well but they are really—well—mean! At times, we may have been fed empty spiritual calories in some meals with Bible portions. The soup might have been watered down. The broth could have been from time to time a bit weak but the cook had added some interesting spices that made it taste good but it wasn't as good for us as it tasted. We had been starving for Truth; so, we listened and ate!

Much of what we are fed is good for us because it does just what food is suppose to do. It brings back our strength; it revives us. We get up from the table—leave the service—ready to go back to work, back to living the life for Christ. Truth is the spiritual protein that we take in and it is transformed into faith—the muscle of the soul.

But we eat too many chips and drink too much soda pop. We all may have a few doctrines not shared by fellow believers in other Christian groups. As a result, we don't want to go to their parties—their fellowship-unless they serve—these beliefs—our favorite snacks.

Admit it. We would rather talk about mode of water baptism, what the infilling really means, how far you can stray from God without losing sight of Him or if you can, when He is going to return, and on and on instead of our common faith. God has prepared a spiritual banquet for us in His Word in the message of salvation and we bring junk food to the gathering!

I would shame us if I didn't think that inappropriate for this work. The simple idea is this: If your understanding of God's Word strengthens your faith and helps you to live for Him; if you see the grace of God in your understanding of what God is saying in His Word, yes—please by all means —believe it and live it. It is part of your testimony. It is a part of your life! It is you!

But if any of your—our—beliefs are simply arguments that serve no purpose unless we are privileged to discuss them; if they are the substance of debate only, the manuscript that supports our contentions, the position we hold to in our theology but nothing more, we have the wrong recipe! It is an uneatable concoction and I am trusting God's people to leave the dish untouched at the picnic table.

I think if you made it this far in your reading, you must agree with me. Man shall not live by bread alone but by every—I like "every"—word that proceeds from the mouth of God. Matthew 4:4.

3. And it is my fondest hope that we become more and more aware of God's heart between the lines as we read Scripture. See the thread of grace running through it. See the plan of God as it unfolds. See the revelation of our great God and Savior, Jesus Christ, from Genesis to Revelation as it progressively becomes clearer.

Even the chronologies point to Him. All those strange sounding names that we can't pronounce, that we hope pastor never calls on us to read, offer a lineage from Adam to Jesus. It is a genealogical tree. Most of the time we are on a branch that leads to Mary but once in Matthew it ends at Joseph, but always and only at Jesus. No Scripture lacks continuity. No portion is a tangent to the main message. All of it speaks of the Salvation Plan and the Savior!

* * *

One evening late I decided to read one of the minor prophets; so, I opened my Hebrew Bible to—I think was—Haggai. I am not sure. What I do remember is a strange feeling that came over me as I read. It can only be described as a growing excitement deep inside that was turning into a burden, a cry, a longing, to go further, to read on, to learn more. It began to—well—burn! I think I understand what the two on the road to Emmaus were describing. Luke 24:32: Were not our hearts burning within us while he talked with us... As I read, it was as if His Word spoke to me.

In my thoughts, I sit somewhere in the back row unseen and unknown by anyone there, for their minds are not on me—and stomp my feet in excitement—that's my style—listening to Paul say—Philippians 3:10, ...that I may know Him..!

I sit on the train and begin to read Scripture only to pause on a word or a phrase. I say to myself, I have all eternity to read the rest of this book, but for now I want to talk to Him, to God, about this word or this phrase. I don't need answers. I don't have questions. I only want to talk because something in this portion of Truth has arrested my attention and taken me away into a place of richer meditation, a place of more exciting and inspired possibilities.

I hear David in Psalm 25 say, Show me your ways, O LORD, teach me your paths; guide me in your truth and teach me, for you are God my Savior, and my hope is in you all day long. This Scripture might even be worth reciting in the Hebrew! What a prayer!!

It is my prayer. I know it is yours as well.

My sincere prayer is that in some small way something said here might be God's opportunity to speak and we will be able to say while on our road to Emmaus as in Luke 24:32, Did not our heart burn within us, while he talked with us by the way, and while he opened to us the scriptures?

He still does.

Appendices

Appendices are included to offer additional material which like a footnote needs to be separated out to avoid a lengthy tangent from the idea presented in the chapter it is referencing.

New Testament Greek: I put this as an appendix because it is a lengthy quote or section taken from The Vocabulary of the Greek New Testament, which is a dictionary compiled by Professors, James Moulton and George Milligan, copyrighted in 1930. Before passing this off as too technical to be interesting, keep in mind that it relates an interesting find. Prior to Dr. Deissmann's discovery (1908), which this article will go into, the Greek words and language used in the writing of the New Testament was considered a spiritual language because it was different in meaning, spelling and nuance from the Greek used in the Classical writings of the Greek philosophers and playwrights. Some words are first introduced in the Bible like the familiar word agápê, love.

For me, Dr. Deissmann's discovery is interesting because it supports one of my premises that God with focused intent choose and developed the languages He would use for His most singular and inspired work, the Bible, the record and revelation of what He does and Who He is in relationship with His people.

* * *

The Inspiration of Scripture addresses some of the challenges scholarship has in determining exactly what should be considered canonical.

* * *

I Said "No" is a further breakdown of words used to describe or define real sin, the act or thought that disrupts and inevitably would destroy relationship.

* * *

One should not study God and His Word without at least a glancing interest in the language.

New Testament Greek

D r. Milligan writes in his Introduction to The Vocabulary of the Greek Testament,
Alike in Vocabulary and Grammar the language of the New Testament exhibits striking dissimilarities from Classical Greek; and in consequence it has been regarded as standing by itself as "New Testament Greek." In general it had been hastily classed as "Judaic" or "Hebraic" Greek; its writers being Jews (with the probable exception of Saint Luke), and therefore using a language other than their own, a language filled with reminiscences of the translation-Greek of the Septuagint on which they had been nurtured.

[The Septuagint, the name means 70 or in Roman numerals is LXX, is the translation of the Old Testament from Hebrew into Greek around 250 years before Jesus' birth. The Greek of this work and the New Testament appears the same. Professor Milligan continues...]

But true as this may be, it does not go far enough to explain the real character of the Greek which meets us in the New Testament writings. For a convincing explanation we have in the first instance to thank the German scholar, Adolf Deissmann, now Professor of New Testament Exegesis [exegesis means to derive from or is the study of or reading out what is actually written in the Bible, instead of reading into the Bible what we wish it said—eisegesis. It is the and art of biblical interpretation which we concur takes also and primarily the Spirit of God to reveal.]

...While still a pastor at Marburg, Dr. (then Mr.) Deissmann happened one day to be turning over in the University Library at Heidelburg a new section of a volume containing transcripts from the collection of Greek Papyri [papyri is made from the read plant found along the Nile river in Egypt. It is laid out in stripes and pressed together to make sheets for writing.] ...And as he read he was suddenly struck by the likeness of the language of these papyri to the language of the New Testament. Further study deepened in his mind the extent of this likeness, and he realized he held in his hand the real key to the old problem.

So far from the Greek of the New Testament being a language by itself, or even as one German scholar called it, "a language of the Holy Ghost," its main feature was that it was the ordinary vernacular Greek of the period, not the language of contemporary literature, which was often influenced by an attempt to imitate the great authors of Classical times, but the language of everyday life, as it was spoken and written by the ordinary men and women of the day, or, as it is often described, the Koine or Common Greek, of the great Graeco-Roman world.

Professor Mason, at one time Professor in the University of Athens, writes: "The diction of the New Testament is the plain and unaffected Hellenic [Greek] of the Apostolic Age, as employed by Greek speaking Christians when discoursing on religious subjects... Perfectly natural and unaffected, it is free from all tinge of vulgarity on the one hand, and from every trace of studied finery on the other. Apart from the Hebraisms—the number of which have, for the most part, been grossly exaggerated—the New Testament may be considered as exhibiting the only genuine facsimile of the colloquial diction employed by unsophisticated Grecian gentlemen of the first century, who spoke without pedantry—as ..'private persons', and not as ...'adepts'."

... Professor (afterwards Bishop) J. B. Lightfoot is reported to have said: "...if we could only recover letters that ordinary people wrote to each other without any thought of being literary, we should have the greatest possible help for the understanding of the language of the N(ew) T(estament) generally."

There are many examples where the meaning behind a New Testament word becomes clear when we listen to ordinary people in their day to day conversation and correspondence use the same word. Let me offer one such example.

The word parousia which Christians know refers to the Second coming of Christ, is an anglicizing of the Greek word of the same spelling which means in Greek literature, presence. But in later Greek it came to mean or refer to a visit of a king or a great man. Thus, in the ordinary language of the time of the Greek Old Testament it carried the meaning visit. Now let's quote Professor Milligan.

It would seem, therefore,that as distinguished from other words associated with Christ's Coming, such as His 'Manifestation' of the Divine power (2 Tim 1:10) and His 'revelation' (1 Peter 4:13) of the Divine plan, the 'parousia' leads us rather to think of His 'royal visit' to His people, whether we think of the First Coming at the Incarnation, or the Final Coming as

Judge.

Is the Bible Inspired?

Is the Bible the inspired Word of God? By "inspired" I mean "the revealed Word of God." You must know by now that I affirm that it is, but I think I need to make a few more comments to clarify and support that belief. The reason why I think I need to do this is because we are living in the days of scientific inquiry. Science is now a final authority in the minds of liberal scholarship and I don't say that in sarcasm. It may become harder and harder for people of faith to defend that faith against the historical-critical method of today's hermeneutic of interpreting Scripture.

If we argue that the inspiration of Scripture cannot be affirmed because of the human intervention that brought it to us, we lose altogether our desire to study it as the written voice of God. It becomes mere literature for studying the languages. The trouble with this theory is the message itself. It works! It does change lives! It does offer promises that God does fulfill! It is a message that transcends human thinking. It advances the use of language to a higher level of thought, yes, bringing it into a divine place until it leads us up the very path to heaven's gate.

Recall the chapter titled *I Can't Believe You Said That*. I reference 2 Peter 1 and detail an explanation of the text that even I thought was lofty speech for a fisherman. Some of today's scholars have come to believe Peter didn't write the epistle and that it is a forgery. This is a shocking accusation for someone claiming to apply historical or scientific methods to determine the genuineness and authenticity of a book of the *Bible*.

Determining the value of a scripture—at least for me and regardless of its authorship—was much easier when I assumed every word was God breathed and all I had to do was study those words and the phrases and context they were in to get God's message. When I learned that here and there a small portion was spurious or not original, I simply left it out of my sermons and studying. Even the famed Martin Luther didn't want to include the letter of James in his Bible.

Now scholarship—and it is generally known and accepted—has identified some parts of our Bible as forgeries, has claimed that the Bible is filled with contradictions and historical inaccuracies, and liberal scholarship has discredited the Bible—as we know it—as the inspired word of divine Truth. I, of course, continue to challenge this conclusion in my personal studies and in my writings. I still maintain the Bible is God's Word! I don't say that blindly but as best I can by study and research find that some of the liberal conclusions are challengeable. A few are simply wrong if you ask me.

I have no problem accepting the idea that some things preached in evangelical pulpits are misrepresentations of truth. What else is new! When a major doctrinal position is based on a rare grammatical usage or a word written so few times as to deny plausible meaning in the context it is written becomes the sole support for a denomination's distinctive theology, I don't panic and discredit my Christian experience.

When I am told that there are thousands of differences in the many manuscripts or sections or pages of our New Testament, I accept that as a fact because it is a fact. But these differences only encourage and excite my interest in researching and learning more about the Bible. My theory which cannot be proven wrong—no more than my faith—is that somewhere in all those variations we have a message from God. But we must be careful what perspective we have on this. To say the Bible is just a collection of writings by human authors—no more nor less than any work of literature—makes it less than a divine message and discredits the plan of Salvation which I maintained in chapters like *Apples and Oranges* and *Impossible* had to be God breathed. To go the other way and say that the Bible we hold in our hands is absolutely and correctly and totally, unalterably, what God intended to share with us word for word goes off the deep conservative end of things. I know some say only the ideas are inspired but I don't know how to extract ideas without the words and their meanings; so, I have to continue to study words and maintain that the inspirational message is in there. It is verbal and I have to look at all the words—plenary. So I have a twist on the verbal plenary theory of inspiration that keeps me involved.

* * *

If you read anything that challenges your faith—even in the name of science or open research—keep in mind, also, that there is a reason why the writer is writing what he is writing. No one can write without bias. There is a heart or passion or impulse directing one's pen that in turn directs their thoughts and provides a continuous flow of ideas all psychologically—if not logically-connected. It is this underlining reason for writing anything that an author must own if they are going to be completely honest with their readers.

If I write about the Bible as an atheist, my view and interpretation will be quite different from what it would be if I write with a belief in God. If I write with a heart to share the excitement of discovery, the end result will be quite different than if I write to discredit another's thoughts.

Almost any idea can be documented given the natural ambiguity in resource material that lends itself to a writer's cause. Said in plain English: we can probably see just about whatever it is we want to see in the Bible—-believe whatever we want to believe about the Bible and have resources to prove it—and this goes for the liberal as well as the evangelical.

I maintain the conviction that our Bible must be authored by God—-somehow and in someway. The assumption was and remains that words matter, especially in the Bible. I have been seeking knowledge about the God I believe in and I treat this knowledge as historical and autobiographical—it is God's involvement in the history of man. It is not a literary pursuit to learn about some author who penned a myth and lost his way in the historical or geological maze of a fictitious story he was trying to relate.

If, however, all this is troubling, I guess the place to start is with the textual critic. Let me introduce you to a couple and hopefully without passing judgement on their work. Dr. Howard Eshbaugh, a graduate of Pittsburgh Theological Seminary, was a friend. We pastored in the same town. Dr. Bart Ehrman, a graduate of Princeton Theological Seminary and author of a few best sellers including *Misquoting Jesus*, Harper Collins Publishers, 2005 and *Jesus Interrupted*, Harper Collins Publishers, 2009 which are referenced in this appendix, is a professed agnostic and has a less inspired view of the Bible.

* * *

I met Dr. Howard Eshbaugh in the small Pennsylvania town of Burgettstown during the 1970's. We pastored churches across the creek from each other for what seemed at the time forever. Those days had to be beyond busy for the good doctor since he was in the PHD program for textual criticism while he took care of one of the Presbyterian congregations in town. In that program for his doctorate Rev. Eshbaugh's dissertation was on P46, one of the earliest manuscripts written on papyri that contains most of Paul's writings.

Why tell you this? Dr Eshbaugh's research exemplifies the task of the textual critic. The work of the textual critic will hopefully strength our faith by showing after comparing the hundreds of thousands of differences and filtering out the forgeries that what remains points to one common and original source—the originally inspired Word of God. Somewhere, we want to believe, in all that ancient writings is revealed that true Word of God! Prof Ehrman in *Misquoting Jesus* wrote, "The task of the textual critic is to determine what the earliest form of the text is for all these writings."

Sifting through virtually countless documents takes generations of scholars revisiting fragments and comparing snippets of works from a small directory of authors and redactors. So it is work that is never done but always on going. Liberal scholarship simply concludes that trying to identify an inspired text in all of this is like looking for a needle in a haystack—a needle that, to them it is obvious, cannot be there else God would not have made this such an impossible quest. I alluded in chapters such as *Perfect* and *I Want to Speak in Tongues* the task God must have had in getting His message to us. Because of the "language barrier" as well as the simple way we think in contrast to His thoughts, this task was near impossible. Impossible, that is, for man. My hope is that the research of the textual critic—nevertheless—approaches a focal point that says, "God is here!"

Dr. Eshbaugh compared P46, papyri number 46 dated around 250 CE, with a number of other fragments or pages of the Pauline text, lining them up chronologically—that was what he endeavored to show, that they did have a chronological order and that order pointed back to P46 as closest to what Paul actually wrote. The changes my friend and colleague wanted to show were due to changing theological thought. The historical development of Christian theology influenced the redactors or copyists so that they actually edited the sacred text to reflect their changing beliefs.

Yes, developing doctrine, changing theologies! Scholarship is not blind. It is easy to see that many of the changes or much of the editing over the centuries was due to changing dogma and yes, as I have pointed out elsewhere, some of this dogma could not be clearly stated in Greek so even Latinisms worked their way into Christian thought. None of this is questioned. We even pointed out in *Soteriology* that three of the five basic doctrines that define Christianity are not clearly defined in Scripture. Dr. Eshbaugh might be the first to agree since his dissertation was written to show this very point with regard to Paul's works.

A simple example might be found in—say—Galatians 4:7, the Authorized reads: an heir of God through Christ, but the NIV correctly, after P46, says, God has made you also an heir [leaving out the words *through Christ*]. What do we do with Philippians 2:30 where the phrase *the work of Christ* found in P46 was read later in a few manuscripts, *the work of God* which could be a theological note underscoring the Deity of Christ. The words *of God* might have been for theological clarification but they were not original. In Colossians 3:16, P46 reads *the word of Christ* but some manuscripts have *the word of God*. Here is the verse: *Let the word of Christ* [P46; others: God] *dwell in you richly in all wisdom; teaching and admonishing one another in psalms and hymns and spiritual songs, singing with grace in your hearts to God* [P46; others: the Lord]. I can't say Dr. Eshbaugh used these particular Scriptures to prove his theory but it points out the work of the textual critic. He has the task of deciding for us which is more reliable, which is closest to what was origin-ally written.

My youngest son thought that since this book is being written to Chris-tians, why go into a talk about textual criticism and why—which I am about to do—bring up the writings of critics who have used their knowledge to—seems so—discredit the inspiration of Scripture? Christians don't need to hear argument in defense of the inspiration of God's Word. They already believe that it is inspired! It is as if this section is written to the skeptic or the critic. I think, however, Christians need to know that even if they haven't studied it for themselves that there are explanations for the many—so called —discrepancies found in comparative manuscripts—explanations—that can support our cherishing the Bible as God's Word.

We need to know that there are Dr. Eshbaughs out there, textual critics whose faith remains intact and who can believe—not in spite of their work but because of it—that there must have been an original which we can accept as God's message to us, and that we have enough of it brought down to us to be able to say that we get the message! That message is one of divine Grace which the preacher knows well. I know, I am boldly marching in where most Christians fear to tread. I am not a textual critic. I am only sharing my thoughts with—I believe—others of like faith and I hope that faith remains a strong bond between us and our God.

* * *

From the earliest times there has been controversy over the real meaning of some Scriptures. The right of some verses to be called inspired has been chal-lenged as a necessary part of any research that takes the Word of God seri-ously. What has been controversial is what to make of the fact that the original writings are not in the possession of scholars. It is the task of biblical scholarship to sift through all the variations and attempt to reconstruct as best they can what we might call "the closest" to that inspired text.

Some, incidentally maintain that even if we had the originals that doesn't make them inspired! In that case the problem of not having them would become moot and goes away. But the search for the autographs, as they are known, goes on. It must mean that we are still looking for God's inspired sayings in the language of common man. It has been the work of the textual critic to sift this all out and not until recently did I discover that some of them are liberal enough in their thinking that in the spirit of open-minded-ness and scientific enquiry they have come to discredit the Bible as God's inerrant and literal Word.

Dr. Bart Ehrman is an agnostic by his own confession. In his work *Jesus*

Interrupted he wrote:

"I started to doubt that God had inspired the words of the Bible... I started seeing discrepancies... I saw that some of the books of the Bible were at odds with one another... And I began to see that many of the traditional Christian doctrines that I had long held to... were not present in the earliest traditions of the New Testament... and had moved away from the original teachings of Jesus." (page 16)

These thoughts, no doubt, represent a couple underlining issues that many an honest and scholarly pastor—no doubt—had to wrestle with and then be reconciled to in their pulpit. If the Bible is not inspired and if it is recognized simply as a literary device to map out the historical course of the languages and cultures it is written in—if it is not God's Word—the message of Salvation has been seriously compromised and for some scientifically minded individuals discarded altogether.

Pastors must keep the vision of the Great Commission alive and since that vision is found initially and primarily within the pages of Scripture and since that vision is supposedly the eternal plan of God for man, discrediting a belief in the inspiration of Scripture has turned Bible study on its head. In a totally other sense than Paul meant, it has become the "foolishness of preaching". If we contend that there was no original copy of Truth in the mind of God, or if there had been such a divine thought, God has been unable or unconcerned about somehow getting that message to us despite human imperfection, we have given up on "true" biblical scholarship.

In some sense, Dr. Ehrman appears to agree! In *Jesus Interrupted* he sees "..the Bible as conveying important teachings of God to his people." (Page 16). It is also interesting to note that Dr. Ehrman still refers to a certain group of colleagues "in the guild of New Testament studies" as having "remained committed Christians and "my closest friends" (Page 17). He closed his book remarking: "...two of my closest friends, most intimate...,...both smarter than I, better read than I, more sophisticated philosophically than I... unashamedly call themselves Christian. Ask them if they believe in God, they would say, yes. Think Christ is God? Yes. Think he is the Lord? Yes." (page 278).

In *Misquoting Jesus* he wrote,

> For my part, however, I continue to think that even if we
> cannot be 100 percent certain about what we can attain
> to, we can at least be certain that all the surviving manu-
> scripts were copied from other manuscripts, which were
> themselves copied from other manuscripts, and that it is
> at least possible to get back to the oldest and earliest

stage of the manuscript tradition for each of the books of
the New Testament. (Page 62)

Even the best endeavor of the scientific mind, then, is not absolutely certain. When one reads *Jesus Interrupted* one can get an overall impression that the author might have figured it all out, but even he admits that a slightly different perspective on some of his examples might reconcile them with the major body of Truth. Bear in mind that his main interest in writing the book was not resolving controversy but revealing it. He tells us regarding contradictions, "you will find them in droves." (Page 20).

Keep the faith!

An example that might be worth your time because I already made a big deal out of it is found in Gen 15:7 compared to Exodus 6:3. Genesis: He [God] also said to him [Abraham], "I am the Lord,..." Compare Exodus: I appeared to Abraham, to Isaac and to Jacob as God Almighty, but by my name the Lord I did not make myself known to them. A clear contradiction? Not to me! It isn't the speaking of the name but the significance behind the name—the revelation of its meaning—of which Abraham was not aware. Also, in Genesis, Moses is speaking about a conversation between God and Abraham. Even if Abraham was familiar with the term Jehovah, Yahweh— which later became too sacred to pronounce—the inspired meaning of that name came to Moses—we can believe—at the burning bush.

* * *

Dr. Ehrman writes that his interest—and this is, admittedly, the mark of a good teacher— is "to get students to think." He concludes that what he has to say needs to be said. Our lack of an awareness of biblical controversy "is a shame, and," he maintains, "it is time that something is done to correct the problem." (Page 18).

I only ask, "Why?" Why is this controversy needing to be raised among church goers? Don't they argue enough about other things? The more likely scenario is that people who read Dr. Ehrman's book with a need "to think" ... won't! They will simply accept his conclusions and his view.

I guess if we are going to just accept stuff, we should be accepting what our pastor teaches. Otherwise I, for one, might ask "Why are we sitting there?" Pastors are not stupid for presenting the Scripture as a guide to faith and conduct. This doesn't mean that pastors are belittling their parishioners by "hiding" truth from them. It doesn't mean that pastors don't know about controversy or the many places where variations in the biblical text require a closer look. Ask yourself how you want your pastor to present the Bible: As English literature? As linguistic puzzles of unresolved meaning? As complex truth that requires a little Latin, Greek or Hebrew to explain? As God's Word for life and faith?

* * *

Here is a great example. View this as a sermon for Easter Sunday or a Good Friday Service. In Dr. Ehrman's chapter on *A World of Contradictions,* he asks, "When did Jesus die?"

Dr. Ehrman:

> Noon? On the Day of Preparation for the Passover? The day the lambs were slaughtered? How can that be? In Mark's Gospel, Jesus lived through that day, had his disciples prepare the passover meal, and ate it with them before being arrested... But not in John. In John Jesus dies a day earlier, on the day of Preparation for the Passover, sometime after noon... And so the contradiction stands: in Mark, Jesus eats the Passover meal (Thursday night [Mark 15:42: *the day before the sabbath*]) and is crucified the following morning. In John, Jesus does not eat the Passover meal but is crucified on the day before the Passover meal was to be eaten [John 19:14: *it was the preparation of the passover*]. Moreover, in Mark, Jesus is nailed to the cross at nine in the morning [Mark 15:25: *the third hour*]; in John, he is not condemned until noon [John 19:14: *the sixth hour*], and then he is taken out and cruci-fied. (Page 26-27).

Now compare the studied remarks of a few other scholars.

J. P. Lange says in his *Commentary of the Holy Scriptures,* Zondervan Publishers, 1980, page 154:

> Meyer [another commentator] says: 'Here, accordingly, there is not a trace that this Friday was itself a festival.' [Ehrman agrees with this saying that this is an ordinary week's end or sabbath; the Sabbath begins Friday night at 6PM] The trace is given fully , ch. xiv. 12 [*On the first day of the Feast of Unleavened Bread;* Meyer maintains that there is more than a trace here. Mark says it was the time of the Passover Feast]. If the day mentioned there was the 14th Nisan, then the following day must have been the 15th Nisan. Besides, we know that upon a Passover feast, where the second day of the feast was at the same time a Sabbath, upon this day...the chief feast fell as is *distinctly shown in John* [my italics] xix. 31 [If it was the day of Preparation, the next day, Passover, would be a special or

High Sabbath.]

Frederick Louis Godet, *The Gospel of John*, Zondervan Publishers, 1970, looks at the time difference for the crucifixion and adds,

> It is certainly difficult to bring this hour of noon into harmony with the account of Matthew, according to which at that hour Jesus had been already for some time suspended on the cross [Matthew 27:45: *From the sixth hour until the ninth hour darkness came over all the land*], and still more difficult to reconcile it with Mark [Mark 15:25: *the third hour*].
>
> ...[But note: The] word *about* is also added by John [19:16 **about** *the sixth hour*]. It is certainly allowable, therefore, to take the middle course...especially if we recall the fact, as Lange says, the apostles did not have watch in hand. As the third hour...may include all the time from eight to ten, so the sixth hour...certainly includes from eleven to twelve. ...an account must be taken [also] of an important circumstance, noticed by Lange: ...Matthew and Mark, having given to the scourging of Jesus the meaning which it ordinarily had..., made it the *beginning* of the punishment... [Matthew and Mark] therefore united in one the two judicial acts [scourging and crucifixion] so clearly distinguished by John ...*scourging*... and final *condemnation*.

Dr. Ehrman, then, takes the Gospel writers' reckoning of time as exact, where it is more reasonable to recognize what John confessed that it was *about* 12. Also Mark used the Greek word for *before the sabbath* which has been elsewhere in Scripture only in Psalm 93:1, where it probably does denote the *weekly* Sabbath but didn't have to. Mark found it necessary to explain: *it was the preparation*. This could refer to either a weekly sabbath or the day before a feast, i.e. Passover. Dr. Ehrman interprets this as the weekly sabbath which unnecessarily—in my opinion—contradicts the apostle John's account.

Did you think and decide for yourself what the flow of events was?

You can go back and read it again. I had to read it multiple times before I decided that it was possible that the Sabbath spoken of in Mark was a High Sabbath corresponding to Passover and in total agreement with John's account. And what about the third hour or sixth hour controversy? John's way of reckoning time is based on the actual time Jesus was suspended on the cross whereas Mark starts the clock at His trial and scourging. Matthew only mentions darkness between noon and 3PM which is a detail easily synchronized with all accounts.

Remember Isaiah 53? "By His stripes we are healed." From Matthew 8:17 we know that Matthew was cognizant of Jesus ministry as in some way a fulfillment of Isaiah 53. His theology might have been at the time lacking depth of meaning according to Christian doctrine but the point here is that seeing the process of Jesus' trial and crucifixion as one event starting his reckoning in the AM was not beyond reasonable possibility.

* * *

But a sticky matter is what Mark appeared to say. Mark 15:25 says, It was the third hour... What isn't evident in this translation is the word *and* in this sentence: ***And** it was the third hour...* Recall the chapter on *And... And What!* This *and* is a different word from the word *and* used in the verses immediately preceding and following which suggests to me a mild break in the narrative. Also some copies of this text in error read ***when** they crucified him*. The word *when* would probably fix the crucifixion time starting mid morning, the third hour, but the actual reading does not say *when*. Add to this what we read in the *Morphological Greek New Testament*. This text is sometimes referred to as the "critical text" or the "eastern manuscript tradition," and is the most widely used today, it is the basis for nearly every modern Bible translation in the past one hundred years, This Greek text is identical to the Nestle-Aland 27th Edition. (http://www.logos.com/ebooks/details/NA27). The MGT reads in verse 24 *And they are crucifying him* instead of *And when they crucified him*. What are we to make of a present tense here? You might want to read or reread the chapter on *December 21, 2012*.

We are almost done collecting information about Mark's text. You may want to consider also that if numbers were used for the hour, a 6 would be the Greek letter Ϝ whereas 3 is a Γ. Several patristic writers, Ammonius, Eusebius and Jerome, claimed that this was the confusion. I have my doubts, though. The manuscript evidence is overwhelmingly in support of *about the sixth hour* in John's Gospel and *the third hour* in Mark's.

What this all means to me is that I can agree with Frederick Godet and hear Mark relating the general description of Jesus' trial and then His crucifixion. The Third hour is when it begins in Mark's mind. It is actually around that hour or mid-morning. We do not need to ascribe to Mark's description the exactness of legal language in this case since his wording does not warrant it. He started verse 25 with a Greek word for *and* that loosely connects this verse with the preceding which suggest a summary of sorts—a way of repeating what he had previous reported and then continuing. Verses 19-22 are mid-morning events. The smiting and mocking of Jesus along with the walk along Via Dolorosa took time. Verse 24 uses a present tense for vividness not for chronological accuracy. By the time Jesus was actually hoisted up into the air and the cross was set in the ground it was between eleven and noon. I know, we assumed Jesus hung on Calvary's cross for six hours but it might have been three or four. Nothing in the plan of Salvation denies that possibility and it would reconcile John's account with Mark's. Dr. Ehrman thinks this is too much twisting and turning to wedge a round idea into a square theological hole.

You decide.

* * *

What about our theology? We already used Dr. Eshbaugh's research to indicate that copies of the New Testament were tweaked to represent changing theological thought. What about the end result of our study to learn about God through the medium of Scripture? Here's a shock: No one's theology can possibly be without contradiction. The reason for this is simple. Theology is a study of God and if our logic is complete it means we have Him figured out. So, a part of what we need to know about God to complete the picture of His plan and person necessarily is yet to be discovered. Somethings God chooses not to reveal, at least for the time being. Deuteronomy 29:29: The secret things belong to the Lord our God, but the things revealed belong to us and to our children forever. Daniel 2:14: ...close up and seal the words of the scroll until the time of the end.

This means simply that our present level of knowledge, scientific or otherwise, is not sufficient to explain all that needs explaining. In fact we may go as far as to say that our logic by the very nature of the process of deduction is not capable of understanding some truth. Perhaps, this is what Paul meant in 1 Corinthians 2:14: The man without the Spirit does not accept the things that come from the Spirit of God, for they are foolishness to him, and he cannot understand them, because they are spiritually discerned.

Living it explains it. Believing is seeing. These are not cliché but real working principles not shared by the agnostic or atheist whose science and logic necessarily must fall short. After all, the book is about GOD. The—so-called, liberal—critics focus on the letter and not the spirit of what is written. They fail to look beyond the copyist errors in the manuscripts but claim the Scripture as an imperfect literary piece which should be studied only for its literary value.

* * *

Again, we do not need to conclude that our copy of Scripture is perfect. We maintain only that once a perfect copy did exist—yes, even if only in the mind of God—and we are looking for that copy in the manuscripts we do have. I know; that's a statement of faith and it is frustrating because it cannot be challenged. You must let me believe what I want to.

Well, maybe pieces are missing—say, Enoch's or Clement's, whose work interests me personally. But we must trust God to have said enough in what we do have. What else can we do? And yes, mere men tried to set the canon in place, and we know something isn't totally right since the Catholic branch of Christianity sees more books to read than do the non-Catholics. We have to let that go for now. It is not an argument for discrediting those writing which we share a common interest in.

My point here is that we cannot see what we are not really looking for. We cannot see the work of God in the Bible if we are engaged in looking for controversy and contradiction. How can we see God if we are not looking for Him! How can we approach—we only need approach—an academic position of honest investigative work unless we start with the theory that somewhere in all those words is something God said—God wrote—through the agency of human personality

If we relegate the Bible to a place—honored as it might be—only of English literature, up there with Shakespeare's, no doubt—what happens to our faith? On "A Crisis of Faith" (Page 272) in *Jesus Interrupted*, Dr. Ehrman says, "My personal view is that a historical-critical approach to the Bible... can in fact lead to a more intelligent and thoughtful faith..."

* * *

Is it possible that some contradictions are not contradictions at all because they represent a developing thought? The chapter *Threads* shows us, for example, that the word or concept of God's grace was developed over biblical time—if I may say it that way. This doesn't explain all differences in comparative Bible texts, of course not, but it makes sense to me to believe that some of God's ideas needed to be taught through generations of interrelating, centuries of prophetic outcries and providential directing. Israel, for example, couldn't appreciate the One God concept until after the Babylonian Captivity. After all this, Israel finally captures the meaning of the *Shema* of Deuteronomy 6:4: Hear, O Israel: THE LORD our God [is] one LORD. (KJV)

The big example from Dr. Ehrman's *Jesus Interrupted* would be the differing point of view—alleged—between Matthew and Paul on the subject of "the Law." This is in more general terms a contrast between the Jewish view and Paul's view of justification. Dr. Ehrman writes, "I have often wondered what would have happened if Paul and Matthew had been locked up in a room together and told they could not come out until they had hammered out a consensus statement on how followers of Jesus were to deal with the Jewish law. Would they have emerged, or would they still be there, two skeletons locked in a death grip?"

This is in fact the general controversy that had to be hammered out at the Council at Jerusalem in Acts 15. The chapter on *Whose Fault Is It?* references this general controversy. Simply said, Paul was God's man of the hour to reveal the message of Grace which was to include the gentiles. Before Paul, the message was not clear. It is the grace thread we spoke of earlier and to me no mystery; the historical development of the concept would go through Israel somewhat undetected or unrelated until the time was right. Of course Israel would have a different interpretation of Isaiah 53.

Dr. Ehrman makes an interesting statement on page 94 in *Jesus Interrupted*, "...aren't atonement and forgiveness the same thing? Not at all." Dr. Ehrman understands that in Mark Jesus dies to (10:45) give his life a ransom for many. This is atonement. But Luke in Acts says nothing about atonement but instead blames Israel for rejecting Jesus and declares them to be in need of forgiveness.

Acts 2:36-38: "Therefore let all Israel be assured of this: God has made this Jesus, whom you crucified, both Lord and Christ." When the people heard this, they were cut to the heart and said to Peter and the other apostles, "Brothers, what shall we do?" Peter replied, "Repent and be baptized, every one of you, in the name of Jesus Christ for the forgiveness of your sins. And you will receive the gift of the Holy Spirit." A contradiction or a developing thought?

The Bible record begins from a discussion of atonement or sacrifice, the sacrifice of Christ, and then talks through the subjects of forgiveness and repentance—two sides of the same coin. To say that atonement makes forgiveness unnecessary, which I believe is Prof. Ehrman's point, totally disavows the part we play in the divine plan. In the example of a parent-teen relationship, if the teen gets into deep debt, the parent first assumes the debt, pays it for them, but then should want the teen to agree never to get into that financial situation again—repent. Forgiveness is parental recognition of this relationship. I see no contradiction.

* * *

Many of our principles and quite a few of our ethical norms are from the Bible and it is no small concern that we hold to these thinking they are divine wisdom. But wait up before you say, "Amen." Do we pick through the Wisdom of Solomon and take whatever we want if we want? Dr Ehrman correctly observes that Christians do this anyway. He points out that when a scriptural idea—as we translate it—suits us, we adopt it as a principle for living. "Husbands love your wives" has to be a favorite among married women. "Wives submit to your husbands" is the married man's refrain. But when was the last time we stoned an incorrigible teen? (Deuteronomy 21:19) That instruction *is* in the Old Testament. It is a fact of preaching that not just the ceremonial law is discarded in the name of Christian teaching. There are, doubtless, hundreds of laws in the Old Testament that governed relationships and social behavior which we have let slide as irrelevant to modern life.

So where do we draw the line? If the Bible is just literature, picking and choosing is an OK thing to do, but if it is God's Word...! Some Old Testament laws have been given a different perspective thanks to Jesus. Divorce and remarriage comes to mind. This is also explained in the chapter on *Threads*.

Some evangelicals might add that the message of Grace in the New Testament by its very nature supersedes and even abrogates many laws written in Old Israel. After all, Love covers a multitude of sins. 1 Peter 4:8. At this point the liberal scholar throws his hands up in disgust and walks away mumbling, "Whatever...!" And I don't blame him. He is looking for the hermeneutic or rule by which we interpret Scriptures that will filter out the verses we—seemingly—don't like and keep the ones we do like.

Do we have such a hermeneutic? By what rule of interpretation do we allow bad kids to live and—say—the ten commandments are O.K? Maybe we can start with John Calvin's rule of thumb (I'm told it is his): The Scriptures are their own interpreter. I doubt, though, that this covers everything.

Another line of reasoning offered in evangelical circles is that we must obey the spirit of the law not the letter. 2 Corinthians 3:6: He has made us competent as ministers of a new covenant–not of the letter but of the Spirit; for the letter kills, but the Spirit gives life.

Maybe it is time to stone a few people—the criminal law of the state not withstanding. You know I don't mean that. And since you would agree that this is not an option, even the liberal scholar knows that some Scripture like the ten commandments are worth consideration but killing children is out.

For my part—and here is not the place to detail my remarks—the progressive revelation of Divine grace does tell a few rock hurlers to stand down. This was probably the message of John 8:1-11. Even though these verses are spurious—not part of the original—they are an example of what I am saying. The proof hermeneutically and theologically is a grammatical study that takes another book. It is not fair of me to ramble out too much here—email me on this if you wish—but let me say that a study of Hebrew or Old Testament forms and what we call "verb stems" compared to the historical development of some Greek modes and tenses—are you bored yet? —tell me that the Old Testament language was more social and relational than theological. It shows through historical narrative what God wants to document when we get to the New Testament and Paul, in particular. Under-standing the theological development of "grace" in the context of biblical history is a necessary part of understanding what hermeneutic to use in interpreting God's thoughts.

For me, the Bible can be studied word by word, phrase by phrase, in the language common to the time and culture that is its context. I can hear God in such a study and see the hand of providence in the development of thoughts within its pages that point to grace and to Calvary. I can overlook scribal errors and not consider them a flaw in God's design. I can learn new things about my Bible I didn't know as I remain teachable. Prof. Ehrman has shown me a few and for them I am grateful without having my faith threatened. I know the textual critics are still hard at work mulling over ancient scripts trying to figure things out a bit clearer historically. And I say, "Keep up the good work."

Some may think the Bible is in danger of being set aside for more productive texts on how to live. Some think that Christianity as an invention of man's mind is going to morph eventually into something theologically harmless and that the world will—as far as religion goes—head off in another direction. If you are anxious and worrisome you must read Lee Strobel's The Case For The Real Jesus Zondervan Press, 2007. Mr. Strobel admirably refutes Dr. Ehrman's conclusions.

As long as I have my Greek and Hebrew texts plus a few more study books, I will sit alone in the silence of my study, oblivious to what is happening around me, and meditate on the message that has been from my youth: my joy, my profession and my life. Join me there.

I Said No!

For the scholars who prefer to acquaint themselves directly with the language and the words, here is a closer view of Galatians 5:19-21 which, all should be agreed, are absolute no-nos and which overview clearly what God is not about. I leave it to the reader to have the insight and the conscience necessary to explain this. One note, since this is an appendix, let me footnote, so-to-speak, in place. One more note—a preacher's prerogative—truth be told, I just wanted all those loose leaf pages scattered about in my office to finally have a home.

Galatians 5:19-21 reads,

When you follow the desires of your sinful nature, the results are very clear: sexual immorality, impurity, lustful pleasures, idolatry, sorcery, hostility, quarreling, jealousy, outbursts of anger, selfish ambition, dissension, division, envy, drunkenness, wild parties, and other sins like these. Let me tell you again, as I have before, that anyone living that sort of life will not inherit the Kingdom of God.

Sexual immorality: adultery, fornication. The term is a general term referring to promiscuity of all kinds, fornication, John 8:41; marital infidelity, Hosea 3:3; prostitution, incest,I Corinthians. 5:1; and homosexuality, I Tim 1:10. "The New Testament is characterized by an unconditional repudiation of all extra-marital and unnatural intercourse... A further result of this is a basically new attitude to women. She is no longer man's chattel but a partner of equal dignity before both men and God. (Kittel, Gerhard. Theological Dictionary of the New Testament, Vol VI, Pg 590)

Impurity: uncleanness .The term is a synonym of sexual immorality. It has the added emphasis of profligacy. It denotes a promiscuous life style, an indulgence in iniquity, Romans 1:24; 6:19.

Lustful Pleasures: lasciviousness. The term signifies a "lawless insolence and wanton caprice (Trench Synonyms of the New Testament pg 58). It speaks of someone who acknowledges no restraints, who dares whatever his or her caprice and wanton petulance may suggest. (Trench Synonyms of the New Testament pg 56). It is a certain brazen, bold, brassy—what can I say—shameless display of sin. It is a harmful display of self-will blaring an undisciplined maliciousness. It is also a synonym of sexual immorality, but it emphasizes shameless indulgence and its harmful affects or results. It is a display of desire with no constraint, unbridled and gluttonous., Jude 4; I Peter 4:3; 2 Peter 2:2; Romans 13:13. (Thayers, Joseph. Thayer's Greek-English Lexicon Page 80).

Idolatry: idol worship. The term signifies the worship of false gods, being fully explained in the first commandment, Exodus 20:3-5; I Corinthians 10:14; Colossians 3:5.

Sorcery: witchcraft. This is the use or administration of drugs or poisons and as such in Bible days it meant sorcery or magical arts. (Thayers, Joseph. Thayer's Greek-English Lexicon Page 649). The Latin is "witchcraft" from which we get our word venom. A curious reference is offered by Milton and Mulligan (Moulton, James Hope and Milligan George The Vocabulary of the Greek Testament. Page 664), where a wife "solemnly promises she will not mix noxious drugs with her husband's drink or food." The word is in the New Testament in the Revelation, 9:21; 18:23; 21:8; 22:15, and definitely condemns witchcraft and wizardry. Might we include an illicit use of drugs?

Hostility: hatred. The word is emnity, James 4:4; Romans 8:7 (Thayers, Joseph. Thayer's Greek-English Lexicon Page 265). It has been freely translated "quarrelsomeness" (Moulton, James Hope and Milligan George The Vocabulary of the Greek Testament. Page 269). It has been translated "hostility" (Kittel, Gerhard. Theological Dictionary of the New Testament, Vol II, Page 811)—a personal hatred for an individual, mostly (Ibid. page 815). The plural in Galatians 5, may suggest private skirmishes, word battles, an inner disposition that places one member of the body of Christ at odds against another. The word is also found in Luke 23:12; Ephesians 2:14, 16. The Latin word from which we get "inimical" can simply signify something said or done in an unfriendly way.

Quarreling: variance. The Latin of this word from which we derive the word "contention" means competition, struggle, dispute. It is a heart unconquerable when hate takes hold of it. It depicts a rivalry, a jealous striving after (Moulton, James Hope and Milligan George The Vocabulary of the Greek Testament. Page 254). Now we know we are not talking about kids soccer; so, please don't go there. Every adult knows the subject before us. The word means striving or wrangling, I Timothy 6:4; Titus 3:9.

Jealousy: emulations. This is zeal and it does have a good side but it has what scholars call a partem malem, a bad or evil meaning. Like a lot of feelings and expressions, zeal misplaced can cause irreparable damage. Trench has much to say, (Trench, Richard C. Synonyms of the New Testament.) It is "a desire to make war on the good which it beholds in another, and thus to trouble that good and make it less... where there is not the... energy enough to attempt the making of it less; with such petty carping and fault-finding as it may dare to indulge in..." [He asks us to listen to the English poet:} "Envy, to which the ignoble mind's a slave, Is emulation in the learned and brave."

We may understand this word in a bad sense in Acts 5:17; 13:45; Romans 13:13.

Outbursts of Anger: wrath, rage. The Latin gives us the word "ire" which means wrath and resentment. It signifies a turbulent commotion and boiling agitation of the feelings. (Trench, Richard C. Synonyms of the New Testament. Page 131). In English we say, "boiling mad!" "...like fire to straw quickly blazing up, and as quickly extinguished (Ibid., Page 132). It is our word "rage" Study Luke 4:28; Acts 19:28; Ephesians 4:31; Hebrews 11:27; and Revelation 19:15. This last verse references He treads the winepress of the fury of the wrath of God Almighty. I guess we must concede that if God can show rage, it can't be all that bad, but bear in mind that this word is used here not because God's feelings are out of control but because what His anger must do, it must do quickly—fire to straw. We cannot ever accuse God of doing anything without intense and passionate feeling. Half-heartedness or pulling one's punches can never describe Him. For us, however, I maintain rage is something we best think twice about before responding.

Selfish Ambition: strife. The Latin means "a brawl". A fight, quarrel, squabble, fisticuffs. The Greek word signifies more personal ambition. It speaks of those "who demeaning themselves and their cause, are busy and active in their own interests, seeking their own gain and advantage." (Kittel, Gerhard. Theological Dictionary of the New Testament, Vol II, Page 660). They have a readiness to do things only for profit. (Ibid., Page 661). It is an ambitious self-interest leading to factions, partisanship and contention. In Romans 2:7 we see those who with a "despicable nature... do not strive after glory.. and immortality ... but ... think only of immediate gain. " (Ibid.) You might choose to also glance at 2 Corinthians 12:20; Philippians 1:1, 2:3' and James 3:14 and 16.

Dissension: seditions. Our word comes from the Latin "dissension" and "discord" In the New Testament it signifies disunity in the community or general parties (and we don't mean suppers or banquets, here but political) within the church. (Kittel, Gerhard. Theological Dictionary of the New Testament, Vol I, Page 514). It joins to words like schism, disturbance, and contention. Study romans 16:17; I Corinthians 1:10 and 3:3. One can see clearly that a rift between believers is never in God's favor.

Jon Meacham in American Lion, a biography of President Andrew

Jackson, gives us a good definition of partisanship. It was in a debate in the Senate, March 1830, that the distinguished senator from Louisiana, Edward Livingston—yes, brother to the famed Dr. Livingston—gave a passioned plea for unity and union. "The cost of partisanship for partisanship's sake," Meacham related the senator's thoughts, "—of seeing politics as blood sport, where the kill is the only object of the exercise—was, Livingston said, too high ..to pay. Differences of opinion and doctrine and personality were one thing." Livingston called these "necessary ...and legitimate..." And then the Senator waxed eloquent and what he said—for me—describes the sin of dissension.

"The spirt of which I speak, [arguing against zealotry,] creates imaginary and magnifies real causes of complaint; arrogates to itself every virtue—denies every merit to its opponents; secretly entertains the worse designs ... mounts the pulpit and in the name of a God of mercy and peace, preaches discord and vengeance; invokes the worst scourges of Heaven, war, pestilence, and famine, as preferable alternatives to party defeat; blind, vindictive, cruel, remorseless, unprincipled, and at last frantic, it communicates its madness to friends as well as foes; respects nothing, fears nothing." (Meacham, Jon. American Lion, page 133)

Division: heresies. The Latin means "sect" In both Greek and Latin represents a school of thought or a political party (Kittel, Gerhard. Theological Dictionary of the New Testament, Vol I, Page 182). I Corinthians 11:18 and following forbids such divisions within the church. If a body of believers endorses a particular philosophy or school of thought it will not be supporting the Pauline spirit that maintained that there is neither Jew nor Greek. The word, thus, means division on doctrinal grounds. See Acts 26:5 and 2 Peter 2:1.

Envy: envying or a displeasure over another's good. I think the Italians call this the MAL OCCHIO or evil eye (Trench, Richard C. Synonyms of the New Testament. Page 89). Matthew 20:15 and 1 Samuel 18:9 should be helpful. This is an envy which attempts to depress the envied to the same level of misery and spiritual poverty as the envier. "Sick of a strange diseases", Phineas Fletcher said, "of another's health." I have a few more verse to offer, Matthew 27:1; Mark 15;10; Titus 3:3 and James 4:5.

Drunkenness: inebriated. In Greek there are three words signifying drinking. One means drinking alcoholic beverage but not to the point of a drunken stupor (I don't know if this is less than .09 blood alcohol.) It is almost like our phrase "a social drink". The next word means drunk enough to stagger and reel. It is the point where our troubles are temporarily drowned in the liquid. This is our word "bombed." This is the word used here in Galatians. There is a third term akin to our idea of becoming addicted or an alcoholic, but in biblical days this was not identified as a sickness only an insatiable thirst. (Trench, Richard C. Synonyms of the New Testament. Page 226). For those interested. The first word "social drinking" is found in Genesis 19:13; 2 Samuel 3:20;Esther 6:14. Being bombed—our word in Galatians—is also found in Luke 21:34; Romans 13:13; Joel 1:5; and Ezekiel 39:19. The last term meaning an addictive use of alcohol may be researched in Deuteronomy 21:21 and Isaiah 56:12.

Wild parties: revelings. This bespeaks of the reveling that could follow heavy drinking. In one instance the revelers "with garlands on their heads, and torches in their hands, with shouts and song—loud noises, not melodious sounds—pass to the harlots houses or otherwise wander through the streets with insult and wanton outrage for everyone whom they meet." (Trench, Richard C. Synonyms of the New Testament. Page 227). The amplified Bible calls this carousing. See Romans 13:13 and 1 Peter 4:3.

* * *

There is a curious word study imbedded in all of this talk or study on things we shouldn't do or become which shows the Bible to be current in its evaluation of human behavior. Psychological schools of thought are forever tweaking their understanding of who we are as humankind. Without intending any disrespect to the discipline, I maintain that their knowledge can only someday catch up to God's and His Word if they stay true to the course of honest scientific inquiry. An example is the terms used in Scripture to map out the path of an undisciplined man.

First, he becomes in tractable through good feeding according to Deuteronomy 32:15. The word here speaks of the insolence of wealth, the petulance from fulness of bread. (Trench, Richard C. Synonyms of the New Testament. Page 55ff). Luxurious living gone amok. See Genesis 19:4 thru 9; 1 Timothy 5:11 and Revelation 18:7 and 9.

This can lead to a wasteful attempt at self-satisfaction, the idea found in Luke 15:13; 1 Timothy 5:6 and James 5:5. Here the language adds the idea of squandering, wasting, using up or the waste of a life in the attempt at easy living.

We are lead next to study the circular path this takes with a desire to satisfy desire. This is found also in James 5:5 or Luke 16:19. Add 2 Peter 2:13 and Luke 7:25. It speaks of luxury abused. It keeps company in the Greek mind with such words as effeminate or soft, sluggishness or laziness. It is the old adage about the lack of callouses on a man's hand which before computers used to signify a life of ease and no hard work. Even now, many consider this a troublesome behavior pattern. It is a spirit broken through self-indulgence. If you have money... well. It produces in some a greedy love for pleasure, meddling with it to excess, enjoying all things without constraint of conscience or regard for the needs of others. Doing one's own thing for one's self alone. You got the picture. I kind-of think these words go together in the order I am relating them. They are marking out the path of the undisciplined.

Beware!

It gets worse. Galatians 5:19 lists one of the works of the flesh, lascivious-ness, which fits in here. We won't go over the same ground twice. Let me add only the word "excess" found in Ephesians 5:18. It can mean buying what one cannot afford. "It is easy to see," says Trench (Trench, Richard C. Synonyms of the New Testament. Page 54ff) "that one who is excessive...laying out his expenditures on a more magnificent scheme than his means will warrant, slides easily under the fateful influence of ...all ...temptations... laying it out for the gratification of his own sensual desires." O.K. I did say that before in the chapter on sin. I was due a little emphasis. Don't you think?

This goes from won't manage to can't manage or addictive behavior. It is the word incontinent found in Matthew 23:25 and 1 Corinthians 7:5. It is ungovernable and uncontrollable self-indulgence.

* * *

2 Timothy 3:2-4 adds to this list.

For people will love only themselves and their money. They will be boastful and proud, scoffing at God, disobedient to their parents, and ungrateful. They will consider nothing sacred. They will be unloving and unforgiving; they will slander others and have no self-control. They will be cruel and hate what is good. They will betray their friends, be reckless, be puffed up with pride, and love pleasure rather than God.

Perhaps, Paul in 2 Timothy 3:4 was summing it all up with the phrase "Lovers of pleasure." I can leave this also to your Bible study groups to hash out, but the bottom line is that the Bible is not so vague after all. It begs the old question which needs from time to time to be asked, "What part of No! don't you understand!"

Oh, by the way, the opposite of all of this—and I take this on the word of scholarship—is "a sound mind" referenced in 2 Timothy 1:7. He is a lover of self and consequently a waste of all his goods and inevitably his time, his faculties, his powers or strength and lastly himself. If you find your life, you in effect, end up losing it, Jesus said. Remember the prodigal son.

* * *

We can find other traits described in Scripture which if correctly studied put them at odds with the Spirit of God. I only list them here because—truth be told—I tire now of writing this appendix. I become a bit sick after awhile squashing bugs or talking about such bad stuff. But here goes, the finale of fire works.

The word "cruel" in Jeremiah 6:23 speaks of pitiless violence, savage behavior, the unmitigated flareup of a hot temper. It is the opposite of "meekness." It is the untamed nature of the lion.

"Despisers of those that are good" is found in 1 Timothy 3:3. The word speaks for itself. There are those who detest the goodness of the Spirit seen in others This engenders a general hatred or animosity against it and this often leads to some form of persecution.

There are those who are "heady", Acts 19:36 and Judges 9:4. Brazen, offensive, inconsiderate, careless with their tongues and actions, insensitive ...oohh! Proverbs 10:14 and 13:3 he who speaks rashly will come to ruin. Amen!

In I Timothy 6:4 Paul adds, he is proud, knowing nothing. This adds the word "high-minded" to the discussion. It means aufgeblassen vor Stolz. That's German for swollen with pride. A cloud of smoke has fogged up a man's intellect. Matthew 12:20. Clouds of conceit and stupidity. 2 Timothy 3:4. There is a lesson in here somewhere.

In this Scripture also we glean from a list of behavioral traits, if I may call them such, that do not belie the heart of a true believer. We must always study to show ourselves approved unto God workmen—work persons—who do not need to be ashamed, rightly dividing the Word of Truth. 2 Timothy 2:15.

Endnotes

Discovering What's in the Bible, Part One
1.   Sayers, Dorothy L. *Creed Or Chaos*, page 9

What's in a Name
1.   Trench, Richard C. *On the Study of the Words Lectures. Page 29ff*
2.   *Genesis 22:14 appears to be a clear contradiction to this verse in Exodus 6:3. In Genesis Abraham calls the Mountain in the land of Moriah where he almost sacrificed his son, Isaac, Jehovah Jireh. How reliable is Exodus 6:3? by my name the Lord I did not make myself known to them*

Liberal scholarship uses this verse to point out multiple authors for the first five books. The claim is that Genesis 22:14 had to be written *after* Exodus 6:3. Another view is that the name Yahweh, Jehovah, was known to Abraham but the *meaning* behind the name was not known. Kiel points out in his *Commentary on the Old Testament*, Volume, Page 468 that "the work of Israel's redemption resided in the power of the name Jehovah." This power Abraham was not familiar with. The problem became a two pronged issue: Why would God introduce a name to the patriarchs and not reveal its meaning until the time of the Exodus—Name changes in the Old Testament were very significant, as Jacob's name change to "Israel", the meaning was given at the time of the name—and how could a name which was so sacred as to lack vowel sounds—it is known as the tetragrammaton, four letters without a pronunciation—be used so casually on the lips of the patriarchs when they didn't even understand its significance? These issues for the conservative interpreter seem to defy explanation. Textual criticism is now positioned to discredit the theory that Moses was the author of these first five books.

Exodus 3:15, however, is a curious verse: *God also said to Moses, "Say to the Israelites, 'The Lord, the God of your fathers—the God of Abraham, the God of Isaac and the God of Jacob—has sent me to you."* Is it possible that God did in fact introduce His name Yahweh or Jehovah to the patriarch only to add to the revelation of its meaning with Moses? The fuller significance of the name in the Exodus was beyond the scope of Abraham's knowledge about God.

Chuck Smith says "Now that is in the sense that the word means "the becoming one", actually Abraham used the term Jehovah-Jireh when his son said, 'Dad where is the sacrifice?' Abraham said, 'Jehovah-Jireh, the Lord will provide'... But yet the Lord is saying, 'By My name Jehovah was I not known.' In other words, they knew Him in a less personal way than Moses was to know God. They knew Him as the Almighty God, the Creator of the heavens and the earth." (http://www.blueletterbible.org/commentaries/comm_view.cfm? AuthorID=1&contentID=4740&commInfo=25&topic=Exodus&ar=Exd_6_3)

Apples and Oranges
1. Trench *Synonyms of the New Testament* pg 197.
2. Lightfoot, J. B. *The Epistle of Saint Paul to the Galatians* Pg 212
3. Lange, John Peter. *Commentary of the Holy Scriptures* Vol 11, Page 139
4. Trench *Synonyms of the New Testament* page 196
5. Ibid.
6. Ibid. Page 198
7. Kittel, Gerhard. *Theological Dictionary of the New Testament*, Vol IX, Pg 486
8. Lightfoot, J. B. *The Epistle of Saint Paul to the Galatians* Pg 213
9. Kittel, Gerhard. *Theological Dictionary of the New Testament* Vol I, page 18
10. Trench *Synonyms of the New Testament* Pg 391
11. Ibid., Page 392
12. Ibid., Page 151
13. Ibid.
14. Liddell and Scott, *A Greek-English Lexicon* Page 1461.
15. Trench, *Synonyms of the New Testament* Page 157
16. Moulton, James Hope and Milligan George *The Vocabulary of the Greek Testament* Page 180
17. Aristotle's *Ethica. Nicomachea.* Vii. 2.
18. C.S. Lewis *The Four Loves.* Page 177

Awakened from a Sound Sleep
1. http://www.blueletterbible.org/commentaries/comm_view.cfm?AuthorID=1&contentID=7132&commInfo=25&topic=Mark&ar=Mar_4_39
2. http://www.blueletterbible.org/commentaries/comm_view.cfm?AuthorID=4&contentID=1628&commInfo=5&topic=Mark&ar=Mar_4_39
3. Lange, John Peter. *Commentary of the Holy Scriptures.* Vol 8, Page 133
4. cp.. ftnt. 2
5. http://mog.com/music/The_Collingsworth_Family

Impossible!

Endnotes

1. Sayers, Dorothy L. *Creed or Chaos*. Page 8ff
2. Strobel, Lee. *The Case for the Real Jesus*. Page 126.
3. Trench, *Synonyms of the New Testament* Page 262ff. Trench affirms that although "form" doesn't mean "being" like the German "gestalt" is signifies "the inner life" or "mode of being" and "only God could have the mode of existence of God."
4. Ehrman, Bart. *Jesus Interrupted. Page 247.* Ehrman maintains that the theology of Jesus' divinity was introduces into Scriptures through scribal corrections in the fourth century and later. He understood the original doctrinal belief of early Christians was only in Jesus' humanity. This is refutted admirably— I might add—by Lee Strobel in *The Case for the Real Jesus*.
5. Boyd, Gregory A. *Letters From A Skeptic*. Page 151.
6. Sayers, Dorothy L. *The Man Born to be King*. Page 290
7. Ravi Zacharias in *Can Man Live without God*.
8. Sayers, Dorothy L. *Creed or Chaos*. Page 8ff.
9. Ibid.
10. Taylor, H. Kerr. *Event in Eternity* "A Bible Timeline" Atlanta, GA: John Knox Press, 1976

Perfect!
1. Burton, Ernest De Witt. *Syntax of the Moods and Tenses in New Testament Greek*. Page 37ff.
2. Boman, Thorleif. *Hebrew Thought Compared with Greek*. Page 31.

Whose Fault is it?
1. Sayers, Dorothy L. *Creed or Chaos*. Page 8ff.

Jot That Down
1. My daughter-in-law suggested you see the Hebrew letters for the words I *love* אֶרְחָמְךָ and I will have *mercy* אֲרַחֵם The reason for the footnote is to explain the form. Mercy is a strengthened form but the middle letter can not have the dot since the dot doubles the letter. It is unpronounceable in Hebrew. So the scribes change the dots and lines underneath the letters to represent the strengthened form. I still maintain that this is a most interesting example of a strengthened form and many words have the dagesh forte or doubling or strengthening dot which alters and often intensifies the meaning, as we see with our word *love*.
2. Lange, John Peter. Commentary of the Holy Scriptures Vol 7, Page 211
3. http://en.wikipedia.org/wiki/Masoretes
4. Gesenius, William *A Hebrew And English Lexicon of the Old Testament*. Page

341.

5.   Kelley, Page H., et al. *The Masorah of Biblia Hebraica Stuttgartensia*, Page 35.

Sin? I'll Drink to That!

1.   Girdlestone, Robert B. *Synonyms of the Old Testament*. Page 76

2.   Trench, *Synonyms of the New Testament* Page 55.

I Can't Say That in Greek

1.   http://www.geocities.com/Heartland/Pines/7224/Rick/Septuagint/spex-ecsum.htm

2.   Ibid.

3.   Robertson, A.T. *A Grammar of the Greek New Testament,* Page 94 . Taken from (Swete, Intr. To the O.T. In Gk., 1900, pp. 381-405).

4.   Trench, *Synonyms of the New Testament* Page 125.

5.   Liddell, Henry George and Scott Robert. *A Greek-English Lexicon,* Page 1115

6.   Moulton, James Hope and Milligan George *The Vocabulary of the Greek Testament* Page 404

7.   Kittel, Gerhard. Theological Dictionary of the New Testament Vol VI, page 722.

8.   Thayers, Joseph. *Thayer's Greek-English Lexicon,* Page 692ff.

9.   Kittel, ibid. Page 779.

10.   Trench, ibid.

Thy Speech Bewrayeth Thee

1.   Robertson, A.T. *A Grammar of the Greek New Testament, Page 103.*

2.   Lange, John Peter. *Commentary of the Holy Scriptures.* Vol 8, Page 498

3.   Robertson, A.T. *A Grammar of the Greek New Testament, Page* pg 104

4.   Ibid. Page 97.

5.   Ibid. Page 100.

6.   Ibid. Page 98.

7.   Ibid. Page 108

8.   Ibid. Page 101.

9.   Ibid. cp .Churton, Infl of the LXX Vers., 1861, p.1.

10.   Ibid. Page 102. cp. in Die Hellen. Des Semit. Mon., p. 174

11.   Ibid. Page 93. cp. Expositor, Oct. 1907, "Philology of the Greek Bible, p. 294)

12.   Ibid. Page 100.

13.   Ibid. Page 88.

14.   Ibid. Page 107.

15.   Ibid. Page 94.

16.   Kittel, Gerhard. *Theological Dictionary of the New Testament,* Vol I, Pg 475

Endnotes

17. Moulton, James Hope and Milligan George *The Vocabulary of the Greek Testament* Page 79.
18. Ibid.
19. Gesenius, William *A Hebrew And English Lexicon of the Old Testament*. Page 815.

I Can't Believe You Said That!

1. Kittel, Gerhard. Theological Dictionary of the New Testament Vol IV, page 735.
2. http://en.wikipedia.org/wiki/Alcoholics_Anonymous

Let Me Underline That

1. Lange, John Peter. *Commentary of the Holy Scriptures* Vol 8, Page 176

A Particle Of Truth

1. Thayers, Joseph. *Thayer's Greek-English Lexicon,* Page 616ff.
2. Ibid. Page 131.
3. Gesenius, William *A Hebrew And English Lexicon of the Old Testament*. Page 635.

And ... And What!

1. Driver, S. R. *A Treatise on the Uses of the Tenses in Hebrew.* Page 94
2. Ibid., page 95.

December 21,2012

1. Burton, Ernest De Witt. *Syntax of the Moods and Tenses in New Testament Greek*. Page 29.
2. Ibid.
3. Ibid. Page 30.

Threads

1. Kittell, Vol IX page 377
2. The word *compassion* here is our word *mercy* in the chapter *And—And What!*
3. Kittell, Vol IX page 380
4. Ibid.
5. Ibid..
6. Ibid., Page 381
7. Ibid., Page 382
8. Lange, John Peter. *Commentary of the Holy Scriptures* Vol 1, Page 288

9. Botterweck G. J., et al. *Theological Dictionary of the Old Testament.* Page 88
10. Ibid. Page 89
11. Ibid. Page 94

Soteriology

1. Nunn, H.P.V.*A Short Syntax of New Testament Greek.* Page 125
2. Taken from: D.F Payne, "Semitisms in the Books of Acts," W. Ward Gasque & Ralph P. Martin, eds., Apostolic History and the Gospel. Biblical and Historical Essays Presented to F.F. Bruce. Exeter: The Paternoster Press, 1970. Hbk. ISBN: 085364098X. pp.134-150. Page 15
3. Trench, Richard C. *On the Study of the Words Lectures.* Page 23
4. Ibid. Page 25
5. http://alencon13.blogspot.com/2006/02/graf-wellhausen-theory.html
6. Unger, Merrill F, and Wiliam White. *Nelson's Expository Dictionary of the Old Testament.* Page 17
7. Thayers, Joseph. *Thayer's Greek-English Lexicon,* Page 150
8. Deem Michael J. *A Christological Renaissance: The Chalcedonian Turn of St. Anselm of Canterbury* wrote: 'The Council of Chalcedon was summoned by Emperor Marcian during the autumn of 451 to respond to an extreme model of monophysite Christology that threatened to eclipse the moderate teaching of Ephesus. The Fathers of Chalcedon sought to establish a norm-ative teaching on the Incarnation, confessing "one and the same Son, our Lord Jesus Christ, the same perfect in human nature, truly God and the same with a rational soul and a body truly man . . . acknowledged in two natures . . . combining in one Person (*prosopon*) [The Greek word which doesn't say what the tenets of faith should say] and substance (*hypostasis*), not divided or separated into two persons, but one and the same Son only begotten God Word, Lord Jesus Christ." While the Council was profoundly influenced by the Christologies of Cyril of Alexandria and John of Antioch, it was under the sway of Pope Leo the Great's *Tome to Flavian* that the majority of conflicting parties at Chalcedon were reconciled. The bishop of Rome provided the decisive polemic against the false Christological doctrines threatening the orthodox faith, marking **the first instance of a Latin solution to a peculiarly Eastern controversy.** [My bold italics] But Leonine Christology was not exhausted through its service to the Chalcedo-nian formula. Rather, as a system it goes much further than the Council with regard to the prerogatives Christ's natures, exemplifying a refined Latin tradition of the twofold consubstantiality of Christ.' (http://www.an-selm.edu/library/saj/pdf/21deem.pdf)
9. Thayers, Joseph. Ibid.

Endnotes

10. DuBose, Francis M. ed. *Classics of Christian Missions.* Page 336.
11. Ibid. Page 337.
12. Ibid. Page 339.
13. Ibid. Page 343ff.
14. Ibid. Page 342.

I Want to Speak in Tongues
1. Trench, Richard C. *On the Study of the Words Lectures.* Page 56
2. Ibid. Page 24
3. Ibid. Page 83
4. Kittel, Gerhard. Theological Dictionary of the New Testament, Vol I, Pg 88
5. Ibid. Page 122
6. Ibid. Page 91

Bibliography

Boman, Thorleif. *Hebrew Thought Compared with Greek*. New York, NY: W. W. Norton & Company, Inc. 1960.

Botterweck G. J., et al. *Theological Dictionary of the Old Testament*. Grand Rapids, MI: Wm. B Eerdmans Publishing Company, 1975.

Boyd, Gregory A. *Letters From A Skeptic*. Colorado Springs, CO: Cook Communication Ministries, 2004.

Burton, Ernest De Witt. *Syntax of the Moods and Tenses in New Testament Greek*. Edinburgh: T. & T. Clark, 1898.

Driver, S. R. *A Treatise on the Uses of the Tenses in Hebrew*. Oxford UK: Oxford Clarendon Press, 1969

DuBose, Francis M. ed. *Classics of Christian Missions*. Nashville, TN: Broadman Press, 1979

Ehrman, Bart. *Jesus Interrupted*. Harper Collins Publishers, 2009.

Gesenius, William *A Hebrew And English Lexicon of the Old Testament*. Boston, MA: Houghton, Mifflin and Company, 1882.

Girdlestone, Robert B. *Synonyms of the Old Testament*. Grand Rapids , MI: Grand Rapids Book Manufacturers, Inc. 1974

Kautzsch, E and Cowley A. E. eds. *Gesenius' Hebrew Grammar*. UK: Oxford Clarendon Press, 1969 1974. 2nd edition.

Kelley, Page H., et al. *The Masorah of Biblia Hebraica Stuttgartensia*. Grand Rapids, MI: Wm. B Eerdmans Publishing Company, 1998.

Kittel, Gerhard. *Theological Dictionary of the New Testament*. Grand Rapids, MI: Wm. B Eerdmans Publishing Company, 1974.

Lange, John Peter. *Commentary of the Holy Scriptures*. Grand Rapids, MI:

Bibliography

Zondervan Publishing Company, 1980.

Lewis, C.S. *The Four Loves*. New York, NY: Harcourt Brace Jovanovich, 1960.

Liddell, Henry George and Scott Robert. *A Greek-English Lexicon* Oxford: At The Clarendon Press, 1968.

Lightfoot, J. B. *The Epistle of Saint Paul to the Galatians*. Grand Rapids, MI: Zondervan Publishing Company, 1974.

Meacham, John. *American Lion*. New ork, NY: Randon House, 2008

Metzger, Bruce M. *A Textual Commentary on the Greek New Testament*. New York, NY: United Bible Societies, 1975.

Moulton, James Hope and Milligan George *The Vocabulary of the Greek Testament*. Grand Rapids, MI: Wm. B Eerdmans Publishing Company, 1974.

Nunn, H.P.V.*A Short Syntax of New Testament Greek*. Canbridge at the University Press, 1956.

Ravi Zacharias in *Can Man Live without God*. Thomas Nelson, Inc. Publisher, 1990.

Robertson, A.T. *A Grammar of the Greek New Testament*. Nashville, TN: Broadman Press, 1934.

Sayers, Dorothy L. *Creed Or Chaos*. Manchester,NH: Sophia Institute Press, 1974.

Sayers, Dorothy L. *Man Born to be King*. San Francisco: CA: Ignatius Press, 1943.

Strobel, Lee. *The Case for the Real Jesus*. Grand Rapids, MI: Zondervan Press, 2007

Taylor, H. Kerr. *Event in Eternity* "A Bible Timeline" Atlanta, GA: John Knox Press, 1976.

Thayers, Joseph. *Thayer's Greek-English Lexicon*. Hendrickson Publishers,

1996.

Trench, Richard C. *Synonyms of the New Testament*. Grand Rapids, MI: Wm. B Eerdmans Publishing Company, 1975

Trench, Richard C. *On the Study of the Words Lectures*. New York: W.. Widdleton, publisher. Unknown.

Unger, Merrill F, and Wiliam White. *Nelson's Expository Dictionary of the Old Testament*. Nashville, TN: Thomas Nelson Publishers, 1980

Translations

The Authorized Version or King James Version (KJV), 1611, 1769.

New American Standard Bible® (NASB), © The Lockman Foundation 1960, 1962, 1963, 1968, 1971, 1972, 1973, 1975, 1977, 1995

NEW INTERNATIONAL VERSION® (NIV®) © 1973, 1978, 1984 by International Bible Society

New Living Translation, (NLT) © 1996, 2004. Tyndale House Publishers, Inc., Wheaton, Illinois 60189.

New King James Version (NKJV), © 1982 by Thomas Nelson, Inc.

Revised Standard Version (RSV) containing the Old and New Testaments, translated from the original tongues: being the version set forth AD 1611, revised AD 1881-1885 and AD 1901: compared with the most ancient authorities and revised AD 1946-52.—2nd ed. of New Testament AD 1971.

Young's Literal Translation (YLT), translated by Robert Young, public domain.

Tanakh: The Holy Scriptures, The New JPS Translation According to the Traditional Hebrew Text (NJPSV), © 1985 by The Jewish Publication Society.

Websites

On Aristotle's Ethica Nicomachea:
http://etext.virginia.edu/toc/modeng/public/AriNico.html

For Bible references see:
http://www.blueletterbible.org/

For SBL literature
http://www.sbl-site.org/publications/journals_jbl_noLogin.aspx

The Septuagint in the New Testament
http://www.geocities.com/Heartland/Pines/7224/Rick/Septuagint/spex-ecsum.htm